D1548126

Academic Archives

Managing the
Next Generation
of College and
University Archives,
Records, and
Special Collections

Aaron D. Purcell

Neal-Schuman
Chicago

The Archivist's and Records Manager's Bookshelf

No. 1 *Archives and Archivists in the Information Age,* by Richard J. Cox
No. 2 *Understanding Data and Information Systems for Recordkeeping,* by Philip C. Bantin
No. 3 *Leading and Managing Archives and Records Programs: Strategies for Success,* edited by Bruce W. Dearstyne
No. 4 *Academic Archives: Managing the Next Generation of College and University Archives, Records, and Special Collections,* by Aaron D. Purcell

Published by Neal-Schuman, an imprint of ALA Publishing
50 E. Huron Street
Chicago, IL 60611
www.neal-schuman.com

Cover photo by Steve Tatum.

Printed and bound in the United States of America.

The paper used in this publication meets the minimum requirements of American National Standard for Information Sciences—Permanence of Paper for Printed Library Materials, ANSI Z39.48-1992.

Library of Congress Cataloging-in-Publication Data
Available at http://catalog.loc.gov

ISBN 978-1-55570-769-9

For
Laura Marie Stevralia Purcell,
editor-in-chief, writer of the family,
and instigator of my happiness

Contents

PART II: BUILDING AND UPDATING AN ACADEMIC ARCHIVES PROGRAM

List of Figures

Preface

So what are academic archives? In the past, this term referred to college and university archives programs, which collected, preserved, and provided access to material that documented their institution's history. Today, however, the field of academic archives is more expansive and complex. In addition to college and university archives, academic archives encompass records management programs, special collections departments, and other campus archival repositories. This new definition of academic archives programs has also redefined the role, and training, of academic archivists.

Today's academic archivists differ from their predecessors. Most of today's archivists working in higher education have access to education, training, and technology that were not available to previous generations. Demand for services and information by diverse user groups has also changed the mission of many academic archives. Academic institutions are the home to many archivists, and for good reason; nowhere is there such a need for talented people to contribute to an understanding of the past and help inform the future.

The majority of today's academic archivists work in programs with direct connections to a campus library system. Academic archives have taken many cues from academic libraries on redesigning reference services, creating collaborative spaces, reaching users with new technology, and merging units into larger departments. Likewise, academic librarians have learned from academic archivists the importance of building unique research collections, primary source education and instruction, and contributing to scholarly communication, both in print and electronic formats. This influence is most evident in the dramatic changes in special collections departments, the most common location for archives programs within academic libraries.

Academic Archives: Managing the Next Generation of College and University Archives, Records, and Special Collections examines the changing world of academic archives. It defines today's academic archivists and the future of their work. Academic archivists, who may be special collections librarians, records managers, reference archivists, manuscripts

processors, college or university archivists, and curators, are integral to
the ever-changing academic library. In the face of limited resources and
campus downsizing, academic archivists must wear many professional
hats, assume multiple roles and titles, and develop new skills to meet
the research and technological needs of their researchers. No longer
can academic archives programs remain isolated, committed to narrow
missions, limited to tiny constituencies, and without a true vision. To
accomplish this transformation, academic archivists must keep their programs relevant, growing, and connected to other parts of their campus
environment, especially the academic library.

Academic Archives is designed to appeal to archivists of all ranks and
experience, archivists working outside of academic libraries, archivists in
training, other information professionals, library directors, historians (who
often describe themselves as archivists because of their research skills), and
members of the academic community. Readers wanting to start an archives
program (academic and non-academic), update an existing archives program, begin a career in academic archives, or remain current on recent
developments, will find this timely reference source valuable.

At its heart, *Academic Archives* examines big-picture, practical issues of
working as an academic archivist and managing the next generation of
academic archives programs. It is not focused on just college or university archives but conceptualizes academic archives more broadly, with a
particular focus on merged departments in academic libraries, such as
a special collections unit. The major themes include choosing a career
in academic archives, working with other information professionals
in an academic library, defining and articulating the vision, connecting the program with the goals of the institution, integrating records
management functions into the archival program, building collections
with help from donors and dealers, presenting unique material to many
audiences, determining the best approaches to processing and organizing collections, digital opportunities, explaining the role of archivists in
twenty-first-century academic libraries, and defining what it means to be
an academic archivist.

ORGANIZATION

Academic Archives is divided into three parts. The first section, consisting
of three overview chapters, defines the academic archives environment.
Chapter 1 begins with a definition of today's academic archives and ar-

chivists. It describes career paths to academic archives, some of the most common traits evident in today's academic archivists, and how academic archivists remain current in such a dynamic environment.

Chapter 2 analyzes the current trends in academic libraries and how technological developments have redefined the role of the college or university library in the lives of students, faculty, and researchers. Understanding academic libraries is critical to understanding academic archives. Chapter 3 focuses on special collections, a significant counterpart to academic archives, which often serves as the home department for an archives program. It describes how these often misunderstood departments fit into the academic library, the kinds of collections found in these units, the training and preparation for special collections librarians, recent initiatives in this subfield, and finally how academic archivists fit into the special collections model. This first section emphasizes that by knowing the landscape, trends, and expectations of academic libraries and higher education, archivists have ample opportunities to make themselves and their programs an indispensable part of the academic environment.

The second section is more prescriptive and explains how to build and update an archives program in an academic library. Academic archivists must be resourceful and generate support for their collecting efforts on campus, while often seeking collections with little or no funding. These chapters examine the internal operations of academic archives, processes that have significant implications for the development of public and research services.

Chapter 4 examines practical approaches to maintaining a mission and charting a vision for academic archives. Successful academic archivists must exhibit broad leadership, manage and share resources, keep current in several fields, identify stakeholders, and target users for their collections and services.

Records management programs are a crucial part of academic archives. Chapter 5 examines how records management programs work within an academic environment, how to launch or revamp a records program, the importance of records management programs, and their relationship with an academic library's archival program.

Without a clear collecting policy, academic archivists run the risk of overextending their programs and duplicating the efforts of others. Chapter 6 describes why and how academic archivists define their collection scope and some of the internal and external sources they might target for collection building. These sources can document a wide variety of campus functions, its history, and other non-campus historical topics that support the mission of the institution, the academic curriculum, and the archival program.

Processing, organizing, and managing collections is the focus of Chapter 7. It describes the steps of accessioning, the common procedures for processing collections, and how academic archivists manage their collections and spaces. These "behind-the-scenes" activities also include preservation and conservation concerns, providing security, disaster planning, and creating tools for discovery such as archival finding aids.

Chapter 8 examines the public face of academic archives and the people who use them. More than just delivering efficient reference service, academic archivists must target their users, prioritize their services, develop and assess instructional sessions, create a public awareness for the program, and work closely with others in the library to ensure consistency.

Chapter 9 describes complicated technological issues faced by academic archivists, including managing electronic records, digital projects, providing online access to archival collections, and virtual collaboration with others. As more information becomes available electronically, academic archivists have adapted to technological shifts and obsolescence. The ability to harness the power of new technologies for greater public services, program awareness, and outreach efforts offers academic archivists great challenge and opportunity.

The final section consists of one chapter and is focused on the future. Chapter 10 reviews emerging trends in academic archives and describes the future of the subfield. Changing technology, research needs, and the role of the academic library in the campus community are significant factors in understanding the trends of the next decades. Academic archives programs that exhibit an understanding of collaboration, academic libraries, the emphasis on usage and access, the need for resource sharing in difficult budget climates, digital endeavors, and awareness building, are better able to function within their institution and thus find appropriate channels to create opportunities. This final chapter, more than any other, offers readers a window into the next generation of college and university archives, records, and special collections.

The book is not about the past; it is about the future. Today's academic archives are much more than repositories for institutional history and official records. In recent years, the mission of many academic archives has expanded to include collecting other formats and research areas, reaching a much broader audience of researchers, and taking a more active role in serving the information needs of the campus community. Recent trends in academic libraries have had many positive effects on the evolution of academic archives. In 2012, academic archives represent a dynamic subfield poised to influence many changes on campus, within academic libraries, and across the archival and related professions. The next generation of academic archives programs will be built on technological advances, a new array of campus and library resources, born-digital collections, collaborative partnerships that share and best utilize resources, and the skills of professional archivists with broad experience and training.

Acknowledgments

My interest in archival work emerged from a love of primary sources, research, history, and organizing information. I have University of Louisville history professor Thomas C. Mackey to thank for pushing me toward a career in history that best utilized my talents as a researcher. Solid training at the University of Maryland's College of Library and Information Services (CLIS) put me on the road to a career in libraries and archives. While the name of the college may have changed, those of us who chose Maryland for our archival education will always know it as CLIS, and as the preeminent program for archival training.

My first steps as a professional archivist were guided by retired CLIS professor Bruce W. Dearstyne. He taught me that archivists are managers, leaders, and sometimes visionaries. His courses emphasized user needs, effective approaches to archival appraisal, and how to run an archives program without running away the archivists. Instead of merely trying to dazzle students with stories from the archival trenches, he presented us with the realities, challenges, and opportunities for archivists in the twenty-first century. Over a decade after I finished library school, he contacted me without any warning to suggest that I write a book on archivists who work in higher education. He deserves praise for entrusting me with such an important project. I hope he finds my perspective on archivists working in college and university settings valuable.

Before embarking on this project I contacted a few of my professional colleagues. I have been fortunate to have the wise eyes of Kate Theimer, the founder of the ArchivesNext blog, David McCartney, University Archivist at the University of Iowa, and Betsey Pittman, the University Archivist at the University of Connecticut, to read my drafts and to improve the discussions of what academic archivists face on a daily basis. Other support came from members of the 2010 cohort of the Archives Leadership Institute, held at the University of Wisconsin in Madison. When I attended the program in July 2010 I had only completed the first chapters of this book, but what I took away from those discussions helped me move quickly on incorporating new ideas, practical approaches, and realistic situations into the text.

In early 2010 Neal-Schuman connected me with Sandy Wood as an editor and also a timekeeper. While not a trained archivist, she kept me on track and picked up on many things in my narrative that needed more explanation. Neal-Schuman also supported this project with editorial and production assistance, wise comments of outside reviewers, and great flexibility.

My few years in Blacksburg, Virginia, have been fruitful ones. My library colleagues, the archivists in our department, dean of libraries Tyler Walters, and retired dean of libraries Eileen Hitchingham, have provided me with an unyielding base of support and encouragement. The illustrations and graphics for the book could not have been completed without help from Marc Brodsky, public outreach and instruction archivist at Virginia Tech Special Collections. Kira Dietz, processing and acquisitions archivist at Virginia Tech Special Collections, also assisted with locating images. The interlibrary loan staff at Virginia Tech played an important role in gathering many of the sources for this book.

Most important in this endeavor, however, is the ongoing support from my family, especially from my wife, Laura, who understood that the benefits of this book far outweigh the many late nights of reviewing drafts and listening to my ideas on archives. This book is dedicated to her and her patience with an over-active and sometimes impatient academic archivist. Finally, I want to thank my six-year-old son, Sam, who frequently tells me that when he grows up he wants to be an archivist, just like his daddy.

Part I

Archives and the Academic Environment

1

The Path to Academic Archives

INTRODUCTION

Academic archivists are one of the largest groups of professional archivists. For the purposes of this book, academic archivists are defined as: professionally trained archivists, curators, records managers, special collections librarians, and digitization specialists who work within or are affiliated with an academic library. Their ranks are not limited to university archivists who work mostly with official records. Instead, academic archivists are part of a larger umbrella of professionals, who work in special collections departments, records management units, rare book libraries, audiovisual archives, and other repositories found within the academic environment. They provide access to unique or sometimes problematic materials for students, scholars, administrators, and the general public. The numbers of these archivists are growing; they are the budding leaders of academic libraries and the larger archival profession.

This chapter provides a description of the path to academic archives, who today's archivists are, and the challenges they face. It seeks answers to the following questions:

1. What is an academic archives program?
2. What is an academic archivist and how do I become one?
3. What are the expectations and opportunities for today's academic archivists?

DEFINING ACADEMIC ARCHIVES

Traditionally academic archives have consisted of an on-campus unit called the college or university archives, often situated within an academic library and sometimes part of a special collections department. Other archives programs had their origins within their school's upper administration, such as the president's office, or the public relations department. A college or university archivist led the initiative and focused on collecting official records and historical materials about their institution from campus and off-campus sources. These units had a strong connection to their school's records management program, either cooperating with a separate records management unit on campus or operating a records management program as part of the archives.

From these traditional origins, academic archivists carved out programs and services that best served their institution. Some archives programs focused on collecting official records, while other units expanded into the role of a campus information center concerned with the history of the institution. Archivists also diversified their reach, with many becoming records managers while others assumed the role as a college or university historian. At the professional level, college and university archivists active in the Society of American Archivists (SAA) formed the College and University Archives Section, which is one of the largest and most active sections of the organization. This group developed general guidelines for college and university archives in an effort to help clarify what an academic archives program does and the most common roles that academic archivists assume within their institutions (SAA, 2005).

During the past two decades several factors have redefined and broadened the definition of academic archives. First, technological developments have resulted in the creation of born-digital archival records, online tools for improved access to archival collections, and stronger connections between academic archivists and the campus constituencies that they serve (Burckel, 2008). The increased use of electronic methods of communication (e-mail and Web 2.0) and the creation of electronic-only documents has put the archives program in closer collaboration with records management programs and IT departments.

The need to collect and preserve electronic records and rescue digital records from obsolete formats

> **Reasons for Changing Definition of Academic Archives**
>
> - Technological advances and demands
> - Merged archives programs
> - Shrinking resources in academic libraries
> - Need for closer cooperation with records management units
> - Overlap of archival work into other fields and professions
> - Wider range of archival materials available

has fostered collaboration between academic archives and campus experts on computer systems, information technology, and systems administration (Tibbo, 2008). Rather than avoiding technological developments and the challenges of electronic records, academic archivists have taken an active role in using technology to provide greater access to material. Further, academic archivists were largely responsible for creating archival standards such as Encoded Archival Context (EAC), Describing Archives: A Content Standard (DACS), and Encoded Archival Description (EAD), which have greatly improved access to archival collections, in both electronic and paper formats.

In recent decades, academic archives have played a more prominent role within their libraries. The emphasis on research and the unique holdings of academic libraries have placed a higher value on archives and special collections departments. No longer are academic archives departments seldom visited "outposts" in a campus library, where only scholars once dared to tread. Instead, academic archives have developed instructional sessions and public programs that are integral parts of the outreach activities of their academic library. Acquiring, processing, and providing access to archival collections, which were often behind-the-scenes activities, now involve other departments in the library, such as technical services, development, reference and instruction services, and digital library departments. As a result of this new interest, other library departments are much more aware of what academic archives have to offer.

However, interest in academic archives from library leaders has not been enough to overcome the challenge of fickle allocation of resources. Private fundraising has been one approach to offset the costs of expanding services, renovating public and collection storage spaces, building new collecting areas, and creating new programs in academic archives. Merging and integrating academic archives programs into larger units such as a special collections department has become a common approach to balancing library resources and operational demands. In many academic libraries, archival materials are available through one public reading room or through one main webpage, instead of through scattered physical and virtual spaces in the library. As a result, academic archives have become an important segment of the research library concept, which provides researchers access to official records, archival materials, other primary sources, numerous formats, and secondary sources. Finally, cost-cutting measures have brought records management programs closer to academic archives, either as collaborators or as merged units.

Academic archives programs have responded to the call from archivists, institutions of higher education, and the research community to document a wider range of voices and perspectives. Many archives programs collect far beyond the official records of their institution by actively seeking material from unscheduled departments, student and campus organizations, papers from faculty, collections from alumni, and items from dealers. Many programs collect off-campus material, such as historical collections related to the nearby town or community or prominent subjects that directly support their institution's academic mission. This expansion has diversified the topics, viewpoints, and formats found in the collections of academic archives. By collecting a fuller range of resources, academic archives document a wider swath of campus life, provide researchers with a fuller picture of history, and support collection uniqueness in academic research libraries (Burckel, 2008).

In the past few decades, academic archives have changed tremendously and are no longer on the periphery of their campus and the archival profession. Academic archives programs have the ability to influence their campus, their library, their researchers, and their archival peers. These programs contribute to the development of new technology, services and outreach in academic libraries, national archival standards, integrated library and campus functions, and documentary techniques to better understand the institution's history.

The role and presence of academic archivists in the past few decades has been just as noticeable as the changes in academic archives. The once small field of academic archives has emerged as a significant area of archival study, even though there are few sources and no known organized courses offered on the subject. The duties of academic archivists have grown to encompass other aspects of documenting their campus. In the process, academic archivists are no longer the traditional college or university archivist. In fact these titles do not adequately reflect their responsibilities, talents, and integrated nature of their work.

Today's academic archivists include those working as special collections librarians, records managers, reference archivists, manuscripts processors, curators of collections, and, of course, college and university archivists. Whatever

---

Types of Professionals Working in Academic Archives

- College or university archivists
- Special collections librarians
- Records managers
- Reference archivists
- Processing archivists
- Outreach archivists and librarians
- Curators
- Rare books experts

their official title or designation, these professionals work within an integrated framework that involves other library and information professionals in many departments and at many administrative levels across campus. The majority of academic archivists work within an academic library. Most often they work within large merged departments, such as special collections and archives units, rather than as a stand-alone archives program. Academic archivists are well poised for library and professional leadership because of their understanding of the research process, strong skills in providing access to nonstandard library resources, connections to campus departments and donors, and technical expertise. While the efforts of academic archivists are often unrecognized and misunderstood by many on campus, these professionals have become an integral part of academic libraries, the college and university community, and the archival profession.

PREPARING FOR ARCHIVAL WORK IN THE ACADEMIC ENVIRONMENT

Academic archivists face the same challenges as other archivists. Changing technology, decreasing funding, heightened user expectations, and strong competition within the job market have become common realities for archivists of the twenty-first century. A combination of graduate education and practical experience has become the most common path to archives, especially for those entering the ranks of academic archives. The best way to prepare for working in an academic archives environment is to understand the changing face of the profession and recognize how those trends affect the work of academic archivists. That big-picture perspective of archival work in the academic environment will help better prepare the academic archivists of today and tomorrow.

A Snapshot of A*CENSUS

The best overview of today's incoming archivists and the profession as a whole comes from the 2004 A*CENSUS survey. Supported by a grant from the Institute of Museum and Library Services (IMLS), this 2004 survey provides a fascinating snapshot of a changing field. Of the 12,000 archivists solicited, just over 5,600 responded, which puts the survey at a respectable 47.2 percent response rate (Walch, 2006). Most important for this discussion is that the majority of the survey's respondents

(36 percent) came from archivists working in academic settings; the second largest group came from government archivists (32 percent) (Walch, 2006). Those figures indicate that academic archivists may in fact be the largest group of professional archivists, or at the very least those figures support that academic archivists are the largest group within SAA. The survey gives a solid overview of today's academic archivists (their backgrounds, their education, and their working experiences). But more important for this discussion, the results of that far-reaching study frame the common questions of how to prepare for academic archival work and which challenges affect their work.

> **Demographics of A*CENSUS Survey**
>
> - 12,000 archivists solicited, just over 5,600 responded, 47.2 percent response rate
> - Academic (36 percent) and government archivists (32 percent)—the two largest groups
> - 2/3 of profession female, with 4 in 5 archivists under age 30 being female
> - 1/2 of profession over age 50
> - Only 7 percent minority archivists, up from past surveys but still far too low
> - Over half reported that archives was not their first career
> - Nearly 3/4 hold a master's degree; 15 percent hold two master's degrees
> - Decline in number of PhD holders

The survey assessed the demographics of the archival profession and compared its findings to previous surveys. One of the most remarkable trends is the gender shift. In 1956, historian and archival educator Ernst Posner surveyed the archival profession and he reported that of the respondents, 67 percent were male and 33 percent were female. However, the 2004 survey recorded the complete reverse with 34 percent male and 64 percent female respondents (Walch, 2006). Figure 1.1 compares the results of the two surveys. Those numbers are even more striking when looking at the age of the survey group. The survey groups respondents into five-year age categories, beginning with under the age of 25 and ending with the age of 65 and over. Female archivists are the majority in all of these age groups. Most striking, for all respondents under the age of 30 beginning their first archival job, nearly four out of five are female (Walch, 2006).

In addition to pinpointing the significant gender shift, the survey's breakdown of archivists according to age and experience reveals other significant trends of the profession. Most striking is the large numbers of archivists approaching retirement age. Nearly half of the survey's

Figure 1.1
Gender in the Archives Workplace

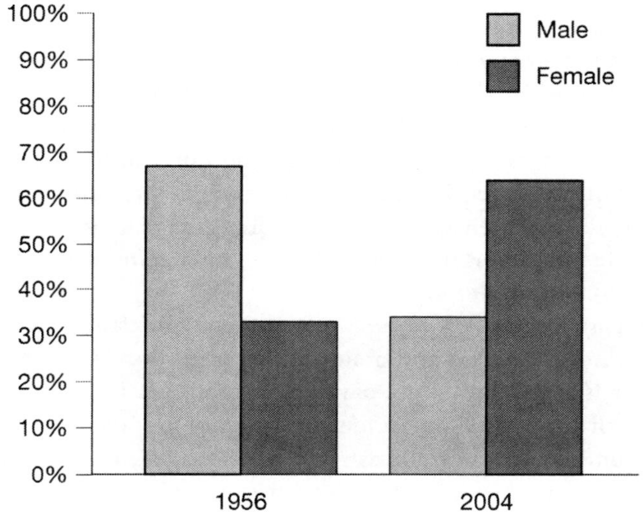

Source: Graphic by Marc Brodsky; data from Walch, 2006.

respondents were over 50 years of age, more than one-third were be-tween the ages of 45 and 60, and the approximate mean age was 48 (Walch, 2006). While some of the archivists in these age groups are beginning second or even third careers, a majority have been practicing archivists for at least two decades. These age trends are not unlike other professions, but the problem is that there are too few incoming archi-vists, and even fewer archival educators, to replace the large numbers of archivists who will retire in the next two decades.

Generational Waves

Approximately every 30 or 40 years the archival profession experiences a significant generational transition. In the twentieth century, the last major influx of archivists and archival programs occurred in the 1970s. That wave of new professionals challenged the archivist-historian ap-proach to entering the workforce, as many attended library schools in-stead. During that period, archivists took special interest in documenting diversity, the underrepresented, and social movements. The bicentennial celebrations of the decade created not only new interest in the nation's history, but led to the founding of many new historical societies, museums, and special collections departments on college and university campuses. Those new repositories provided incoming archivists their first professional experiences and opportunities to define their archival programs. But today that generation of archivists and their predecessors are nearing retirement age. Many of these now "graying" archivists rose to supervisory roles or entered the teaching ranks to train future archivists. In both cases their institutional knowledge, their understanding of archival work, and their experience building and managing archival collections must somehow be conveyed to the next generation of archivists moving into and up the ranks.

In the early twenty-first century, the archival profession is undergoing another wave of interest and generational transition. An influx of new professionals is redefining the parameters of archival training and practices. Not all are twenty-somethings fresh out of graduate school; in fact, a large number of new archivists are middle-aged, transitioning from many years in another job field. The survey reported that archival work was not the first career choice for 58 percent of all respondents (Walch, 2006). Many of these "accidental archivists" bring valuable job experience from the corporate or business world into their work as archivists. Another trend is that the numbers of minority archivists have grown in the past two decades, from 2.8 percent in 1982 up to 7 percent in 2004 (Banks, 2006). The percentage, however, is woefully low for a field that attempts to document underrepresented groups.

Building on the trends from the 1970s generation, graduate training has become the primary entry point to the profession. The 2004 survey reported that 71 percent of respondents hold at least one master's degree, and 15 percent hold two (Walch, 2006). For the profession as a whole, there is no predominant master's degree program. However, for the newer archivists just entering the field and for the specific group of academic archivists, the master's degree in library and information sciences is the most common credential. The number of archivists with PhDs has declined since the 1980s, largely because fewer newly minted PhD historians take a direct path to the archival profession, and because academic libraries and government archives have embraced the concept that a master's degree is in fact the terminal degree. These new archivists are perhaps more technologically savvy than the previous generations of archivists; however, this new group may not have as much subject knowledge or historical research experience as their predecessors.

Pressing Trends for Today's Archivists

As a response to this transition, archival leaders have identified several areas for improvement of the archival profession. The survey data indicates that the top priorities for the profession are recruitment of new practitioners to replace retiring archivists; attracting archivists who represent and reflect the diversity of society at large; strengthening technical skills; and transferring existing archival knowledge and values to the next generation of archivists (Walch, 2006). To address these challenges, the survey investigators suggest that archival leaders should: expand continuing education and delivery options; ensure the viability of graduate archival education by recruiting more archival teaching faculty; and maintain an active statistical record of archivists, repositories, and archival collections (Walch, 2006).

All of these trends and action items are relevant for academic archivists, with the issue of incoming and outgoing professionals being one of the largest. In the past decade, a large number of archival positions have been advertised and filled. The most notable turnover has been at the entry and senior administrative levels. The number

> **Trends and Challenges from A*CENSUS Survey**
>
> - Recruiting and training new practitioners to replace retiring archivists
> - Attracting archivists who represent and reflect the diversity of society at large
> - Strengthening technical skills
> - Transferring existing archival knowledge and values to the next generation of archivists
> - Expanding continuing education and delivery options for training
> - Recruiting more archival teaching faculty
> - Maintaining an active statistical record of archivists, repositories, and archival collections

of applicants for entry-level academic archivist positions has been rapidly increasing. In this case, the supply of jobs is much less than the demand. While large numbers of recent library and information school graduates with some kind of archival training are seeking their entrance into the academic ranks, funding for professional positions has been decreasing. In many institutions when archivists vacate a position, a lack of funding or interest from the administration may make it impossible to refill. The salaries from those unfilled positions may be used for other purposes or different positions, with the too-common reality that the salary line for an academic archivist disappears.

At the other end of the spectrum, a large number of department heads, directors, and archivists in deanship roles have recently changed positions or retired. This turnover creates great transition for the repository or program, for all the associated librarians, archivists, and records managers, and for the on-going continuity of the collections themselves. The demand for effective leaders in academic archives has far exceeded the supply. Some of this is due to the fact that a large number of mid-level academic archivists have been in "comfortable" and satisfying positions and are not interested in moving up into a more administrative role. At the same time many mid-level academic archivists have not been allowed enough opportunity to gain administrative experience in their current roles. Without some kind of mentoring or grooming from supervisory archivists, most mid-level academic archivists are unable to rise to the new challenges that are only accessible by having the right kinds and amounts of professional experiences. As a ripple effect, without mid-level archivists moving up or moving on from their positions (which would most likely be reclassified and refilled as an entry-level position), there is a logjam for incoming archivists and an absence of new senior administrative archivists to lead programs.

Improving education and training seem to be the simplest answers to the interconnected problem of recruitment and advancement for academic archivists. The number of applicants for entry-level archivist positions has grown concurrently with the increasing number of library and information schools offering archival training. While the 2004 survey called for increased numbers of archivists, it also called for increased quality of archival education. Quite simply there are too many institutions claiming to offer students a graduate degree program with a strong archival component. In fact most of these graduate programs provide no more than two or three courses devoted to archival work, and those courses are usually taught by adjuncts and not by tenure-track faculty within the department. This lack of course offerings is a significant problem in gaining basic archival skills and more advanced technical training. For prospective archivists, it is important to not only choose a graduate program with a demonstrated focus in archives, but to make sure that the archival concentration is being led by a full-time faculty member. The best programs have two full-time archival educators and also offer archives courses in appropriate topics taught by knowledgeable adjunct instructors. These archives-centric courses will expose students to big-picture issues such as electronic records, archival standards, repository management, appraisal and processing theory, and records management functions.

First Steps to a Career in Academic Archives

The lack of a recognized degree in archives in the United States makes an American Library Association (ALA)–accredited library degree from a program with a recognized archives track the best option for future academic archivists. All library school programs require every student to complete a core curriculum for librarianship, focused on reference, cataloging, and technology (all valuable skills for academic archivists). Thereafter, students attending a library school with an archives concentration can take mostly, if not all, archives-related courses to best prepare for the profession. Any available course on records management will also be useful for academic archivists, as many institutions operate their university archives concurrently with a records management program. Courses that require students to complete group or individual projects at repositories are excellent methods to gain practical experience. To expand their breadth of knowledge, future academic archivists should consider taking library courses that focus on academic librarianship, collection development, website and database design, and management. Library school can be a rich experience for future archivists, especially if the student already knows that they want to focus in academic archives.

Most academic library searches list a MLS as a minimum requirement, meaning that candidates without that credential will not even be considered for the position. The tightened job market for academic archivists makes the choice of graduate programs and available practical experiences even more important. The advice of many librarians that "it doesn't matter where you go to get your library degree as long as you get it," does not ring true for archivists heading off to library school. Picking a recognized program with well-known faculty and a solid curriculum carries great weight with job search committees. Choosing a program with access to nearby archival repositories is another important consideration. Institutions with several on-campus archives or with other nearby colleges and universities, increases the chance of landing practical experience in an academic archives. The best graduate archival programs offer students potential work opportunities as student assistants, funded graduate assistants, internships, field placements for course credit, or even as volunteers.

For incoming academic archivists, gaining practical archival experience is crucial. Too often graduate students in library schools focus on archival theory and may complete their program without ever processing a collection or writing a finding aid. Whether gained during a graduate program or outside of formal education, practical archival experience should include facets of technology, archival arrangement and description, reference service, and interaction with other archivists. A diversity of experience may require work at more than one repository. At the least, all future academic archivists should have the experience of processing archival collections, writing an EAD-compliant finding aid, answering incoming patron requests by researching in the collections, shelving materials, and shadowing an experienced archivist. The best practical experiences provide student exposure to the realities of archival work; the worst practical experiences put students in front of a photocopier to languish.

Having the right balance of education and practical experience is the clearest path to academic archives. While archival training through an ALA-accredited library school is not the perfect solution to the issues of archival education it has become the preferred method of entry into academic archives. At the very least, completing a library program will provide new archivists with a greater understanding of the user's needs, using technology to create access to information, the reference process, the importance of standardization, and the vocabulary of librarianship. Having that degree will make it easier for academic archivists to connect with their library

> **A Common Path to Academic Archives**
>
> - ALA-accredited master's degree in library and information science
> - Master's degree with an archival concentration
> - Practical archival experience
> - Strong technical skills
> - Understanding of the academic environment
> - Familiar with the trends in academic libraries

colleagues and to be recognized by the faculty as a professional. Completing a library degree is a solid choice for those with a subject master's degree or even a PhD, as it demonstrates their commitment to the field of academic archives. For nonarchivists who have a library degree the best way to transition into archival work is to gain practical experience working in academic archives and taking basic archives courses and workshops.

Archivists United

Regardless of age, gender, and education, we are all twenty-first-century archivists. The 2004 A*CENSUS survey provides us with valuable data

about the present state of the profession and it also challenges us to prepare the future leaders. Impending retirements, technological shifts, and
the need to better document the whole of society are just a few of the
significant challenges for archivists. On college and university campuses
a new wave of archivists are addressing those larger challenges. Unlike
other archival settings, the academic environment offers these archivists
unparalleled opportunities to collaborate with faculty in other departments, students, library colleagues, and institutional leaders. While
education and practical experience prepares archivists for the academic
setting, the first significant hurdle is to actually secure a position as an
academic archivist.

EXPECTATIONS AND OPPORTUNITIES FOR ACADEMIC ARCHIVISTS

Once on the job and on campus, academic archivists realize that their
work and profession is ever changing. In addition to remaining current
on developments in the archival world, academic archivists must follow
trends in higher education, technology, and research. Academic archivists
are part of the institution's professional workforce and must be committed
to the larger purpose of higher education: to promote inquiry, research,
and scholarship. At all levels of experience and responsibility, academic
archivists are expected to contribute to the institution, the profession,
and to the scholarly community. In many academic institutions, academic
archivists are part of the tenure-track system and are measured in the
same areas of other campus faculty. While making progress in their daily
work and becoming active scholars, academic archivists are also expected
to continue their education and develop their skills. These core values of
ongoing education, scholarly pursuits, and professional involvement form
the building blocks of academic archival work.

Continuing Education and Training

Ongoing training for new and well-seasoned archivists has become much
more of a necessity in the past decade. Changes in technology and
standards have made it imperative to seek new training and education.
The results of the 2004 A*CENSUS survey confirmed the importance
of continuing education for professional archivists. For those without
a master's degree, continuing education or self-instruction remains the
primary method of education. But even for archivists with a master's

degree, participation in formal training or continuing education programs is on the rise. The survey reported that nearly two-thirds of the respondents listed some kind of continuing education as their most recent form of archival education (the remainder listed graduate school as their last form of education) (Zimmelman, 2006). According to the survey, the largest barrier to continuing education for archivists is cost, but many institutions and professional organizations are overcoming that barrier by selecting training opportunities that can be administered through webinars, self-directed tutorials, or distance education programs (Zimmelman, 2006).

The survey suggests that because continuing education is so important for archivists, national and regional groups should offer training opportunities in both core and specialized areas. Archivists must also look to other fields for training in areas that are intersecting their work. Technological training workshops including managing electronic records, and creating finding aids using standards such as Encoded Archival Description (EAD), Encoded Archival Context (EAC), and Describing Archives: A Content Standard (DACS), are in great demand. Basic archival skills programs devoted to topics such as preservation, copyright law, arrangement and description, and managing repositories are constantly being updated and remain popular. National and regional professional organizations, especially SAA, have a wide range of training workshops, preconferences, and multiday or even week-long sessions to provide archivists with continuing education. Other related professional groups, such as ALA, offer training sessions in photographic restoration, digital projects, leadership, and collection development, all relevant programs for archivists, especially those working on a college or university campus. Specialty programs such as Rare Book School at the University of Virginia offer archivists a range of continuing education programs, including courses on the history of printed materials, digitization for archivists, and fundraising training.

> **Continuing Education and Professional Development**
>
> - Technical training programs
> - Basic archival skills workshops
> - Related skills programs outside of archives field
> - Professional programs offered at home institution
> - Formal graduate programs supported by home institution

By being part of an institution directly involved in the educational process, academic archivists have unique access to opportunities for ongoing education and training. Some academic libraries offer their employees internal training programs to help cross-train their faculty across departments, but the opportunities outside of the library or department are even more significant. Colleges and universities sponsor training programs in a variety of areas, such as management courses, instruction on using software programs, working with donors and fundraising, and learning how to design departmental budgets. These programs not only provide important skills, but allow academic archivists to network with other faculty and staff, represent their department, and explain to others the work of archivists.

Formal graduate programs are another alternative for academic archivists. While institutional policies vary, many college and universities offer tuition assistance for their employees. This very attractive perk makes it possible for an archivist with a MLS to begin work on a second master's degree in a subject area such as history, a technology-based program such as computer science, or even an MBA or a PhD degree program. Being a part-time student and a full-time archivist is a difficult balance, but having additional credentials beyond the standard "terminal" MLS degree allows upward mobility, increased responsibility, and an expanded skill set. Extra degrees and training do not ensure a salary increase, but may lead to a more diverse role with different responsibilities and opportunities for development.

Evaluation and Performance

As with other professionals, academic archivists undergo annual evaluations and work with their supervisor to set new goals and expectations. Employees should be evaluated on clearly documented expectations, such as an annual work plan, rather than last-minute or previously undisclosed documents that appear at the time of evaluation. While the process and rubrics for evaluation varies by institution, the most common areas for review are job performance, research, and service. Measuring job performance is by far the most important part of the review. Simply put, an archivist must meet the basic expectations of their job and demonstrate progress in their position. Without appropriate attention to the major responsibilities of their job, academic archivists are unable to meet the other professional demands of research and service.

Evaluations of job performance are especially crucial in the first few years of an archivist's career. Archivists who receive poor or mediocre assessments of their work should seek assistance from others in the department, the institution, or the profession. While mastery of an academic position can take time, new archivists typically have a very short probationary period to demonstrate their skills. Seasoned archivists with more job security should also strive to focus on their daily work before other obligations. Poor evaluations of job performance may indicate that the archivist is not meeting potential or that he or she is not the best fit for that position. Other times, poor job reviews stem from miscommunication or personality conflicts. If a case of extreme inequity is demonstrated during a performance review, the archivist should carefully seek remediation or appeal the decision to the institution. Archivists who manage archivists should take serious precautions to be professional, equitable, and honest during employee evaluations. Clearly communicated expectations and goals make the evaluation process much easier and more effective.

Criteria for Evaluation

- Job performance
- Research, publications, and professional involvement
- Service to the institution, profession, and academic community

The job duties of academic archivists cover a wide range and will be discussed in greater detail in later chapters. Most commonly, archivists will be responsible for a combination of reference duties, processing collections, and digital projects. Many archivists will assume the duties of a records manager, by working with campus office and departments to schedule materials for retention or disposition. Some positions will include direct supervision of students, staff, volunteers, and other faculty. Depending on the position and institution, a teaching component may be part of an academic archivist's responsibilities. For example, a public services archivist responsible for outreach and exhibits may also be asked to teach introductory sessions to graduate students on how to conduct archival research. Other positions may focus on donor work and fundraising, collection development, records management, grant-funded projects, leading a research program for scholars, or planning public programs. The best positions offer archivists a wide range of responsibilities, opportunities for growth, and the ability to define and redefine their work.

Developing a Research Agenda and Producing Scholarship

Academic archivists are expected to perform their duties while being active scholars and professionals. Similar to teaching faculty on the campus, academic archivists are responsible for engaging the scholarly community through publications, presentations, and other forms of research. The amounts and kinds of scholarly research for archivists vary by institution; however, new and seasoned archivists should expect to develop and maintain a research agenda throughout their careers. Many second-career archivists may enter the field with a pre-existing research interest, often in a subject outside of librarianship, such as history or English. Because librarianship has become so interdisciplinary, taking a more subject-based research project is common and often preferred. Archivists who came to the profession because of their own love of research or have a subject master's degree may have few problems meeting this expectation, but they may have difficulty limiting their area of study. Archivists from a technical or a library background may prefer to conduct research that involves user studies, assessment tools, and practical analyses. Combining library, technical, and research skills is the most effective approach to scholarly engagement.

Developing a research agenda can be daunting for all archivists, regardless of their background or research interests. However, academic archivists are not alone in the research world. Most research libraries sponsor some kind of mentoring program, whether formal or informal, for library faculty. Collaborators may also come from outside the library in the form of faculty who are already working on related research and need assistance from a trained archivist. One example of such collaboration would be with an English professor who is interested in scanning eighteenth-century poetry and creating a website for scholars to meet and discuss the original sources. Archivists with a background in English and an understanding of digitization could easily become part of such a project, and later publish or present about their role in the project for various professional audiences. Some archivists may choose to complete their own projects without collaborators, but one caveat is that research can take many years to complete and additional years to show results. If academic archivists are in a tenure-track position with a limited probationary period, they must work quickly to produce some kind of evidence of their research.

The most beneficial research projects for academic archivists relate to some aspect of their jobs and generate a large amount of material or data that can be used in many ways for many audiences. A large research initiative should have the expected results of a publication, a presentation, funding sources, and possible expansion into other areas. Using the above example, an archivist should consider writing a short article about working with humanities faculty for an archival newsletter, writing a co-authored article on literary analysis of online poetry for a peer-reviewed interdisciplinary journal, or writing a chapter on archival digitization experiences for a book, blog, or website. Research and writing demonstrate the ability to communicate effectively in print, but an enormous time lag occurs in publishing. Presenting that same material to audiences at professional conferences is a much faster way to deliver results and demonstrates the ability to effectively communicate to the scholarly community. Again, the different parts of the project can be presented at a campus research event, at a regional archives meeting, or at a national humanities conference.

Scholarly research can be disseminated in a variety of ways. Within the academic community, peer-reviewed publications are the most valued. Books published by university presses and mainstream commercial publishers rely on outside reviewers to assess the quality of the work. In most cases the reviewers are anonymous and in many cases the authors remain anonymous to the reviewer. By preserving anonymity, the book manuscript can be reviewed in a much more unbiased way without personal or professional conflict of interest. Academic journals also follow the same peer-review protocol for selecting articles. Writing peer-reviewed articles is most often the expectation for academic archivists, but archivists may author academic books or chapters in edited volumes. Other kinds of publishing such as book reviews, solicited articles in non-peer-reviewed journals, encyclopedia articles, essays for popular press publications such as a school's alumni magazine, and internal publications are also worthwhile. For academic archivists unsure about how much and where to publish, the best approach is to present your research in a variety of ways for different audiences. While peer-reviewed publications are the most highly recognized by the academic community, supplementary publications in other forms demonstrate a range of abilities and scholarship.

> **Professional Engagement**
>
> - Developing a research agenda
> - Collaborating with colleagues
> - Publishing peer-reviewed books or articles
> - Presenting at national, regional, and local conferences
> - Serving in a leadership role in a professional organization
> - Serving on college or university committees
> - Serving on library committees

Service to the Profession, the Institution, and the Community

Academic archivists are also expected to contribute to the profession and to their campuses through service activities. Professional conferences allow archivists to network, exchange ideas, collaborate on projects, and learn about new trends and developments. But one of the most important parts of scholarly conferences is the meeting of committees, roundtables, sections, and other sub-groups of the membership. National organizations, such as SAA and ALA, have numerous subgroups, while regional and state groups are much flatter organizations. Just like determining a research agenda, archivists should choose service obligations that relate directly to their jobs or professional interests. As a possible example, entry-level academic archivists might find their service time best spent on committees for regional groups such as New England Archivists or the Society of California Archivists while veteran archivists might find a leadership role in a SAA section or roundtable more useful. At some point most archivists will serve on temporary committees, such as nominating or election subgroups. The work of those short-term groups can be tedious and sometimes called "thankless" work, but the experience is valuable for archivists at all levels.

Service to the institution is another important expectation for academic archivists. All research libraries have standing committees that work on issues such as governance, promotion, digital initiatives, collection development, and administrative policies. An appointment or election to these groups can yield important insights into the internal workings of a library. Serving alongside library colleagues and representing the department may be just as important as the accomplishments of the committee. Participation in more short-term internal committees, such as a position search or a special task force, means a great deal of sudden work, but oftentimes the results are greater than the work of a permanent committee. Larger departments may have subgroups working on projects, policies, or technology. Committee work allows archivists to serve with library colleagues from different departments and to interact with people that they may never work with directly in their jobs.

Beyond the walls of the library are innumerable service opportunities. Each campus has its own method of governance, policy creation, and oversight. Some have formal committees or commissions, while others have groups at the college or school level that are opened to members from external departments. Service on university or college committees is often considered part of campus outreach, which for librarians and archivists means ongoing interaction with other departments. For example, academic archivists may be part of a campus committee that discusses electronic records management practices. Work on a university committee exposes not only the archivist to other members of the faculty, but it passes along the message that academic archivists are professionals dedicated to the same principles of higher education.

The larger goal of professional engagement is central to ongoing education and being part of the scholarly community, but archivists must carefully balance research and service obligations with actual job duties. Many new archivists are afraid to say "no" to committee work or suggested research projects. The best advice is to consult with a mentor or supervisor and then pick commitments carefully, especially after reaching a critical mass of responsibilities. The overall expectation is that academic archivists find a balance between their daily work and their professional obligations, without losing sight of emerging changes. Although the challenges seem immense, academic archivists have the ability to create their own professional and research niche by simply doing their job each day.

CONCLUSION

Academic archivists are one of the largest subgroups of the profession, most often working in academic libraries. Their preparation for the field has come from graduate education and practical experience. In the past two decades a number of archival concentrations have emerged from within ALA-accredited library and information science programs. However, more qualified faculty members are needed in these programs to train the next generation of archivists. To remain relevant, today's academic archivists must be connected to trends in higher education, technology, academic libraries, and archives.

The overall expectation for academic archivists is to be an active part of the scholarly community, while continuing their education and professional development. Achieving goals and making progress in their daily work as an archivist is the first important part of that expectation. The second part of the equation is engaging with and contributing to the profession. Archivists do not have to be prolific scholars, but they do need to develop a research agenda, publish or present their findings, and collaborate on projects with other colleagues on campus and in the larger profession. Service opportunities are not to be taken lightly, especially being part of a search committee for a professional position.

Working as an academic archivist is an exciting and rewarding career choice. Being a member of the university or college community, alongside students, staff, and teaching faculty, has distinct advantages. It is defining the role of academic archivists within their institution that is the most challenging part. One of the best ways for academic archivists to broaden their perspective is to make strong connections with librarians and consider the evolving world of academic libraries in the information age. The next chapter looks at academic libraries and how archivists can play a role in determining that future.

REFERENCES

Banks, Brenda. 2006. "Special Section on A*CENSUS (Archival Census and Education Needs Survey in the United States): Part 6 A*CENSUS Report on Diversity." *American Archivist* 69, no. 2 (Fall/Winter): 396–406.

Burckel, Nicholas C. 2008. "Academic Archives: Retrospect and Prospect." In *College and University Archives: Readings in Theory and Practice*, edited by Christopher J. Prom and Ellen D. Swain, 3–26. Chicago: Society of American Archivists.

Society of American Archivists. 2005. "Guidelines for College and University Archives." Society of American Archivists. Last revised May. http://www .archivists.org/saagroups/cnu/cuguide2005.pdf.

Tibbo, Helen. 2008. "The Impact of Information Technology on Academic Archives in the Twenty-First Century." In *College and University Archives: Readings in Theory and Practice*, edited by Christopher J. Prom and Ellen D. Swain, 27–51. Chicago: Society of American Archivists.

Walch, Victoria Irons. 2006. "Special Section on A*CENSUS (Archival Census and Education Needs Survey in the United States): Parts 1-3, Project Overview, General Data Analysis, and Highlights of General Data Analysis." *American Archivist* 69, no. 2 (Fall/Winter): 294–348.

Zimmelman, Nancy. 2006. "Special Section on A*CENSUS (Archival Census and Education Needs Survey in the United States): Part 5, Continuing Education." *American Archivist* 69, no. 2 (Fall/Winter): 367–395.

2

The Mission of College and University Libraries and Academic Archives

INTRODUCTION

Today's campus libraries are much more than the brick-and-mortar buildings, books on shelves, and sponsored websites with access to on-line databases and articles. Instead, academic libraries have embraced the concept of being information centers for their campuses and communities. The stereotypical view of campus libraries as a place for only serious scholars, with rows of dusty stacks, and prim-and-proper librarians shushing noisy patrons, has been replaced with a more service-oriented environment. Technology is the main engine for this change, with emerging trends consistently challenging the needs, equipment, and spaces in academic library buildings. A generation of forward-thinking library directors and deans has transformed academic libraries into relevant physical and virtual "places" for students and faculty. But one of their biggest challenges is to convey the importance of the library and its resources to the rest of the campus and the community. In a period of difficult economic times, academic libraries can no longer embrace the "if you build it they will come" attitude; the resources and services of a campus library are only as good as how well they are used and acknowledged by their patrons.

The majority of academic archivists work within a college or university library system, which makes it imperative for archivists to understand the larger picture of academic libraries. While graduate programs in library science may prepare archivists for understanding the work of librarians, few graduate programs offer insights into the inner workings of an academic library. Using technology to provide access to material is a shared issue for librarians and archivists, which indicates the importance of cooperation and shared understanding.

This chapter describes the current state of academic libraries and the most significant challenges. It will analyze how technological developments have redefined the role of the college or university library in the lives of students, faculty, and other users. The chapter includes discussion of library assessment, determining who the users are and what they want, and other current trends in academic libraries, with a particular focus on the issues that most affect academic archivists. This chapter seeks to answer the following questions:

1. What are academic libraries?
2. What technology needs does a campus library provide?
3. Which changes and trends in academic libraries most affect academic archives?

MODERN ACADEMIC LIBRARIES

At the beginning of the twenty-first century, academic libraries at colleges and universities across the nation share the common characteristic of frequent change in the face of uncertainty. The demands for more services, staff, online resources, and space are counterbalanced with shrinking resources. The needs of modern academic libraries are diverse, but there are a few concurrent trends that affect all of them, whether located within a research university, a military academy, or a liberal arts college. Academic archivists must understand these challenges in order to successfully position their departments to meet the larger goals of their academic library.

Generations of Users and Librarians

Understanding and reaching users is a primary component of librarianship. Likewise archivists must have some idea of the intended users and uses of the material that they are acquiring, arranging, describing, and to which they are providing access. Academic archivists and librarians have the further challenge of connecting with their primary users: students, graduate and undergraduate; teaching and research faculty; and other members of the campus community. Within that large population there are a variety of information needs. Secondary users of academic libraries may include local residents, genealogists, visiting scholars, and primary or secondary schoolchildren. Depending upon the mission of the institution, it may be difficult to determine exactly who the primary and targeted users are. For some academic libraries the primary audience is everyone, but a well-articulated statement of the primary user group from library administrators makes the goals of academic libraries much more achievable and manageable.

Recognizing the different generations of people who are part of a college or university campus is the first step to reaching primary and secondary library users. There are at least four distinct generations in society, and they are often in the library at the same time. These groups are roughly defined as the following: Veterans, born before World War II ended; Baby Boomers, born between 1945 and 1965; Generation Xers, born between 1965 and 1980; and the Millennials, born between 1980 and 2000 (Lancaster and Stillman, 2010). Scholars, sociologists, and human resource professionals indicate that the needs and skills of these four distinct generations are different.

> **The Predominant Generations of Academic Library Users**
>
> - Veterans
> - Baby Boomers
> - Generation Xers
> - Millennials

These four generational groups understand, approach, and use academic libraries in different ways. While the following are generalizations, it is important to recognize these patterns of academic library usage. Although most members of the Veteran generation are no longer in the workplace, as retirees or emeritus professors they are frequent users of library resources. Their research skills are often limited to print-only resources and have more trepidation with using computers and online sources. However, their campus connections and decades of using library resources should be respected.

The Baby Boomers are still very much a part of the academy, with many long-since tenured professors making frequent visits to the library. Many members of this group have embraced technology as a way to further their own research, and may recognize the library as an important access tool for information. Although professors have a tendency to retire much later than in other professions, large numbers of Baby Boomers will retire during the next decade, which may in fact bring them, physically and virtually, more often to the library.

Large numbers from the Generation X category work in the academic environment as professors, staff, administrators, and in technology positions. As retirements and departures occur, this group is likely to assume a more active role in their departments, colleges, schools, or offices. This computer-savvy generation continues to use the library, but they are increasingly more dependent on online library resources.

Currently, the Millennials are the largest group represented on college and university campuses. As students, this generation may have the least training with traditional library resources and may have an unclear understanding of the research process. However, the strength of the Millennials is their adoption of technology, online resources, and virtual communication—all key elements of the modern academic library. For most academic libraries, the students from this generation are heavy users of the library and are the primary audience.

These generational groups and patterns have enormous implications for those who work in an academic library, whether faculty or staff. As the Veterans and the Baby Boomers retire, there will be numerous positions at all levels to fill within college and university libraries. Most significant will be the retirement of library deans and directors, and the succession of new leadership and redefining programmatic priorities. Other key library positions in the areas of instruction, subject fields, systems, collection development, and human resources will also suffer great losses of institutional memory and practice. Perhaps one possible solution to this impending transition of leadership is that the experience of the Generation Xers can be complemented by the technological skills of the Millennials to redefine the purposes and services of academic libraries.

Identifying and Surveying Success

Academic archivists must be aware of how patrons use academic libraries in order to plan for services, collection building, access to materials, and patron needs. Since the middle of the twentieth century, academic libraries have relied on surveys and assessments to determine their effectiveness and measure their progress. Professional organizations, such as the Association of Research Libraries (ARL) and the American Library Association (ALA), collect wide sets of library data from members and institutions. These groups take the results and publish the collected data, making rankings, and summarizing emerging library trends. These surveys measure the inner workings of academic libraries (size of collections, numbers of employees, overall budgets, salaries, etc.) as well as the habits and needs of many of the targeted users of academic libraries. The published statistics help the leaders of academic libraries to recognize trends, make adjustments to their programs, and consider the work of their peer institutions.

In the past two decades, a significant increase occurred in the number of libraries participating in professional surveys, monitoring

Approaches to Library Assessment

- Focus groups
- Usability studies
- Online surveys
- Assignments with pre- and post-tests
- Tracking online usage

user behavior, and launching their own assessment initiatives. Most of the assessment programs in academic libraries began in-house during the early 1990s and were designed by librarians to help better understand their users and identify needed services (Wright, 2007). Librarians collected data using a variety of instruments including user studies, web usability testing, focus groups, in-person conferences with librarians, online assignments that featured pre- and post-tests, and software to track usage of electronic resources. By the early 2000s, many academic libraries had expanded their assessment activities by designating a coordinator for assessment, who planned for measuring and collecting, assessing the data, and then reporting the findings. Internally, the results of those studies could then be used to make programmatic changes to the academic library, such as re-vamping websites or adding new copying services for graduate students. Externally, the reported data could be used by other peer academic research libraries to design similar programs or implement new initiatives.

By the early 2000s, academic libraries embraced a more comprehensive evaluation tool to supplement their home-grown assessment activities and basic reporting of statistics. In 2000, 13 ARL libraries tested the quality of their services with an emerging assessment instrument called LibQual (Kyrillidou, Cook, and Rao, 2008). Developed by ARL and Texas A&M, the web-based LibQual survey collected data from participants about library perceptions, and measured the overall quality of library service. Following the success of the pilot program, LibQual surveys quickly became an annual event for academic libraries. Participants in LibQual surveys also have access to the data from other institutions, which makes it possible to recognize larger trends in users of libraries that could not have been gleaned from the results of other assessment tools, internal studies, or published annual statistics. Within only a decade, LibQual has become a standard assessment tools for academic libraries.

Collecting information about web usage and electronic downloads has become an important part of library assessment. Free tools such as Google Analytics and other tracking programs allow libraries to record much more than just visits to their websites. The results of Google Analytics data can lead to the elimination of unused electronic databases, conclusions on how to better structure and display information on the library's webpages, and identify clear patterns on peak times of use. While Google Analytics was primarily designed for business uses, academic librarians can use the program to gather large amounts of data about how virtual patrons are accessing the library's electronic resources and make decisions about collection development.

> **Areas of Assessment in Academic Libraries**
>
> - Physical facilities
> - Print and online collections
> - Library website, catalog, and databases
> - Reference and instructional services
> - Document delivery or interlibrary loan services
> - Number of employees, salaries, and their educational backgrounds

Whether collected by an internal or external survey mechanism, the most frequently assessed components of the academic library include: using the library's electronic resources and websites; access to computer equipment or software; the layout and design of the building; the number of study, quiet, group, and "comfortable" spaces in the library; the usefulness of reference and instructional services; available library collections; document delivery or interlibrary loan services; and overall satisfaction with, or quality of, the library. It is beneficial for academic archivists to understand these measurements, trends, and components of modern academic libraries, some of which will be discussed further in the following sections.

The Quest for Better Spaces

Today's students demand more usable and appealing library spaces for quiet study, group interactions, and examining library collections (Figure 2.1). As one result, academic librarians have focused their attention on viewing the library as "a place" (Aldrich, 2008). To make that transformation, librarians have embraced the concept of creating a learning or information commons—cleverly designed spaces in the library where students interact, learn, and collaborate, oftentimes over a cup of coffee.

Figure 2.1
Collaborative Library Space

Source: Photograph by the author.

For decades, academic libraries offered students standard amenities such as study carrels, a few rooms for group work, and access to computers with indexes and software. But during the past 20 years, two factors made librarians rethink the spaces in their buildings. First improved technology—better, faster, and cheaper—gave students instant access to much of the library's online resources from their own equipment or from a computer elsewhere on campus. Many students also perceived that Internet sources in general were "good enough" for their purposes. Thus the standard research visit to the library, while highly recommended by their instructors, became more optional for students. Second, other spaces for quiet study and group work appeared on campus. As a result, students found refuge elsewhere in renovated student centers, campus-operated coffee shops, or 24-hour study lounges in dormitories or other campus buildings.

Beginning in the late 1990s, academic librarians reconsidered their buildings, stacks, and floor plans to better accommodate the needs of students. New technologies required a different approach to library reference service and spaces, which has become known as the "commons" phenomenon (Cowgill, Beam, and Wess, 2001). Primarily aimed at undergraduates, the library commons movement consisted of several components, focused on redesigning spaces and rethinking the role of the library in providing students with access to technology and information resources. Librarians first selected a centralized place in the library, cleared the stacks, offices, etc., and refitted it with moveable and comfortable seating. Various floor plans, anchored by public access computers

> **Academic Libraries and the Commons Movement**
>
> - Create spaces for students to better interact with faculty and with technology.
> - Redesign and reconfigure spaces for user needs.
> - Combine reference service with technology assistance.
> - Provide comfortable seating, more computers, group study areas, and coffee shops.
> - Make collaborative agreements with information technology departments and others.

and at least one centralized service point, featured group study rooms and open tables for multipurpose use by students. As one result, more volumes from the reference and circulation collection found their way into off-site storage facilities or compact shelving units.

Many libraries added coffee shops and cafés near their commons area, which negated the decades-long concept that food and drinks are not allowed in libraries. In most cases, the institution planned to operate coffee service with some kind of cooperation with the library. Potentially large profits generated by coffee sales made such an endeavor attractive for vendors, the library, and the institution. User demand for meeting spaces and a coffee supply have made library cafés popular and informal gathering places for faculty and students. As library users filled these coffee shops, a subsequent demand for longer operating hours of the library increased, which is a reversal of the trend for fewer operating library hours because so many library resources are available electronically.

Another component of the commons concept is hands-on use of new technology to access information resources. Librarians working in the commons area focus on the technology and reference needs of the target user group, and are not restricted to the traditional confines of a centralized reference department. Oftentimes, a library commons is a collaborative venture between the library and the campus information technology department. Sharing new equipment with students, such as loaner laptop or iPad programs, is yet another way of integrating technology with a library commons.

By the mid-2000s many academic libraries redefined their information commons as learning commons. While similar, the latter designation indicates a more developed or mature approach to providing students with information technology and library services. In a learning commons, students have access to a number of previously separate services including computer support, library reference, writing assistance, tutoring, media services, and online resources (Seal, 2010). Such collaborations and centralization of related but often distant services located outside of the library, allow academic libraries to be a viable part of campus technology and the lives of students. While some detractors have described library commons as glorified computer labs with comfortable chairs, these collaborative spaces are heavily used in hundreds of academic libraries.

Academic Libraries and the Campus

Even academic libraries with broad missions focus the largest amount of resources on providing services and outreach to their campus constituencies. Rather than being a passive warehouse for print sources and workstations, academic libraries have increased their efforts to reach out to students, faculty, and staff. Academic libraries have become more attuned to the way that scholars and students interact with information, more focused on how information is structured and accessed, and more of a presence outside of the physical buildings than ever before (CLIR, 2008).

The most obvious form of library outreach is through the concept of librarians as liaisons to departments, programs, college, and other campus units. In these liaison programs, librarians develop strong ties to their faculty and students. Some liaison librarians are fully embedded within departments, often participating in departmental activities, maintaining office hours, advising students, and teaching courses (Williams, 2009). Other outreach programs involve library instruction for large numbers of students within each program. Simply put, academic libraries are being redefined as less of a physical location for students, staff, and faculty to visit. Rather, academic libraries offer their on-campus constituencies a cadre of resources, services, and tools that foster collaboration, learning, and research.

Maintaining and Building Collections

Even with comfortable seating and good coffee, academic libraries are still measured by their collections, both print and electronic. In only the past few decades, collection development activities have become a standard part of academic librarianship. Some institutions centralize their collection building through just a few or even one individual, while others distribute the work between subject-focused librarians. No matter what structure is used, collection development work is crucial to the relevance and sustainability of any academic library program. Collection development for academic archivists will be discussed in detail in Chapter 6, however, that work is impossible and limited without a fuller understanding of how academic libraries approach the complicated task of building collections. In particular, budget restraints and soaring costs of subscriptions for print and online materials, make collection development a careful balancing act for academic librarians and archivists.

During the 1970s, collection development emerged as a specific area of professional specialization for academic librarians (Johnson, 2004). These librarians took leadership roles in academic libraries and established collection development departments or distributed the work of selection to other librarians. Their work initially focused on selecting materials, managing budgets, and allocating funding to selecting titles. Collection development librarians assumed responsibility for conducting user assessment, gathering statistics on collection usage, developing outreach programs to academic departments, and planning for expansion of the collections. Collection development librarians also took the lead in determining the number and kinds of books, newspapers, microforms, journals, and other resources held by their institution. As a result, many academic libraries during the late twentieth century measured the quality of their collections by the number of volumes, often celebrating the addition of their one, two, or three millionth volume.

Publishers and book suppliers responded to the concept of bulk buying of titles for academic libraries. Book wholesalers and publishing groups developed the concept of designing "approval plans" for academic libraries, meaning that books are automatically sent to libraries based on their preferences—mission, budgets, programs, and publishers (Johnson, 2004). As part of the approval plans, librarians can review the titles (either from a generated list or by examining the books directly) and select titles that most fit their needs. Approval plans do not cover all selection activities by academic libraries, but a majority of printed books in academic libraries continue to be acquired through this process.

During the 1980s, collection development librarians expanded their work to include collection management. Instead of merely adding new titles, collection development librarians became responsible for canceling or renewing periodicals, weeding the circulating stacks, moving infrequently used titles to storage units, and taking responsibility for repairing damaged books (Johnson, 2004). To better manage their collections, collection development librarians conducted frequent surveys of their stacks to target the areas with the least and most growth. That data helped determine the available growth space for incoming titles, justified weeding and storage projects, and helped library administrators make arguments for more building space for library materials. Collection development librarians also relied heavily on national surveys, from ARL and ALA, to compare their budgets, expenditures, collections, and decisions to peer institutions (Casserly, 2008).

> **Collection Development Responsibilities for Academic Librarians**
>
> - Selecting printed sources, with help of an approval plan and selectors
> - Managing stacks, subscriptions, and collections budget
> - Evaluating electronic resources and aggregator databases
> - Negotiating with vendors
> - Exploring consortial projects to share costs and resources
> - Assessing user and collection needs

By the end of the twentieth century, the growth of electronic library resources had redefined the playing field of collection development librarianship. As commercial publishers began distributing their content online and companies developed databases for information resources, collection development librarians were increasingly dealing with intermediary vendors and not just with publishers. In an effort to maximize funding, these librarians developed their negotiation and budget skills, oftentimes developing interinstitutional collaborations and consortia to share expenses and resources. The costs of electronic resources quickly outpaced the allocation for print resources in shrinking library budgets. The commons movement of the past decade also resulted in fewer print volumes in main libraries to manage, which further directed collection development librarians toward managing and acquiring electronic resources.

Collection development responsibilities have grown far beyond simple selection of books, journals, and electronic resources. In today's academic library, collection development is still a very active part of professional librarianship. This work now includes more active promotion of the campus library through developing marketing strategies, stronger liaison services to departments, community outreach efforts, and consortial relationships. The management of the library's digital assets (either purchased through expensive subscriptions or home-grown digital collections) has become a large part of the collection development equation. The area of library assessment is also a growing area of responsibility for collection development librarians, especially the need to understand the information and technology needs of today's students. However, the more traditional part of collection development—refining an approval plan, allocating funding to selectors, trimming budgets without significant losses to program support, collection analysis in light of institutional needs, and monitoring the growth or contraction of the stacks—is a crucial part of understanding how library collections are growing and are being measured.

The Challenge of Support

Budget cutbacks and rising tuition have been an ongoing epidemic in higher education for decades. Academic libraries as a whole have learned to "do more with less," for more than a generation. ARL statistics during the past 20 years indicate that library budgets, numbers of full-time staff and faculty, and subscriptions (journals, serials, and databases) are generally declining. At the same time, user needs assessments and other surveys indicate increased demand for more library resources and assistance. Academic libraries have responded to these concurrent and divergent trends by seeking support from campus, local, state, and federal sources.

Historically, nearly all college and university libraries have relied primarily on annual appropriations from their institutions to pay their employees, buy new materials, and operate their buildings. In many cases these annual allocations gave libraries adequate funding to maintain their operations without significant gains or losses. Periods of economic prosperity brought more funding to campus libraries, while economic downturns often resulted in a decline of base budgets. This uncertain boom-and-bust cycle has resulted in a "slow growth" of library budgets, and an uneven expansion of library

Approaches to Academic Library Funding

- Petitioning state governments
- Cultivating private donors
- Working with a development officer
- Starting or maintaining a library friends group
- Appealing to alumni supporters
- Applying to federal or state grants
- Consortial partnerships with peer institutions

services and collections. Further, as other campus programs and emerging initiatives attracted attention and funding from the institution, campus libraries were often relegated to a lower level of priority. At the same time, many academic libraries have become over-dependent on institutional funding to support their operations.

Whether public or private, all institutions of higher education have learned to rely on alternative sources of funding to maintain their operations. Even in the best of economic times, academic libraries must develop outside funding sources to enhance their library operations. The most common approach to building other sources of funding at academic libraries is through private donations coordinated by the institution. Nearly all public and private colleges and universities have development or advancement departments—often separate entities loosely affiliated to the institution, such as an alumni foundation. Development had become a big business for colleges and universities. In the past few decades, fundraising campaigns have become a central part of campus activities with development departments coordinating the efforts.

The structure of development efforts in higher education varies, but the approach is generally to identify, court, and develop ongoing relationships with potential donors. Development departments work closely with alumni groups, business leaders, athletic supporters, and philanthropic organizations to first identify potential donors. Employees of development offices are generally assigned to colleges, schools, or specific programs within the institution, which means that identified donors are often assigned to individual development officers.

This standard approach to development often puts academic libraries at a disadvantage. First, since libraries do not sponsor academic programs there are technically no library alumni to court and no prebuilt constituency. The clever response to this reality is that "no one can graduate without using the library"; however, most alumni are devoted to their academic program, department, or college. Another challenge is that the assignment of a development officer to the campus library is a relatively recent trend, which means that most library development efforts are in their infancy. Many times development officers work for multiple departments or part of the campus, which may diffuse their efforts. Turnover in development positions is quite high, which makes it difficult to maintain consistency in a library development program. The concept of giving money rather than books to the library is a frequent point for library development officers to address. While donations of collections are welcomed, it is more desirable to secure donations of unrestricted funding, which can help cover costs of new acquisitions, initiate renovations, or even endow positions.

Libraries have other methods of fundraising that are unconnected to their institution. Some libraries have created national or regional advisory groups to help raise awareness and support fundraising. The library friends group is most common approach to supporting academic libraries through a noninstitutional group. These groups have traditionally organized events to showcase the collections, resources, people, and spaces of libraries. Library friends groups raise money for libraries through membership drives and collecting yearly fees. Such organizations can successfully locate potential donors not identified by development officers and help facilitate donations of collections and funding. One advantage of working with a library friends group is that those groups are nonprofit and noninstitutional, which allows them to generate funding through various events and then donate the proceeds to the library. Such unrestricted gifts can then be used by the campus library for purposes, programs, and equipment not covered by institutional funding. There are some disadvantages of library friends groups, most notably when leaders of the group attempt to dictate library priorities or have over-ambitious expectations. Further, the most active friends groups need library staff to coordinate activities and perform the work. On the whole, however, library friends groups are valuable programs for academic libraries.

Other external sources of funding for academic libraries include grants and collaborative programs. Funding for technology or computer equipment is often much easier to obtain from an outside source than a donation to purchase a new series of books. Federal agencies prefer to fund grant projects that include interinstitutional participation and cutting-edge technologies. However, many of those funded grants do not include support for hiring new staff to do the actual work. Staffing and finding spaces for such projects are left to the campus library to determine.

Regardless of where the funding originates—from a state legislature, a private board of trustees, a wealthy donor, or from a government agency—academic librarians must understand how their institution plans to spend its money. It is crucial for campus libraries to be connected to the larger initiatives of the institution, especially those projects that involve fundraising. Capital campaigns often exceed their goals, which may result in funding other efforts. In difficult budget times, campaigns may become the only source of financial relief for institutions facing significant cutbacks. It is crucial for academic librarians and archivists to understanding not only how to budget and spend money, but to understand the potential sources of new funding. Developing creative ways to cultivate new financial support will be a continuing trend in academic libraries.

TECHNOLOGY AND THE ROLE OF THE CAMPUS LIBRARY

While each library program is unique, today's academic libraries provide the students and faculty on their campuses with services, equipment, and assistance related to emerging technologies. The connections between libraries and campus technology units have grown strong during the past few decades. Some academic libraries have merged with technology departments, while others share service responsibilities and develop programs with other information professionals on campus. Students and faculty may not think of their campus libraries as the hub for technology assistance, but for many schools the library is the chief location for access to equipment and to professionals who are familiar with emerging technology.

Academic libraries face the uncertain challenge of remaining on the cutting edge of technology. While many librarians are early adopters of new technology, the expense of hardware, software, data migration, and subscription-based electronic resources make it difficult for all academic libraries to remain current. A few technological developments and approaches to sharing costs make it possible for many academic libraries to be an important part of information technology on campus and in the academic community. These recent trends are very relevant to academic archivists, who are often charged with using technology to provide a new generation of library users greater access to information resources.

Technology Trends in Academic Libraries

- Using Web 2.0 to communicate with students
- Integrating the best parts of search engines into library services and instruction
- Embracing open access for scholarly works
- Tempering the costs of commercial databases and subscriptions through collaboration
- Sharing the costs of technology with other partners
- Utilizing grant and outside funding for digital projects
- Building in-house digital expertise

Web 2.0 and Social Media

The explosion of the Internet in the 1990s brought new methods of seeking information and changed the way academic libraries approached reference work. Online access to information through database searches, links to full-text content, and greater capabilities for virtual reference mark some of the main features of modern reference services in academic libraries. As a continuation of this shift to a more online environment, during the past five years many academic libraries have utilized Web 2.0 technologies to better connect with their users.

In the mid-2000s a new suite of web-based tools and software made the Internet more interactive, user-driven, and networked. Web 2.0 technology approached communication as a collaborative endeavor. Through blogs, wikis, RSS feeds, Twitter updates, and podcasts, users could more readily receive, create, share, and comment on information (Theimer, 2010). Digital content, such as images and videos, could be widely shared in this more dynamic web environment. Websites such as YouTube, Flickr, and Delicious, allow users to post digital content for viewing, for comment from other users, and for storage. Social networking sites such as Facebook and MySpace quickly became international phenomena with millions of users. All of these sites and technologies could be accessed through new mobile smartphones, such as iPhones and Blackberries, which made communication more portable and instantaneous with Web 2.0.

Keeping current with these emerging technologies is challenging, but colleges and universities are excellent testing grounds for such experimentation. While much of the content on these and other Web 2.0 sites is for personal or entertainment purposes, scholars realized the potential to use similar technologies for research and collaboration. Academic librarians also understood that through Web 2.0, they could better reach their target audiences, share information with colleagues, and promote the library in new ways.

The use and extent of Web 2.0 technologies in academic libraries is uneven. Because of the recentness of these technologies, many academic libraries are cautious about investing time and resources into Web 2.0 efforts. Other libraries have developed numerous programs and services with the use of social networking tools and frequent postings to websites. One of the most common and practical uses of Web 2.0 in academic libraries is making announcements through blogs and RSS feeds (Kim and Abbas, 2010). While Millennials may be the most frequent users of emerging technologies, many academic libraries are utilizing Web 2.0 to reach other groups and design more user-driven services (Casey and Savastinuk, 2007). The advancement of the Internet through Web 2.0 technologies is an emerging trend with great implications for academic libraries.

Competing and Collaborating with Google

Part of the expanding web is the omnipresence of Google.com. In a dozen years since it launched, Google has become the Internet search engine of choice. The search algorithm used by Google to mine millions of webpages at the click of a button has proven to be the most preferred, efficient, and convenient method of locating online information. Each day over a billion searches are conducted using Google. The company's other programs, such as Gmail, Google Calendar, and Google Docs, provide users with free online software tools to manage files and schedules. These programs utilize "cloud" computing, which means that software, data, and other information are distributed across multiple servers and gathered through a web-based access point. However, the increased use of Google represents the trend toward proprietary digitization efforts and access.

In addition to these programs, Google has dozens of other online products and initiatives that have become standard Internet tools in the age of Web 2.0 technology. Two specific Google initiatives have enormous ramifications for academic librarians and the role of the campus library for patrons. In late 2004, Google launched a project-targeted web search engine called Google Scholar. Through Google Scholar, users can broadly search scholarly literature in numerous academic fields. The project searches across a variety of formats and sources including: interdisciplinary journals, books, theses, and abstracts; website content from academic publishers, digital repositories, and professional societies; and online materials hosted by colleges and universities (Google Scholar, 2011). Google Scholar, which encourages collaboration with publishers and libraries, ranks results according to relevance, where and who published the material, and how often the result had been cited in the scholarly literature.

Google Scholar encourages collaboration with publishers and libraries to locate and access academic literature. Although still in a beta phase, the project has proven useful for academic librarians. The greatest strength of Google Scholar is the ability to quickly search a vast and growing range of materials including academic journals, full-text books, digital content, and citations indices (Jacso, 2008). Students who might normally begin their library research by going to a general Google search might have the better option of beginning with Google Scholar and proceeding to the library for the information resources not freely available on the Internet. But those findings are incomplete. One analysis of the "scholarliness" of the project compared Google Scholar with several proprietary library databases. The results were that Google Scholar had much wider results and did better with ranking the result by relevancy than many standard library databases (Howland et al., 2009). However, the study noted that most patrons go no further than the third webpage of results in a standard database or Google search, which negates the importance of Google Scholars' ability to retrieve millions of relevant pages (Howland et al., 2009). From the librarian's perspective, the greatest weaknesses of Google Scholar are the software, the unknown parameters of the database being searched, and the inability to customize searches (Jacso, 2008).

On the whole, Google Scholar is a discovery tool, rather than a standalone source of information that is useful for academic librarians and their users. The related Google Books project, however, is a controversial initiative for many academic librarians. In late 2004, Google launched a small project called the Google Books Library project to begin digitizing selected texts from five partner libraries: Harvard University, the University of Michigan, the New York Public Library, Stanford University, and Oxford University (Google Books, 2011a). The five institutions selected the texts to be included in the project and received digital copies for their own purposes. Google scanned the pages of the selected public domain books, used Optical Character Recognition (OCR) software to render searchable text, and placed the bibliographic information into a free online searchable database. By 2005, Google announced that the Google Books project would expand its focus to include public domain texts as well as books still under copyright protection (Jones, 2010).

Unlike library-based digitization projects, the Google Books initiative approached book scanning on a massive scale, with a much more commercial application. Google began digitizing books from library collections in a very comprehensive fashion. The project provides users the full-text of public domain books and selections from titles still under copyright. Similar to websites like Amazon.com, Google Books allows users to preview sections of the recent books, access the references cited, see a list of similar titles, and have options to purchase the print or online version of the text.

By 2006, just as a number of new partner libraries joined the project, the Authors Guild, the Association of American Publishers, and a number of authors and publishers filed a class action lawsuit against Google Books (Google Books, 2011b). The claimants argued that Google had violated copyright laws and could not claim "fair use" for the full digitization of titles still under copyright protection. Three years later, Google and the petitioners reached a settlement about how to handle recent and out-of-print books that are still under copyright. In addition to sharing the revenue from Google Books with the claimants, the settlement required Google to create a nonprofit registry to represent authors, publishers and rights holders. The exact details of the agreement remain murky, but have not hindered the expansion of the Google Books project. In 2010, Google Books had over ten million scanned titles and in the summer the company launched a new online e-book store called Google eBooks, which allows users to purchase electronic books that can be accessed without the use of an e-reader device (i.e., Kindle, iPad, or Nook).

During the legal battles with Google, the public perceived libraries as willing and almost passive partners with the Internet conglomerate. However, academic libraries have been some of the most outspoken critics of the Google Books initiative. The commercialization of library information is perhaps the main reason for this opposition. On the surface Google Books is a "free" resource where users can discover and access printed information that they may not discover by visiting libraries. That discovery of information is the good news for academic libraries. However, the costs of the project include compromising the rights of copyright holders and shifting the initiative to a more fee-based system, which is a proprietary model already used by the publishing industry that academic librarians have long decried. Critics of Google Books also argue that this growing corpus of electronic texts should be in secure locations under the care of nonprofit information professionals, instead of in cloud computer servers being accessed by unknown and carefully guarded search algorithms. Quite simply, academic librarians recognize the usefulness of initiatives such as Google Books, but they are generally in favor of open access to scholarship and the decline of a proprietary approach to accessing digital content.

Scholarly Communication and Open Access

As one response to the problems of proprietary access to information and the rising costs of library materials, academic librarians gravitated to a larger movement in the scholarly community toward open access. While the success of this movement is a vital issue for librarians, open access to scholarly communication has enormous ramifications for all members of the academic community. Minimizing the role of commercial publishers in the process of scholarly publishing will not only decrease library acquisitions budgets, but an open access approach, through Internet sites and projects, will deliver peer-reviewed research (i.e., articles, books, and reviews) to a much wider audience.

The conjoined issues of access and costs are largely tied to the changes in academic publishing since the 1970s. By that time, scholars and professional societies had partnered with commercial publishers to provide wider dissemination of their print publications and a better printed product. During the 1980s commercial publishers merged into only a handful of conglomerates. At the same time, these publishers acquired high-end journals in specific areas, such as science, technology, and medicine, and then packaged institutional subscriptions to these journals for enormous rates (Yiotis, 2005). Studies estimate that the cost of subscription rates for scholarly journals increased 10 percent each year since the 1970s with the greatest spike during the 1990s (Lewis, 2008).

In the past 20 years, the growth of the Internet and the growing reliance on online communication by academics and researchers brought even greater changes to scholarly publishing. Commercial publishers digitized back issues of their academic journals and through intermediary vendors offered online access to older and recently published articles. At the same time, online journals and other digital-only content appeared. Some of these scholarly sources became accessible only through commercial publishers or vendors. These and other developments in scholarly publishing resulted in questions from academics about the management, distribution, long-term access to, and ownership of scholarship.

The Internet also gave academics and professional societies a mechanism to post, deliver, and retrieve scholarly information without the help of commercial enterprise. In the 1990s scholars began a movement toward open access online publishing of scholarly materials and ending the reliance on outside publishers. Their early work involved the development of local online repositories, where scholars could deposit their research findings and preprints. Campus departments such as computer science, information technology, and the library collaborated to develop the software and architecture for these first institutional repositories. As these open access databases of scholarly information grew on many campuses, leaders of the movement established uniform standards for these repositories. This effort became known as the Open Archives Initiative (OAI), which is designed to provide efficient access to and dissemination of scholarly content.

While not the most active voice in the movement, academic librarians played a role in the push for open access to scholarly information. Academic librarians were philosophically drawn to the concept of equal access to information, but there were also pragmatic reasons for their participation. By the late 1990s, most academic libraries could no longer afford expensive subscriptions and were forced to cancel much-needed journal and serial titles. At the same time, many of these same libraries invested resources into developing digital or online publishing projects. Academic librarians understood that a shift in the way their patrons accessed information required rethinking traditional academic publishing models. Reflecting those needs, in 1998 the Association of Research Libraries (ARL) launched the Scholarly Publishing and Academic Resources Coalition (SPARC) to address the growing costs of scholarly journals and explore open access repositories (Yiotis, 2005). In addition to SPARC participation, many academic libraries participated in OAI-based projects, such as developing harvesters (or search engines) to retrieve academic sources with standard OAI search terms.

During the past five years, federal legislation has started to turn the tide away from a commercial approach to academic publishing. Several compliance laws now require that recipients of federal grants must eventually disseminate the findings of their research through open access websites. Most recently, the 2009 Federal Research Public Access Bill would require that recipients of grants from government agencies with annual research expenditures over one-hundred million, must make electronic manuscripts of peer-reviewed journal articles freely available on the Internet (SPARC, 2011). If passed, the bill would be a monumental step for the open access movement, since so much of the research in science, technology, and medicine relies on federal grant funding.

While the transition from a commercial-based publishing model to a more open access approach to scholarly literature is far from complete, academic librarians are part of the equation and may in fact play a crucial role in a future model of harnessing, managing, and distributing academic discourse. As library budgets decline and journal subscription costs rise, it will become impossible for academic libraries to avoid cutting more online and print sources. However, by hosting online open access journals and collaborating in the development of institutional repositories, academic libraries are seeking new ways to become part of the scholarly communication conversation and remain a vital resource for campus research and researchers.

Digitization and Other Collaborative Projects

Since the 1990s, academic libraries have invested significant resources into their own digital efforts to provide access to oftentimes unique information content. Some of these digital projects are home-grown within the library, but often libraries are the leaders in a campus institutional repository or collaborative scanning projects. The largest and most successful digitization efforts sponsored by academic libraries are collaborative and involve other institutions, campus partners, and government agencies. This distributed approach to digitizing material shares costs and responsibilities between several groups, while building rich online collections drawn from sometimes geographically distant repositories. Because of their unique holdings, academic archives are at the center of many digitization projects.

Many academic libraries developed their first digital projects as a way to preserve and provide access to their unique printed or handwritten material housed in special collections and archives units. Digitizing selected manuscripts, ephemera, campus photographs, Civil War letters, sheet music, or pages from early yearbooks were common first digital library projects. This work required academic librarians and other information professionals to become more familiar with emerging technologies, software, and metadata schemas, as well as become active partners in collaborations outside the library. Some of these early projects were inspired by the open access movement and reconsidering the role of the academic library in the new century.

In order to offset costs of expensive databases, acquiring thousands of new books each year, and purchasing expensive computer equipment, many academic libraries formed collaborative groups. Whether based on simple geography, similarity of users and initiatives, or professional affiliations, academic libraries began numerous digital coalitions. Some libraries strengthened interlibrary loan groups to make it possible for only a few institutions to purchase new books, which could then be quickly borrowed by other participating libraries. The rising costs of databases and journal subscriptions were most often shared by coalitions of academic libraries, or by statewide groups. Digital projects were also distributed between academic libraries. A common scenario of shared digital work included one library with the equipment, staff, and expertise, with three other participants sharing their original material for scanning and markup. The result would be a common website for the online material, which could be mirrored by all participating institutions and hosted at any of the libraries.

Grants or outside funding became the main source for these start-up digital initiatives. With rising costs to operate libraries and maintain levels of acquisitions, academic libraries searched for funding to begin digital projects. The most common agencies funding this kind of work included the National Endowment for the Humanities (NEH), the Institute of Museum and Library Services (IMLS), and the National Science Foundation (NSF). Grants from these and other agencies emphasized the importance of collaborations between institutions, preservation of unique materials, clear learning outcomes for the intended users of the online collection, and using emerging technologies. Providing greater access to material, while central to the work of academic librarians, was simply not enough to secure external funding for a digital project. Other funding for digital work came from private groups such as the Andrew W. Mellon Foundation and the Bill and Melinda Gates Foundation, and from state groups such as historical records advisory boards, state libraries, or humanities councils.

As digital libraries matured, these projects become less dependent on grant funding and were incorporated into the functions and services of academic library programs. However, the interinstitutional alliances continued to develop new strategies for managing digital content. Projects such as Lots of Copies Keep Stuff Safe (LOCKSS) sponsored open source software for other institutions to preserve their digital content and keep multiple copies of files in different virtual locations. LOCKSS and other repository projects adopted a "dark archives" model, which limits access to stored digital material. Such efforts to collect and preserve growing digital content led to new collaborations. In 2005, a consortium of academic and public libraries founded the Open Content Alliance (OCA), which hosts more than one million freely accessible online books and other digital content. The OCA represents a counter-offensive approach to more commercial e-book projects such as Google Books.

Digital and collaborative projects in academic libraries are redefining the role of the campus library in the lives of students, scholars, and faculty. The lack of dedicated funds for such digital projects has allowed academic librarians to be creative in ways of developing and managing digital library resources. While some academic librarians have strong technical skills needed for digital projects, other skills such as project management, collection management, analysis, and grant writing experience are just as crucial for the success of such endeavors. The next few decades will bring even greater involvement from academic libraries in the realm of managing digital library content, as the ongoing management, migration, and preservation of digital content become common areas of study for new professionals.

Librarians as Digital Curators

Today's academic libraries are focused on building strong technological infrastructures, unique digital content, and services (Walters and Skinner, 2011). One area with enormous growth potential for academic libraries and academic archives is to take an active role in the creation of digital information. Libraries have historically served as digital repositories with the responsibility for collecting, managing, preserving, and providing access to electronic information. However, academic libraries are poised to be more involved in the creation and curation of digital content on their campuses. This paradigm shift to a more active role of libraries in the information needs of their campus constituents affects the work of academic archivists.

The concept that academic libraries are involved in the entire life cycle of digital information, rather than just serving as the repository for that information, is known as digital curation (Walters and Skinner, 2011). Academic libraries must be able to not only maintain their role as providers of purchased electronic content (i.e., full-text articles, books, and journals), but also be curators of unique digital content produced by their faculty, students, and staff. The role of digital curator requires that librarians collaborate with their on-campus constituents to use technology to produce new forms of research and scholarly communication. For academic archivists, acquiring new and unique materials is a familiar role. Further, academic archivists involved in managing, appraising, and even creating their own electronic records are well positioned to lead their academic library's efforts as digital curators for their campus partners.

CONCLUSION

Modern academic libraries are complicated environments, which hardly resemble the stereotypical view of the campus library as a static place where books are stored. The growth of academic libraries (their spaces, collections, budgets, numbers of staff, and services) skyrocketed in the second half of the twentieth century. Increasingly academic libraries became early adopters of new technology and academic librarians approached their work through more automated methods. The use of technology improved library services and collections, but the rising costs of digital resources and unstable budgets made it difficult for academic libraries to reach parity.

Within a constantly changing environment, academic libraries face the challenge of remaining relevant for today's users. One approach to better meet the needs of students is to re-create the library as a meeting space where ideas are exchanged, also known as the library or information commons movement. The different generations of library users often require different services, use new methods of communication, and have different expectations of what a library can do for them. Meeting those various needs is a requirement for successful academic librarians. Academic librarians have embraced various kinds of assessments and surveys to determine those needs. One commonality for all library users is the desire to have access to a strong library collection, including print and online sources. The challenge of purchasing new and maintaining current library resources in difficult economic times has often been met by fundraising efforts. Development work has become a central part of the success of today's academic libraries.

Many academic libraries have a long history of using technology to improve their processes and work. Today several technological challenges are redefining how the campus library can satisfy the technology needs of its users. Increased use of Web 2.0 technology and hand-held devices by students has resulted in many academic libraries tailoring their services and access to information to the needs of mobile users. The reliance on Google for e-mail, calendars, and library research makes standard library resources (online catalogs, databases, etc.) and search procedures appear antiquated and unfriendly to many students. Understanding the strengths of Google products, such as Google Books and Google Scholar, and integrating those resources into library instruction has become a necessity for academic libraries. The struggles between librarians and commercial enterprises are most severe in the realm of academic publishing, where vendors have increased subscription prices far beyond what libraries can afford. One result is that academic libraries have taken a clear position in the push for open access to scholarly information, by creating institutional repositories, helping develop open source software, and collaborating with other academics to create a new model for accessing academic research. Academic libraries have also created their own electronic content through digital projects, often undertaken in collaboration with other institutional partners and sponsored by external funding sources.

Archivists working in the academic library environment have a variety of challenges and opportunities. The standard tenets of modern academic librarianship—know your users and their needs, provide access to information, and use technology to best achieve your objectives—are also imperative for successful academic archivists. Many academic archivists working in campus libraries are stationed in special collections departments. These often misunderstood units of academic libraries have received enormous attention in the past ten years. The next chapter looks at special collections departments, what they do, why they are important, and how archivists can play a role in the development of the academic library.

REFERENCES

Aldrich, Alan W. 2008. "Outstanding in the Field: Creating Collaborative Workstations for Reference and Public Use in Academic Libraries." *College and Undergraduate Libraries* 15, no. 3: 364–377.

Casey, Michael E., and Laura C. Savastinuk. 2007. *Library 2.0: A Guide to Participatory Library Service*. Medford, NJ: Information Today, Inc.

Casserly, Mary F. 2008. "Research in Academic Library Collection Management." In *Academic Library Research: Perspectives and Current Trends*, edited by Marie L. Radford and Pamela Snelson, 82–137. Chicago: Association of College and Research Libraries.

Council on Library and Information Resources. 2008. *No Brief Candle: Reconceiving Research Libraries for the 21st Century*. Washington, DC: Council on Library and Information Resources.

Cowgill, Allison, Joan Beam, and Lindsey Wess. 2001. "Implementing an Information Commons in a University Library." *The Journal of Academic Librarianship* 27, no. 6 (November): 432–439.

Google Books. 2011a. "About Google Books." Google. Accessed September 20. http://books.google.com/intl/en/googlebooks/history.html.

———. 2011b. "Google Books Settlement Agreement." Google. Accessed September 20. http://books.google.com/googlebooks/agreement/#1.

Google Scholar. 2011. "About Google Scholar." Google. Accessed September 20. http://scholar.google.com/intl/en/scholar/about.html.

Howland, Jared L., Thomas C. Wright, Rebecca A. Boughan, and Brian C. Roberts. 2009. "How Scholarly Is Google Scholar? A Comparison to Library Databases." *College and Research Libraries* 70, no. 3 (May): 227–234.

Jacso, Peter. 2008. "Google Scholar Revisited." *Online Information Review* 32, no. 1: 102–114.

Johnson, Peggy. 2004. *Fundamentals of Collection Development*. Chicago: American Library Association.

Jones, Edgar. 2010. "Google Books as a General Research Collection." *Library Resources and Technical Services* 54, no. 2 (April): 77–89.

Kim, Yong-Mi, and June Abbas. 2010. "Adoption of Library 2.0 Functionalities by Academic Libraries and Users: A Knowledge Management Perspective." *The Journal of Academic Librarianship* 36, no. 3 (May): 211–218.

Kyrillidou, Martha, Colleen Cook, and S. Shyam Sunder Rao. 2008. "Measuring the Quality of Library Service Through LibQual+." In *Academic Library Research: Perspectives and Current Trends*, edited by Marie L. Radford and Pamela Snelson, 253-301. Chicago: Association of College and Research Libraries.

Lancaster, Lynne C., and David Stillman. 2010. *The M-Factor: How the Millennial Generation is Rocking the Workplace*. New York: Harper Collins.

Lewis, David W. 2008. "Library Budgets, Open Access, and the Future of Scholarly Communication." *College and Research Libraries News* 69, no. 5 (May): 271–273.

Scholarly Publishing and Academic Resources Coalition. 2011. "Call For Action by Leaders of Higher Education Institutions (FRPAA)." http://www.arl.org/sparc/advocacy/frpaa/highered.shtml.

Seal, Robert A. 2010. "Introduction." *Journal of Library Administration* 50, no 1: 1–6.

Theimer, Kate. 2010. *Web 2.0 Tools and Strategies for Archives and Local History Collections*. New York: Neal-Schuman.

Walters, Tyler, and Katherine Skinner. 2011. *New Roles for New Times: Digital Curation for Preservation*. Washington, DC: Association of Research Libraries.

Williams, Karen. 2009. "A Framework for Articulating New Library Roles." *Research Library Issues: A Bimonthly Report from ARL, CNI, and SPARC* no. 265 (August): 3–8. http://www.arl.org/resources/pubs/rli/archive/rli265.shtml.

Wright, Stephanie. 2007. *Library Assessment*. Washington, DC: Association of Research Libraries.

Yiotis, Kristin. 2005. "The Open Access Initiative: A New Paradigm for Scholarly Communication." *Information Technology and Libraries* 24, no. 4 (December): 157–162.

3

Special Collections and Academic Archives

INTRODUCTION

A majority of academic archivists working within a college or university library system are part of a special collections department. The material housed in special collections departments is diverse, invaluable, rare, and largely unique. Special collections are being redefined as the locations for valuable research collections in an array of formats that can be used for a variety of purposes by a range of users. Frequently, special collections define and make each academic library unique.

Special collections departments have enormous implications for all archivists. Simply put, understanding special collections is integral to understanding academic archives, because for many academic librarians the special collections department represents the entire field of academic archives. User demand for more original historical sources, whether rare printed texts, historic photographs, or documents from the founding of the institution, have moved special collections departments from the periphery to the mainstream. At the same time, academic librarians are revisiting the purposes and holdings of their special collections departments. This chapter describes the importance of special collections within the context of academic libraries and the larger work of academic archivists. It reviews the development of special collections departments, their common structures and subunits, and relationships with separate archives. The general formats and materials found in special collections will be discussed in relation to how those items can benefit the larger academic library and institution. The chapter also reviews the recent interest in special collections by library directors and deans, and how that focus is affecting the changing nature of special collections work as a much more integrated part of academic libraries. This chapter seeks to answer the following questions:

1. What are special collections departments and why are they important to academic libraries and academic archives?
2. What are some common approaches to special collections librarianship?
3. What efforts are being made to acquire, catalog, and access special collections material?

SPECIAL COLLECTIONS AND THE CAMPUS LIBRARY

A Brief History of Special Collections

In the early twentieth century, many academic libraries recognized the importance of their early printed books, for both their historical and monetary value. Academic libraries protected these rare holdings by separating the volumes and housing them in locations with very limited access, known as "treasure rooms." These libraries also added their original documents, manuscripts, and other unique items to the same location, or at least gave these materials the same status as their rare books. Protection and preservation were the chief reasons for segregation of this valuable material.

By the first two decades of the century, several academic libraries provided greater access to some of the contents of their treasure rooms by opening rare book reading rooms (Joyce, 1988). This move paralleled the approach of independent research libraries and historical societies, to not only build collections but to provide access to select researchers. Academic credentials were often required for permission to use the rare materials. During this period, larger academic libraries (such as Yale, Princeton, and the University

Development of Special Collections until World War II

- Older books and manuscripts deposited at colleges and universities for protection
- Growing "treasure rooms" of material
- Rare books reading rooms at several schools
- Rare books librarianship emerges as a subfield
- Reliance on donors and collections as main source of rare items
- Targeted subject-based collecting areas

of Michigan) created rare book departments, which gave rise to the subfield of rare book librarianship, the concept of endowed funds for books, and library friends groups (Joyce, 1988). It was during this stage of development that many private book collectors and bibliophiles solidified their relationships with academic libraries.

The National Archives movement of the 1930s coincided with growth of manuscript and archival collections in academic libraries. Beginning in that decade, several college and university libraries took interest in making better use of the manuscript holdings locked away in their treasure rooms, and also embraced the concept of collecting new material. Through manuscript and official archival records, academic libraries could better document their institutions, their community, or areas of faculty research. Protection and preservation of only rare materials gave way to methodically collecting unique materials in specialized areas of study. The most relevant example of this shift is the creation of the Southern Historical Collection in 1930 at the University of North Carolina, Chapel Hill. History professor J. G. de Roulhac Hamilton collected manuscript material on southern history throughout the 1910s and 1920s, and petitioned the university to establish a specific library collection focused on the American South (University Libraries, University of North Carolina, 2008). The University of North Carolina recognized his founding efforts in 1930 by establishing the Southern Historical Collection, one of the first targeted collections and departments in an academic library.

After World War II, many academic libraries began to shed their treasure room approach to managing their rare and unique collections in favor of the research library concept— primary sources in multiple formats to access broad and targeted subject areas. With the help of donors, several institutions built specific buildings for their unique materials. The first of these separate buildings came in 1942 when Harvard University opened the Houghton Library, adjacent to the main library, to specifically house rare books and manuscripts (Hamlin, 1981). In the following decades, other separate special library buildings appeared on campuses, including the Lilly Library at Indiana University, the Harry Ransom Center at the University of Texas, and the Beinecke Library at Yale University. These special libraries operated with internal units or departments based on formats, contained exhibition areas for events, served collections to researchers through reading rooms, and maintained strong ties to donors and friends groups.

By the 1960s, most academic libraries had some kind of special library or department specifically focused on unique and rare materials, both for intentional and practical reasons. New areas of scholarship and emerging academic programs (such as area studies) facilitated the growth or founding of many subject-focused repositories on campuses. Many special collections became the designated archival repositories for the official records of professional organizations. As special collections work became more methodical, the collections themselves become more diverse and included a variety of new formats (i.e., audiovisual, photographic, and realia). Special collections often became the "place" where uncommon formats were kept, such as foreign language materials, microforms, or recordings which required equipment for usage. Less frequently used journals published before the 1950s or heavily illustrated printed pieces in danger of theft or mutilation either found a home in special collections or in a storage facility. Unusual items, such as artwork, tapestries, and even weapons often found their way into special collections departments, simply because the institution and the library had no other suitable alternative.

Although the missions and material of each special collections unit varied, there were several common characteristics that marked the growth of these departments during the late twentieth century. First, each special collections was founded and built because of donors, book and manuscript dealers, and at least one special collections librarian devoted to building collections (Rostenberg and Stern, 1989). The collections added to these departments also grew organically, meaning that the available manuscripts, books, and archival materials defined and redefined the collection focus. Many departments began simply because of one significant donation or a large purchase of material made with specified donations.

> **Special Collections since World War II**
>
> - Research library concept is embraced.
> - Special collections are often located in a building separate from the main campus library.
> - Special collections support campus research.
> - Special collections librarianship expands to include manuscripts and archives.
> - Targeted user group becomes much broader than just current faculty and scholars.

Initially, the purpose of special collections departments was to provide some access to those unique materials, while actively preserving and protecting the material from harm. This curatorial approach often mirrored the work of museum professionals, who do much of the interpretation of pieces and construct restricted access points. Special collections departments also developed other standard restrictions of use such as requiring researchers to sign in or be identified, to only use material in a supervised reading room, to place personal items in a locker or other location, and to use pencils and not any kind of pens with permanent ink. These requirements of use often detracted from having an open environment where patrons would be comfortable to visit. Thus the external view of special collections often became that these departments were set aside for only serious scholars and perhaps advanced graduate students.

Even from the internal perspective, special collections departments developed as a murky realm of the library. The lack of clarity and the many challenges of operating special collections departments resulted in a variety of approaches to leadership. The Rare Books and Manuscripts Section (RBMS) of the American Library Association (ALA) began and grew in the 1940s and 1950s, the same time that college and universities formalized their special collections programs (Schreyer, 1988). The early leaders of special collections often had a strong humanities background (advanced degrees, often a doctorate), reading knowledge of several European languages, and a strong knowledge of the history of the book. Library catalogers responsible for original cataloging and other advanced bibliographic work were the most likely candidates to lead these new special collections departments, especially since they had already been working with rare books. Other academic libraries recruited book collectors or humanities scholars to manage their special collections departments. With an absence of professional courses or programs in special collections librarianship, the work was learned by observation, mentorship, and experience rather than in a formal classroom setting.

By the late twentieth century, many special collections departments redefined their services and approach. Rather than becoming marginalized and a neglected part of the library, departments focused their attention on collecting material for audiences broader than just the faculty at their institutions (Byrd, 2001). Supporting the academic programs rather than specific faculty members of the college or university allowed special collections departments to create distinct research collections and reach out to a larger community of scholars. Those initiatives dovetailed well with many of the services and programs emerging from academic libraries.

While archivists have always had some kind of role in special collections departments, only in the past few decades have archivists become crucial to the operations of these academic library units. That shift is largely due to the centralization of other format-based library departments, such as university or college archives, under the larger umbrella of special collections. That combination of collections and functions into one larger department resulted in the need to diversify the experiences of special collections librarians beyond a familiarity with rare books. While archivists may have lacked the training in cataloging and identifying printed works, their skills in researching, organizing, and providing access to archival and manuscript collections worked well in the special collections environment. As the kinds of collections in these departments broadened, the users of special collections diversified and the research needs changed. No longer did special collections just cater to well-established academic scholars, but to undergraduates, genealogists, and alumni—all familiar groups for academic archivists.

The Structure of Today's Special Collections

At the beginning of the twenty-first century, special collections departments are intimately connected to the challenges and trends facing academic libraries. Instead of being isolated from the other activities of their library systems, special collections departments are integrated into the digital and service mentality of modern academic libraries. Today's special collections librarians are charged with building collections during times of poor economic growth, training and recruiting new professionals to the field, adequately replacing a generation of retiring leaders in the profession, creating new development and donor relationships, managing burgeoning collections in often inadequate or inappropriate spaces, designing new facilities, attracting different audiences into the reading room, providing library instruction on how to use primary sources during research, making the most use of emerging technologies to serve more users, and serving as key leaders in academic libraries. While these issues are not limited to special collections, these departments have a unique place in the academic library environment.

The structure of special collections departments varies, but there are a few commonalties. In the past few decades, academic libraries have centralized their services and departments. Operating separate library departments, with separate staff, and separate facilities is an economic challenge for academic libraries. In addition, academic librarians are approaching the reference process as a more holistic experience, which cuts across departmental lines and involves a variety of information professionals. Concurrently, academic librarians are also emphasizing their subject specialties and connections with specific colleges, schools, and academic programs.

Figure 3.1
Common Units of Special Collections Departments

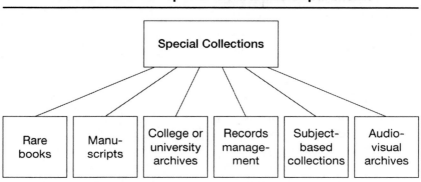

Source: Graphic by Marc Brodsky.

The trend of centralization of library services and the emphasis on specialization has great implications for special collections. As one result, many academic libraries have merged their individual format-based units (i.e., university archives, manuscripts, and rare books) into one special collections department. Figure 3.1 reflects the pattern of combining individual archives and collecting units into a larger department. In today's special collections there may be rare book experts, reference archivists, preservation or conservation librarians, digitization specialists, archival processors, institutional historians, museum curators, records managers, and catalogers all working in the same larger department. Within this larger framework, these special collections professionals still focus on their specialties, whether with a subject, a specific format, or technical software.

The reference process and experience of the researcher has also changed because of this broader environment. Unless units are located in separate buildings, it is most common to have one service point and one reading room for patrons. Directing all in-person research activities to one location emphasizes the research library concept for special collections; meaning that patrons with an interest in a particular topic can view a variety of formats (i.e., manuscripts, archival records, images, and sound recordings) in one location. Generally, standard research room requests, such as making copies, seeking permission to publish, and locating related material, is easier in a centralized reading room. One location also provides greater continuity between staff and students who work on the reference desk. In the process of locating and pulling material for patrons, members of the department become more familiar with all the holdings maintained by special collections.

Managing and conceptualizing all of the potential components of special collections requires a holistic view of academic libraries. Most

---

The Structure of a Special Collections Department

- Specialists working together in a hybrid environment
- Centralized reading room for all inquiries and research
- Subunits led by coordinators all under one larger umbrella
- A director or department head to represent the department within the library

---

commonly, a department head or director is charged with the general administration of all the units under the special collections umbrella. In larger departments, the director may have assistant or associate directors to help manage the subunits. Some institutions rotate their head position in the same way that academic departments elect a chair to serve a term of service. In smaller departments, the director may be the only professional staff member so the director must rely on other full-time employees and students to carry out the daily reference and processing work (Kurtz, 2004).

The director or a designee from special collections usually serves on a library management group and in that capacity works with other library leaders to coordinate services, policies, and initiatives. Because many special collections departments are connected to development (funding and collections) efforts for the library, the leader of special collections may also be at the associate or assistant library director level. The director of the department may delegate responsibilities to the head of each subunit or may take a more "flat" approach to organizing their special collections. Whatever management model is in place, the leaders of special collections must have a clear understanding of funding, collection development, the research process, user expectations, emerging technologies, effectively managing people, and how their department fits into the goals of the academic library and the institution as a whole.

For professional archivists, the most recognizable position in special collections libraries is the university or college archivist. In the era of downsizing and centralization, many college and university archives have become sub-units in special collections departments. In the process of that reorganization, archival and special collections work has become much more overlapping. Often official records are stored alongside manuscript collections, or all inquiries including questions about school history are directed to a reference coordinator who is not necessarily the school's archivist. Thus the college or university archivist has become an important part of the special collections staff, with an area of expertise and a developing understanding of other areas including rare books and manuscripts. The research library concept of having a variety of sources, formats, and perspectives in one location has expanded the role of academic archivists in their special collections departments. This hybrid environment has allowed college and university archivists to retain their designation as the keepers of the institutions' official and unofficial re-cords, while serving much more broadly and visibly in their departments.

Other specialists, such as curators, processors, and catalogers, in special collections have also become integrated into the larger work of the department. While inclusive-sounding job titles such as curator of rare books and cataloger for special formats abound in special collections staff directories, these individuals have become much more connected to the processes and services of their departments. The demands of today's academic libraries make it difficult for special formats catalogers to focus only on rare books. Instead they may be expected to create online records for manuscript collections, upload finding aids into national catalogs, serve a reference desk shift, and teach bibliographic instruction courses to graduate students. The traditional role of a curator—to protect and build collections—cannot fulfill the larger mission of today's special collections departments to provide improved access to a variety of audiences with diverse research needs. The biggest challenge for these specialists, and for college and university archivists, is to use emerging technologies to better serve the research needs of their users (Dooley, 2009).

The Spaces of Today's Special Collections

As academic librarians have embraced the library commons concept and focused a significant amount of resources on redesigning library spaces, special collections librarians have reconsidered their facilities. Typically, special collections reading rooms are arranged with a modern style (simple furniture and few distractions) with an open layout, a more traditional "gentleman's library" style (wood grain furniture, antique lamps, and many items on display) with a museum-like atmosphere, or some combination of the two. Some researchers expect a more "schol-arly" look to the reading room, but that aura of exclusivity can deter users who are unfamiliar with special collections.

The location and design of the main reference desk affects the operations of the reading room. Incoming patrons should be able to register and request material from one central location, most frequently at the main reference desk. Some institutions have automated the request process and require researchers to place online requests for material from a nearby workstation or in advance of their visit. A secure space, such as lockers or a coat room, should be close by for patrons to leave their personal belongings. The placement of the reference desk in conjunction with the researcher's tables should allow archivists to observe patrons in the reading room, be available to assist walk-in researchers, and be close to a computer workstation (Wilsted, 2007).

Whatever the style and layout of the public research area, researchers should have ample access to necessary equipment, enough room to review materials and take notes, wireless or network Internet connections, electric outlets for their computer equipment, and nearby copiers, scanners, or public computer terminals. A nearby reference collection of basic institutional and local histories, duplicates of yearbooks and other school publications, and alumni directories is useful for both staff and researchers. Finally, the planners of reading rooms should select seating that is comfortable enough for long periods of sitting, and tables that are at standard heights. Figure 3.2 shows a special collections reading room with a traditional decor. While those considerations may appear superficial, long-distance researchers using special collections must maximize their time, meaning that they may be in their research zones for multiple hours and multiple days. A comfortable environment means researchers can focus on their task at hand for a longer time.

The layout of the reading room and the need to provide a comfortable and secure environment is only one part of the equation. During the past few decades, a larger number of special collections librarians have participated in the design of entirely new buildings or the renovation of pre-existing facilities for their departments. Construction of a new or remodeled archival facility is an opportunity to address building issues, especially related to collection preservation, storage,

Reading Room Design for Special Collections

- A modern or traditional decor
- One location for registration
- Centralized reference desk
- Separate and secure spaces for personal items
- Access to computer workstations, copiers, scanners, etc.
- Close proximity to collections
- Comfortable seating
- Adequate lighting
- Possible exhibit space
- Staff offices nearby

Figure 3.2
Special Collections Reading Room

Source: Photograph by the author.

security, and access (Pacifico and Wilsted, 2009). The various formats found in the units of special collections often require separate environmental conditions, which make it less likely that one general storage area can accommodate manuscripts, film, blueprints, and audiovisual materials (Ritzenthaler, 2010). Special collections librarians must adequately inform their library colleagues, institutional officials, designers, architects, and construction crews about the weight, climate, storage, and access considerations for their new or renovated spaces.

The proximity between the reading room and the storage space for research collections is important to the design of special collections departments. The most frequently requested material, whether printed, manuscript, or photographic, must be retrievable in a matter of minutes. However, the variety and volume of special collections materials makes it difficult to house everything in one adjoining or nearby space. Storage space has become such a high demand commodity in academic library buildings that special collections librarians have to make choices of what to keep within a short walking distance of the reading room. Often, the large, partially restricted, infrequently used, difficult to catalog, or unprocessed collections are housed in off-site storage units, which may require a day or more to retrieve. Multiple storage locations increase the chances for misplacing material, exposing collections to undue environmental fluctuations, risk of theft, and delay in retrieval; however, the growth of collections and greater demands for space make off-site storage a viable alternative.

The behind-the-scenes decisions about where to store collections directly affects researchers. While large government archives like the National Archives retrieve, or pull, material for patrons on an hourly cycle, most special collections operate on a pull-on-request system. Traditionally, scholars who use special collections contact the department in advance of their visit, with details of their research project. Although not a required part of using special collections, preliminary contact helps identify material, often assists researchers in determining the length of their research visit, and ensures that the material will be available upon their arrival. Walk-in patrons may have equally demanding research needs, and often expect to find relevant material on their topic in a matter of minutes. The realities of off-site storage and the complexities of special collections materials make instantaneous delivery a challenge. Thus patron demands for specific materials have a direct influence on where special collections materials are stored.

In addition to providing researchers with access to original materials, special collections have become increasingly responsible for developing exhibits or public programs for their academic libraries. When renovating or designing new spaces for special collections, there is a common demand for exhibit space for displaying historic or unique materials. Often secure display cases are installed in the reading room, or a separate room near the reading room designated for special collections exhibits (Pacifico and Wilsted, 2009). If such a museum room is built, the space should be flexible enough to meet other needs. This room can be used for public events, external exhibits or traveling exhibitions, instructional sessions, and library presentations (Byrd, 2001). Because special collections units attract scholars, writers, and even filmmakers working on projects, the department is a natural fit for cultivating outreach efforts, such as a public lecture program for the library.

Finally, the layout of staff offices and work spaces in relation to the location of collections and the reading room is an important part of the operations of special collections. Like any office situation, a private office for each full-time employee is preferred, but not always possible. Offices vary in size, but often special collections staff prefer to work with their collections at their desk, instead of a shared workspace. For security and preservation purposes it is best to avoid processing in individual offices. At the very least there should be one private space where discussions with donors, staff, and researchers can occur. That private office should be within very close proximity to the reading room. Reference coordinators should have offices within a short distance from the entrance to the reading room. The staff member responsible for acquisitions is more efficient if located close to stacks and other departmental storage areas.

Most special collections have designated work areas further behind-the-scenes, such as cataloging rooms, storage areas for supplies, and tables designated for processing projects. Sometimes unique projects such as cataloging a large collection of donated books or processing the papers of a famous politician require staff to do their work in an off-site location. Having split work areas and off-site work locations should only be temporary approaches to adding new materials into special collections.

THE COLLECTIONS OF SPECIAL COLLECTIONS

In addition to knowing how special collections operate and how they are spatially designed, academic archivists must also prepare themselves for the variety of materials found in these departments. Archival materials—official documents and institutional or organizational records that are legally required to be retained permanently—are only one part of the whole. Institutional materials that are not required to be retained, personal and financial papers, artificial subject-based collections, and rare printed pieces are key parts of special collections. Materials in special collections vary according to mission, collecting policy, and institutional practices, but there are a few standard formats associated with special collections work. Academic archivists must understand these formats, how they were assembled into individual collections and described, and some of the general characteristics of these unique materials.

Manuscript Collections

The term "manuscript" often has a medieval tone to it—one of monastic scribes toiling away on sacred texts, by the light of a dim candle. While

Figure 3.3
Examples of Manuscripts

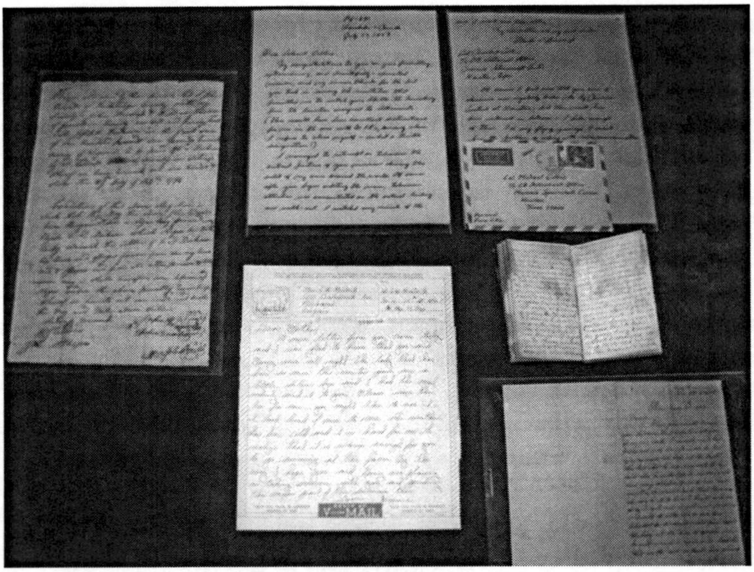

Source: Photograph by Marc Brodsky.

many special collections do indeed have these kinds of pre–printing press items such as illuminated manuscripts on vellum or incunabula (books produced before 1500), the term "manuscripts" in special collections is much broader. For a majority of special collections, manuscript collections refers to a wide range of unpublished material, such as a typescript of an unedited novel, a handwritten letter from a Civil War solider, land grants from the eighteenth century, or a group of documents all relating to one family (Figure 3.3). From the special collections perspective, personal and family papers, and sometimes business records, generally fall within the category of manuscript collections (Burke, 1997). Because of their unofficial nature, historically many manuscript collections in special collections were created as "catch-all" collections of material that fit nowhere else.

Manuscript collections originate from a variety of sources. Most often, individuals amass a corpus of material (i.e., correspondence, personal files, financial and legal documents, photographic and audiovisual materials, and published or unpublished material) throughout their lifetime. When donated to special collections, these manuscripts document the activities of an individual or numerous members of a family (often known as family papers), and may already have a creator determined arrangement, or original order, to them (Burke, 1997). Manuscript collections may also contain legal, financial, and business records, for instance if the individual owned a small company and kept account books detailing the financial history of that enterprise. More common, manuscript collections have a specific focus, such as material documenting a career as an engineer, correspondence with children and grandchildren, or research on family history, rather than documenting an entire life. Thus manuscript collections are organized for specific purposes, begin with some kind of arrangement from the creator or organizer of the material, and are more selective than comprehensive in their contents.

Although all manuscript collections are unique, there are some similarities in formats, organization, and content. American manuscript collections from the eighteenth and early nineteenth centuries frequently share common formats, such as legal documents, receipts for transfers of property or goods, personal and business correspondence, and vital records including wills and birth certificates. On the whole, these documents originated from literate, white, affluent patriarchs who held some level of hegemony over society. Whether businessmen, religious leaders, tradesmen, civic activists, or politicians, they created manuscript collections that document certain segments of society (Burke, 1997). Largely missing from these collections were the voices and perspectives of minorities, most women, the less affluent, and the less educated (Ham, 1975). There are certainly exceptions to these generalities, but not until the Civil War era did the majority of Americans have greater ability to record their thoughts, lives, and activities on paper or through new photographic processes.

American manuscript collections of the modern period (created since the late nineteenth century) are voluminous, diverse, complex, and perhaps more representative of society. Manuscript collections from writers, artists, politicians, soldiers, and labor organizers may include drastically different perspectives on past events. For example, a special collections department with a focus on twentieth-century United States warfare might include material from pacifists who opposed the Vietnam War, an unpublished novel about the subculture of the 1960s, papers from a politician who first supported but later opposed greater American involvement in East Asia, and an oral history interview (recording and transcript) with a decorated military officer who completed multiple tours in Vietnam. While each manuscript collection is a separate entity of unique origins, when viewed as part of a larger focus, these collections and other materials in special collections may form the basis of a research collection.

Modern manuscript collections contain a variety of formats, document types, and objects. For example, a special collections department with holdings on the Civil Rights Movement may have photographic collections of selected local leaders of protests or sit-ins, oral history tapes of interviews with participants in those events, a collection of newspaper clippings from the period, actual signs carried by demonstrators, and material created by white supremacy groups. Manuscript collections often contain material that would not be found or kept in the "official" archival records from an institution or an organization. For example, gray literature, white papers, and internal reports created on campus are ephemeral in nature, but may have significant historical value. The variety of material in manuscript collections requires special collections librarians to be familiar with preservation skills for unusual formats, an understanding of digital technology, and developing logical access points.

Manuscript collections and archival collections are close cousins: both are usually arranged according to the principles of original order and provenance (concepts that guide archivists when processing collections, described in Chapter 7); both contain a variety of formats or series of material; both contain electronic and unstable media files; and the information about both can be made accessible through a finding aid. One important difference is the origin of manuscript collections. While college and university archivists receive most of their new collections from departments, alumni, and donors, special collections librarians are much more involved with the rare books and manuscripts trade for some of their best acquisitions. These and other sources for manuscripts will be covered in detail in Chapter 6 on collection scope and development for academic archives, but it is important to note how purchasing new materials complicates the acquisition picture and requires different skills. Working with the for-profit world for acquisitions means that special collections librarians must understand budgets, know how funding can be spent at their institution, and take an active role in fundraising for their department in order to ensure future purchases. Balancing the budget alongside selecting the "best" purchases for the department and ultimately for researchers can be a challenge for special collections librarians.

While the evidence in manuscript collections is often fragmentary, these materials in special collections are in great demand by researchers. It is the manuscript collections which traditionally have been the basis of scholarly research (Burke, 1997). In addition to official archival records, scholars want access to unpublished accounts, documents, letters, ledger books, diaries, and papers, which traditionally make up the unique research holdings in special collections. These same sources are used by genealogists tracing their family history, undergraduate students researching a local event or campus tradition, or a MBA student exploring early business history. Academic archivists cannot ignore the importance of manuscript collections for research and for collection development purposes.

Institutional Archives

Academic archival work is primarily based on collecting, arranging, describing, and providing access to archival material, most commonly institutional archives. Many academic archivists serve as the college or university archivist, meaning that they have responsibility for working with departments and donors to document the history of their institution, through official and unofficial records. These collections of archival material form the basis for college and university archives collections.

The official records in college and university archives are created by different offices and departments of the institution, such as the president's office, the English department, and the campus publications office, during the course of business. Whether printed, handwritten, or in electronic format, these materials become inactive (i.e., not needed for everyday access) and enter the next phase of the archival records life cycle or continuum (Boles, 2005). Only a small percentage of materials created by an institution will be retained permanently. Academic archivists work closely with campus records managers to develop records schedules for each campus office or entity. These schedules, based on practical, fiscal, and legal considerations, dictate which inactive materials are appropriate for long-term retention in the college or university archives (Maher, 1992). Most college or university archives mirror the arrangement pattern of the record group concept, which is based on an approach to arranging government records. Thus, for many schools the first archival record group in the archives represents the official records of the president's office, the second archival record group may be for the records of the board of trustees or the treasurer's office, and subsequent groupings represent other components and functions of the institution. These record groups provide a sense of the changing organizational structure of an institution, but do not denote hierarchy or importance.

It is most common that only the highest levels of administration at colleges and universities have records schedules. Academic archivists may create other archival record groups, which contain materials that were not part of the records scheduling process. For example, the retirement of the graduate secretary in the philosophy department may result in the discovery of dozens of boxes of material related to the first three decades of that department's history. Proactive, or just lucky, archivists may have an opportunity to accept this material and add selected files to an archival record group related to either the specific department or to the philosophy department's school or college. Those materials may not have been part of the records schedule, but they are still created as part of the functions of the institution and may be invaluable for researchers interested in the development of humanities programs at the school.

Materials created by student organizations or individual students are considered by many as tangential records, but such materials may be quite valuable for documenting the history of the institution. As an example, Greek life is a common part of campus life but is often underdocumented. With the help of campus Greek councils, academic archivists may be able to collect lists of past members, flyers and leaflets, and historic photographs of fraternities and sororities for the archives. Alumni also represent an important source of institutional history. Some of the best historical collections in colleges and university archives are personal scrapbooks from past graduates. Although far from being official records, these items document the daily life of a student many decades past in the form of pasted-in photographs of campus and football teams, grade cards, tickets, corsages, dance cards, and handwritten notes (Samuels, 1992) (Figure 3.4).

Faculty papers are a gray area for many academic archivists. While the research and class material collected over the lifetime of a campus faculty member were technically created as part of the activities of the institution, some academic archivists to not include faculty papers as official parts of the university or college archives. These papers may in fact document other aspects of the faculty member's life and career, and not only their work at the institution. Instead, these papers may often be considered related manuscript collections, housed in special collections.

Figure 3.4
Virginia Tech Football Team, 1894

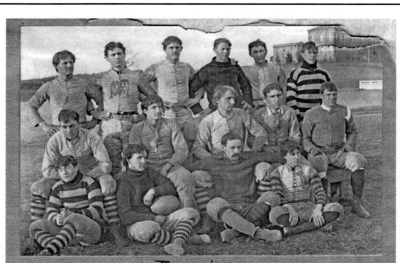

Source: Virginia Tech Special Collections.

College and university archivists are most often integrated into a special collections department and their collections are accessed through a central reading room. Academic archivists responsible for their institution's documentary heritage are also closely connected to some kind of records management office, or may in fact also serve as the records manager for their college or university. The details of organizing and managing a collection of official and unofficial materials of a college or university archives, and the relationship between academic archivists and records management, will be described in later chapters of this book. But from a special collections perspective, the institution's archives are just one piece of the larger research library puzzle.

In addition to the college or university archives, there are other kinds of institutional archival collections found in the holdings of special collections departments. These often ignored archival collections include the records, files, and publications of professional organizations, campus groups, clubs, membership societies, and philanthropic foundations. For example, an officer in a local chapter of the League of Women Voters may donate historical files and publications to a nearby special collections department. The donation could be based on two reasons: (1) the special collections department has a growing collection on international suffrage efforts; or (2) the institution was founded as a women's college. As a common part of this arrangement, groups may donate material incrementally, usually as those files are less needed by the organization. However, sometimes if a group or chapter disbands or completes their mission, their archives arrive in their entirety. Academic archivists approach the processing of these collections in the same way they would arrange and describe official institutional records, most often based on original order or by a simple series and subseries approach.

College and university affiliated groups often donate their official archives to special collections departments. While a campus-based group such as a committee to document the town's bicentennial may receive attention in the correspondence kept by the provost or president of the institution, the details of their work and outcomes may not make it into the school's official records. Thus, at the end of the work of the committee, the boxes of material (correspondence, publications, and digital images) may be donated to the institution's special collections. The interrelated nature of the group and the school, and the fact that the topic fits well within the local history focus of the special collections, makes the records of this bicentennial committee a good fit for the school's special collections.

Institutional archives add great diversity to the holdings of special collections departments. College or university archives and other related collections add tremendous value to a more comprehensive approach to research. Students interested in tracing the history of homecoming activities at their college would find material in the college archives, in the papers of a faculty member who chaired a campus events committee, and in photographic scrapbooks from a female undergraduate of the 1930s. When coupled with multidimensional manuscript collections, these archival holdings provide additional perspectives on the past. Academic archivists, who are trained to collect and manage these kinds of archives, are a crucial part of expanding the documentary reach of special collections departments on the campus, their community, and their region.

Printed Pieces

Traditionally, academic libraries established special collections departments to protect the library's old or rare book collection from harm, and sometimes from the hands of researchers. As a result, most special collections have a significant number of out-of-print books, older journals and serial volumes, and rare or unique printed titles (Cave, 1976). Many of these volumes came from donors, academic faculty, and collectors. These items did not circulate, but were available for use by patient and persistent researchers in a secure reading room. With the merger of rare books units into special collections departments during the past few decades, the area of rare books librarianship expanded to include work with other printed pieces and manuscript collections. At the same time, the number of rare books curators working in a special collection environment has decreased.

Today's academic archivists have little exposure to or training in the subfield of rare book librarianship. Few courses are offered in graduate programs related to rare books and only a handful of noncredit courses in the field exist. Those sparse offerings have resulted in many archivists working around rare books, but not fully understanding their value for research and instruction. Also the process of evaluating, researching, and cataloging rare books is an unclear area for academic archivists. Because rare books are still a central resource for scholars and are found in nearly every special collections department, academic archivists must familiarize themselves with the printed pieces in their repositories (Figure 3.5).

Figure 3.5
Examples of Rare Books

Source: Photograph by Marc Brodsky.

Books destined for special collections are often classified as rare books because they are unique, long out-of-print, valuable on the market, or simply too fragile to circulate. Whether donated or purchased from a book dealer, these rare volumes go through a more rigorous cataloging process (often referred to as "original cataloging") than regular academic library books. Traditionally, the main access and discovery point for a rare book is through a detailed library catalog record, created by a rare book or special formats cataloger. These catalogers record important details about each volume (i.e., handwritten annotations, limited editions, unusual printed markings, or author inscriptions) and include that unique information in the library catalog record. This process of descriptive bibliography is lengthy, requires a great deal of research, and often involves reading ability in multiple languages. The advent of accessible online digital copies of rare books has created new access points to unique printed books, and made it easier for rare books catalogers to locate cataloging information on specific volumes.

To better understand rare books and how they are processed, academic archivists should take an active role in learning more about the basics of book production and the general developments in the history of printing. Understanding basic book history makes it possible for academic archivists to integrate examples of unique printed items from their stacks into instructional sessions. Week-long courses at the University of Virginia's Rare Book School and other continuing education programs sponsored by RBMS provide excellent overviews. Academic archivists who can spend significant time with rare book curators and special formats catalogers have a distinct advantage working in a special collections environment. Reviewing rare book dealer catalogs is another way for academic archivists to familiarize themselves with not only what is available for purchase, but also with the process of researching and describing a rare book.

Printed ephemeral materials, either cataloged as separate pieces like books or treated as part of manuscript collections with finding aids, are common in the holdings of special collections (Clinton, 1981). For many academic archivists, the general term of ephemera often refers to the miscellaneous or leftover material discovered when processing a collection. For a special collections librarian, however, ephemera represents a broad category with subgroups of format-based materials (Young, 2003). Printed ephemera may include broadsides, pamphlets, chapbooks, tickets, theatre posters, playbills, and other limited-run print items that were created for only a short-term purpose (Makepeace, 1985). Because these items were intended to be saved for a very limited period (i.e., a concert, a meeting, a performance, or an auction), collectors, dealers, and researchers seek out scarce printed ephemera (Figure 3.6).

Figure 3.6
Broadside, 1854

Source: Virginia Tech Special Collections.

Academic archivists must take into account the importance of the printed pieces in their repositories. An archivist does not need to become a book history expert or specialize in descriptive bibliography, but a clear awareness of how to research, acquire, catalog, store, preserve, and deliver, these unique books, pamphlets, and broadsides to patrons is an important part of the research library concept. The availability of many of these texts is increasing because of online digitization projects (GoogleBooks, Project Gutenburg, etc.), and several special collections departments are enhancing access to their printed pieces through collaborative digitization efforts.

Other Collections

Nearly all special collections departments have collections of photographic materials (Figure 3.7). The variety of formats can include glass plate negatives, tintypes, ambrotypes, albumen prints, color slides, and perhaps the most unstable, digital images. Whether filed within specific manuscript collections or treated as a separate photographic collection, image materials have enormous research value. However, photographic materials require careful handling and active preservation methods to ensure their longevity.

Historic maps are also another common type of material found in special collections. Often these maps document the campus, the local community, state, and region. Because of their irregular dimensions and frequent use, map collections should be stored flat and placed in protective sleeves. Maps are excellent teaching tools for demonstrating to students and researchers changes in the landscape, population, and campus. Academic archives frequently digitize their map collections to provide greater access.

Audiovisual collections are scattered throughout special collections departments. Outdated formats (i.e., film, betamax, umatic, reel-to-reel audio, cassettes, and DATs) often require special equipment to use and are constantly in need of migration through reformatting projects. These fragile items, however, contain a wealth of research material. Some examples include, a large oral history collection with hundreds of interviews from African American tenant farmers, a complete set of television newscasts from the late 1960s documenting student unrest on college campuses, and dozens of wax cylinders which record Appalachian music from the early twentieth century. Research demand, access to vendors to complete the reformatting, preservation concerns, and interested donors

Figure 3.7
Confederate Soldiers, 1862

Source: Virginia Tech Special Collections.

help determine which audiovisual collections are prime candidates for reformatting.

Artwork, objects, and furniture are often found in special collections, even though typically special collections are not, nor should they be, museums. These nonarchival collections, more suitable for a museum, find their way into special collections for several reasons. Many academic libraries may have developed either gallery space or cultivated donors with an interest in collecting objects of some kind. Because special collections have traditionally had a museum-like quality to their reading rooms, these departments have become the most obvious storage facility for items such as paintings, cadet swords, tapestries, and antique chairs owned by former presidents of the institution. Special collections librarians are often unable to refuse such gifts and their departments become a holding facility for nonarchival material that has little research value for its regular patrons. Some pieces may be useful for display or exhibit purposes, but managing a large collection of objects detracts from the mission of special collections programs.

SUDDEN INTEREST IN SPECIAL COLLECTIONS

The variety of printed and handwritten material found in special collections has long been known by academic librarians. However, during the past decade, special collections departments have become one center of attention in the world of academic research libraries. Library directors and other administrators have taken great interest in providing fuller access to special collections material. Enhanced availability of research collections has made special collections a vital and very relevant part of today's academic libraries (Traister, 2000). At the same time, the question of who will lead special collections departments into the next few decades has become a significant issue. All of this newfound attention and the rise of digital scholarship further

> **Recent Special Collections Initiatives Sponsored by ARL**
>
> - Detailed survey of special collections departments, 1998
> - Task force on special collections established, 2001
> - The hidden collections movement
> - Focus on the education of future special collections librarians
> - Focus on digital opportunities for special collections

integrated special collections departments into the services and mission of their libraries. Academic archivists should be well aware of how special collections are now a central part of many academic libraries.

The "Hidden Collections" Initiative

In the early years of the twenty-first century, academic research libraries examined the status and purposes of their special collections departments. This interest in special collections had its roots in the results of a 1998 survey by the Association of Research Libraries (ARL). The responses to this survey of special collections librarians revealed that archives housed significant unprocessed material which was unavailable and unknown to scholars (Panitch, 2001). A June 2001 symposium at Brown University built on that theme. Attending librarians and administrators expressed concern that many of the unique research collections in their academic libraries were unprocessed, inaccessible, and therefore undiscoverable (ARL, 2007). That fall, ARL formed a task force of librarians, administrators, and archivists to investigate current issues in special collections. ARL charged their special collections task force with seven main areas of investigation, which revolved around making backlog primary resources more accessible to scholars, enhancing the relationship of special collections and academic libraries, and preparing the next generation of special collections librarians (Hewitt and Panitch, 2003).

By 2003 the work of the task force had generated several new initiatives. Early that year, the task force released a statement summarizing their findings. The document emphasized that special collections, which hold unique one-of-a-kind primary sources, are integral to scholarship and the mission of research libraries (ARL, 2009). ARL endorsed their report, and announced that member libraries needed to provide special collections with more resources, such as funding, staffing, and spaces (ARL, 2009).

In June 2003, the task force released a white paper relating to the issue of unprocessed and inaccessible materials in special collections. This document focused on the "hidden collections" in research libraries, which archivists often refer to as the backlog collections. In its white paper, the task force recommended that ARL member libraries address the problems of access to hidden collections by creating basic library catalog entries, finding aids, or other online records (Jones, 2003). Thus, many ARL libraries embraced as a general concept that basic description of an unprocessed collection is better than no description at all, and that patron demand for these "discovered" materials would help prioritize which backlog collections needed further processing attention (ARL, 2008). For many libraries, the actual adaptation of this approach meant that all incoming archival and manuscript collections were given a basic catalog record upon the point of accessioning or acquisition.

The task force's hidden collections white paper encouraged not only a cataloging effort at each individual institution, but a much larger national collaborative project (Jones, 2003). In the fall of 2003, ARL sponsored a two-day symposium for library directors, special collections librarians, and archivists to discuss the growing hidden collections movement. Attendees generally agreed that providing some access, rather than no access, to backlog hidden collections was a worthwhile effort with great scholarly benefits (ARL, 2008). The varied nature of research libraries—funding, staffing, and missions—made it difficult to agree on a standard cataloging approach for all participating institutions. Some research libraries developed practices internally, while others relied on consortial efforts.

Following the 2003 meeting, the ARL task force launched a survey project. Rather than survey all ARL libraries, the task force issued a voluntary call for information. The task force took a thematic approach to identifying unprocessed collections with the greatest immediate research value. The survey searched for collections in the following categories: women's history, advertising, pamphlets and ephemera, material documenting the period from the end of the Civil War until the end of World War I, and collections that highlight ethnic and cultural history (Tabb, 2004). The successful survey—99 institutions submitted descriptions for 466 discrete collections in the five categories—resulted in a grant application to the National Endowment for the Humanities to develop specific cataloging practices for material in the broad category of social and political history (ARL, 2008). Although NEH did not fund the project, the survey resulted in greater efforts to identify, minimally catalog, and provide access to significant research materials hidden in the backlogs of special collections departments.

Academic archivists, who were already developing and adapting minimal processing approaches to backlog collections, were a part of the hidden collections movement. Many archivists took issue with the problems of having researchers use materials that may still have private or protected personal information (e.g., Social Security numbers, student records, and personal addresses). Concurrently, archivists were developing minimal approaches to processing these and other hidden collections. From the perspective of an academic archivist, the hidden collections movement was more of a cataloging project than a processing initiative, which means that many of the components of archival work—preservation, arrangement, description, developing finding aids, and removing sensitive or irrelevant information from collections—were not central to the process.

The hidden collections effort is a worthy and ongoing initiative. Because of the hidden collections movement, academic libraries and their leaders are still interested in special collections materials and the future of special collections. By implementing components of the hidden collection initiative, academic archivists can build support for their backlog processing projects. However, archivists must consider how providing increased intellectual access to backlog materials affects acquisitions, planning, training, and processing.

The Next Generation

In addition to targeting hidden collections, the ARL task force took particular interest in the education of the next wave of special collections librarians. The need to develop core competencies and training models for future special collections leaders emerged as a significant issue during the 2001 special collections symposium at Brown University (ARL, 2007). ARL's task force took up the issue of how to prepare future leaders of special collections and exactly who should be prepared for that enormous task. In November 2003, ARL held a conference in Chapel Hill, North Carolina, to address the question of the education of special collections librarians (ARL, 2008). Attendees identified sets of generic and unique skills that were needed to be successful in special collections, with the overall conclusion that some skills could be learned in a graduate program and others were only obtainable through actual experience (Schreyer, 2006).

The results of the conference and other subsequent discussions appeared the next year in an ARL white paper focused on the future of education and training for special collections work. The document emphasized the need to train, recruit, and retain special collections professionals at all levels, through flexible educational paths to the profession (Schreyer, 2004). While the master's degree in library science has been the standard for academic librarians, the task force indicated that PhD holders might have other relevant skills for special collections work. The white paper also suggested that professionals already working in special collections needed new managerial and technological skills to lead departments (Schreyer, 2004). While some training programs for special collections work did exist, the task force recommended that special collections librarians must expand educational options by collaborating with other professional groups and creating stronger ties with the archival community (Schreyer, 2004).

In late 2004, the task force hosted a special collections symposium in Washington, DC, specifically focused on archivists and special collections. While the meeting did not yield a set of shared core competencies, attendees did note that the lines between archival work and special collections work had blurred significantly (Schreyer, 2004). Common skills such as donor relations, fundraising, and even approaches to processing collections were shared by archivists and special collections librarians. The discussions at the symposium recognized that academic archivists, especially those with a subject specialty and knowledge of primary source education, were strong candidates to lead special collections departments.

During the following years, the special collections task force developed professional ties with leaders of the Society of American Archivists, the Rare Books and Manuscripts Section of the American Library Association, and the Council on Library and Information Resources. These multiple collaborations and the emergence of new training programs hint that the future of special collections and special collections librarianship will not be determined by just one organization or subfield. More likely, technology and the challenges of harnessing scholarly communication in an academic environment will help define the skills needed to lead a successful special collections department (Crowe, 2002).

Future Directions for Special Collections

The ability to use technology to provide greater access to primary source materials is one of the main factors for newfound interest in special collections. Special collections are obvious locations for their library's most unique items, which are ideal candidates for digitization, publication, and online dissemination. In fact, selection of material for possible digitization is becoming a factor in collection development decisions (Taranto, 2009). Digitization projects require a wide range of library faculty and staff. During the course of even small scanning projects, computer programmers, collection development librarians, web designers, reference specialists, catalogers, metadata librarians, and instruction coordinators must interact virtually or physically with special collections material. Close work with special collection librarians on digital projects also results in a greater understanding of how special collections function and what materials are available.

As academic library services have become more virtual and user-centric, many special collections departments have adopted similar approaches. Many special collections are using Web 2.0 applications to create, promote, and manage special collections resources (Whittaker and Thomas, 2009). Web 2.0 tools, such as blogs and RSS news feeds, help reach general users, especially new users unfamiliar with special collections. The use of social networking sites, such as Facebook and Twitter, allow special collections to develop a virtual profile and attract new audiences (Theimer, 2010). Perhaps the most promising application of Web 2.0 for special collections is to create greater access to collections. Web 2.0 features allow users to simultaneously search across library catalogs, finding aids, digital projects, and online open access repositories, instead of merely searching each location separately (Whittaker and Thomas, 2009). Search parameters may also be expanded beyond individual repositories, allowing users to find related archival material at disparate and frequently distant locations.

Special collections departments are redefining library instruction efforts. Instead of reviewing searching procedures and library databases, instructors in special collections use primary sources to teach students about research methods. Quite simply, special collections departments are bringing their collections to the classroom and the classroom to the collections (Smith, 2006). Through primary source education sessions, students discover the power and value of original materials, while learning critical analysis and interpretative skills. For example, allowing a freshman student in an introductory history class to hold an original Civil War diary and attempt to read the handwritten text promotes discovery, engagement, and learning. That kind of supervised instructional exercise also exposes special collections to a wide range of users, some of whom may become repeat users during their years of academic study.

CONCLUSION

Today, special collections departments are dynamic research environments, much more active and cutting edge in the world of academic libraries than just a few decades ago. Within many college and university library systems, special collections departments represent the entire range of academic archives and archival work. Special collections departments have become the locus for innovative instructional sessions, public programs, events and exhibitions, and a central point for scholarly research. This more innovative and integrated approach has resulted in special collections librarians and academic archivists playing a larger role in the leadership of academic libraries.

Special collections—its history, collections, organization, people, and great potential—is at the core of the work of today's academic archivists. There is enormous opportunity for academic archivists to play a significant role in shaping the world of special collections. An understanding of primary sources, the research process, donor relations, collection

development, how an institution functions, and especially new technological tools have put today's academic archivists in a prime position
to lead special collections departments, and influence the direction of
academic libraries.

REFERENCES

Association of Research Libraries. 2007. "Building on Strength: Developing
    an ARL Agenda for Special Collections." Association of Research Librar-
    ies. Last modified November 2. http://www.arl.org/resources/pubs/
    mmproceedings/139brown.shtml.
———. 2008. "ARL Special Collections Task Final Status Report, 2006." Associa-
    tion of Research Libraries. Last modified April 4. http://www.arl.org/rtl/
    speccoll/spcolltf/status0706.shtml.
———. 2009. "Special Collections: Statement of Principles, 2003." Association of
    Research Libraries. Last modified April 6. http://www.arl.org/rtl/speccoll/
    speccollprinciples.shtml.
Boles, Frank. 2005. *Selecting and Appraising Archives and Manuscripts.* Chicago:
    Society of American Archivists.
Burke, Frank G. 1997. *Research and the Manuscript Tradition.* Lanham, MD: The
    Scarecrow Press.
Byrd, Robert L. 2001. "'One Day . . . It Will be Otherwise': Changing the Repu-
    tation and the Reality of Special Collections." *RBM: A Journal of Rare Books,
    Manuscripts, and Cultural Heritage* 2, no. 2 (Fall): 163–174.
Cave, Roderick. 1976. *Rare Books Librarianship.* London: Clive Bingley.
Clinton, Alan. 1981. *Printed Ephemera: Collection Organisation and Access.* London:
    Clive Bingley.
Crowe, William J. 2002. "An Uncertain Trumpet: Developing Archival and Spe-
    cial Collections in the Electronic Era." *Journal of Library Administration* 36,
    no. 3: 73–80.
Dooley, Jackie. 2009. "Ten Commandments for Special Collections Librarians
    in the Digital Age." *RBM: A Journal of Rare Books, Manuscripts, and Cultural
    Heritage* 10, no. 1 (Spring): 51–60.
Ham, Gerald F. 1975. "The Archival Edge." *American Archivist* 38, no. 1 (Janu-
    ary): 5–13.
Hamlin, Arthur T. 1981. *The University Library in the United States.* Philadelphia:
    University of Pennsylvania Press.
Hewitt, Joe A., and Judith M. Panitch. 2003. "The ARL Special Collections Initia-
    tive." *Library Trends* 52, no. 1 (Summer): 157–171.
Jones, Barbara. 2003. "Hidden Collections, Scholarly Barriers: Creating Access
    to Unprocessed Special Collections Materials in North America's Research

Libraries." *RBM: A Journal of Rare Books, Manuscripts, and Cultural Heritage* 5, no. 2 (Fall 2004): 84–105.

Joyce, William J. 1988. "The Evolution of the Concept of Special Collections in American Research Libraries." *Rare Books and Manuscripts Librarianship* 3, no. 1: 19–30.

Kurtz, Michael J. 2004. *Managing Archival and Manuscript Repositories*. Chicago: Society of American Archivists.

Maher, William J. 1992. *The Management of College and University Archives*. Chicago: Society of American Archivists.

Makepeace, Chris E. 1985. *Ephemera: A Book on Its Collection, Conservation, and Use*. Brookfield, VT: Gower Publishing.

Pacifico, Michele, and Thomas P. Wilsted, eds. 2009. *Archival and Special Collections Facilities: Guidelines for Archivists, Librarians, Architects, and Engineers*. Chicago: Society of American Archivists.

Panitch, Judith M. 2001. *Special Collections in ARL Libraries: Results of the 1998 Survey Sponsored by the ARL Research Collections Committee*. Washington, DC: Association of Research Libraries.

Ritzenthaler, Mary Lynn. 2010. *Preserving Archives and Manuscripts*. 2nd ed. Chicago: Society of American Archivists.

Rostenberg, Leona, and Madeline B. Stern. 1989. "Introduction." In *Special Collections in College and University Libraries*, compiled by Modoc Press, Inc., vii–xii. New York: Macmillan.

Samuels, Helen Willa. 1992. *Varsity Letters: Documenting Modern Colleges and Universities*. Chicago: Society of American Archivists.

Schreyer, Alice. 1988. "RBMS at 30: Growing Along with the Profession." *Rare Books and Manuscripts Librarianship* 3, no. 1: 3–7.

———. 2004. "Education and Training for Careers in Special Collections: A White Paper Prepared for the Association of Research Libraries Special Collections Task Force." http://www.arl.org/bm~doc/sctf_ed.pdf.

———. 2006. "What's So Special about Special Collections Librarians?" *RBM: A Journal of Rare Books, Manuscripts, and Cultural Heritage* 7, no. 1 (Spring): 49–54.

Smith, Steven Escar. 2006. "From 'Treasure Room' to 'School Room': Special Collections and Education." *RBM: A Journal of Rare Books, Manuscripts, and Cultural Heritage* 7, no. 1 (Spring): 31–39.

Tabb, Winston. 2004. "'Wherefore are These Things Hid?': A Report of a Survey Undertaken by the ARL Special Collections Task Force." *RBM: A Journal of Rare Books, Manuscripts, and Cultural Heritage* 5, no. 2 (Fall): 123–126.

Taranto, Barbara. 2009. "It's Not Just about Curators Anymore: Special Collections in the Digital Age." *RBM: A Journal of Rare Books, Manuscripts, and Cultural Heritage* 10, no. 1 (Spring): 30–36.

Theimer, Kate. 2010. *Web 2.0 Tools and Strategies for Archives and Local History Collections*. New York: Neal-Schuman.

Traister, Daniel. 2000. "Is There a Future for Special Collections? And Should There Be? A Polemical Essay." *Rare Books and Manuscripts Librarianship* 1, no. 1: 54–76.

University Libraries, University of North Carolina. 2008. "About the Southern Historical Collection." Chapel Hill: University of North Carolina. Last updated September 10. http://www.lib.unc.edu/mss/shc/shcabout.html.

Whittaker, Beth M., and Lynne M. Thomas. 2009. *Special Collections 2.0: New Technologies for Rare Books, Manuscripts, and Archival Collections.* Santa Barbara: Libraries Unlimited.

Wilsted, Thomas P. 2007. *Planning New and Remodeled Archival Facilities.* Chicago: Society of American Archivists.

Young, Timothy G. 2003. "Evidence: Toward a Library Definition of Ephemera." *Rare Books and Manuscripts Librarianship* 4, no. 1: 11–26.

Part II

Building and Updating an Academic Archives Program

4

Mission and Vision Building for Academic Archives

INTRODUCTION

The success of any kind of archival program depends on having a clear direction, purpose, and future. Just like academic libraries and academic institutions, academic archives programs must develop a mission that informs the work they do. The more elusive and difficult challenge for academic archives is to cultivate and strive toward a vision that represents the future for the program. Academic archives with an unclear mission or unknown vision run the risk of becoming less relevant and unimportant to their academic community and users.

This chapter discusses the importance of mission and vision building for academic archives. It reviews the basics for starting an academic archives program, approaches to developing a mission and a vision, and practical approaches to maintaining the mission and vision while operating an archives. As part of building a successful academic archives program, archivists must exhibit broad leadership, manage and share resources, identify supporters, promote their programs, and cultivate users for their collections and services. This chapter seeks to answer the following questions:

1. How does one develop an academic archives program?
2. How does one craft and fulfill a mission and vision for their archival program?
3. How do academic archivists contribute to the mission and vision of their academic archives program?

LAUNCHING AN ACADEMIC ARCHIVES PROGRAM

What Is the Origin of Academic Archives?

Many archivists assume that every academic institution has some kind of archives program (i.e., records management unit, special collections department, college or university archives, or historian's office) somewhere on its campus. While it is true that more than 1,000 academic archives programs exist, there are still many colleges and universities in the United States without an archives program of any kind (Cox, 1992). Some schools are either too new, too poorly funded, or too focused on other initiatives to start an archives program. Other schools have eliminated their archives units for budgetary or political reasons. In these situations, historical materials exist but are not available through any kind of formal academic archives program. Instead, collections and official records are often maintained by the school's administration, specifically to serve the needs of the institution's upper administration. Other times, the school's administrators place the accumulated historical materials in the care of someone in the campus library who is not an archivist or special collections librarian.

The need to document the institution's history, to manage official records being generated on campus, to inform difficult lawsuits, and to preserve the existing historical materials before they disappear from attics, closets, or offices on campus are just a few of the reasons that lead colleges and universities to establish or reestablish an archives program (Cox, 1992). Interest in starting an archives program sometimes comes as a result of a significant anniversary or celebration for the institution. Typically, the academic library is the place where campus archives begin. Often the creation or expansion of a special collections department (with at least one dedicated staff member) within the campus library signals the real beginning of an archives initiative. Records management may be a component of a new archives program; that relationship and the details of establishing and operating a campus records program is the focus of Chapter 5.

The beginning of an academic archives program evolves from discussions at many levels across multiple units. The formation of an archives program may either come from the administration or from within the academic library itself. The actual charge and support for the program most frequently comes from the institution's upper administration in the form of a basic policy statement, while the details of the unit are left to the implementers in the academic library. Stable funding, at least one full-time position, physical spaces for researchers and archival storage, and other dedicated resources represent a clear institutional commitment to an academic archives program (Yakel, 1994). Once that commitment is in place then the actual planning and implementation may begin. A common example is that a new archives unit is created within the campus library and the task of starting the archives falls to a new or repurposed information professional, such as a humanities librarian. Ideally, the

> **First Steps in Developing an Academic Archives Program**
>
> - Campus needs to collect, preserve, and create access to institutional history.
> - Campus units, most often the academic library, agree to maintain an archives program.
> - Administration supports an archives initiative.
> - Develop an official charge or policy document, which formally establishes the program and outlines its location in the institution's administrative structure.

leader of the new program reports to the dean or director of the library and is responsible for the development of the archives.

Central to the operation of an academic archives program is an official statement of responsibility or charge from the institution (Yakel, 1994). The institution's top administration, such as a president or provost, issues the document, which is then signed by other administrators, deans, and the director of the academic library. Such a document outlines the basic expectations, structure, and understood purposes of the unit (Dearstyne, 1993). Academic librarians and archivists are often the authors of the document's content. This opportunity allows the first leaders of the program to clearly state what the archives will collect, who it will serve, where it will be located in the hierarchy of administration, and how it will generally benefit the institution (Hunter, 2003).

Even long-standing campus archives have some kind of original charge on file, which is often updated and amended as conditions and support changes. The charge establishes authority to collect, as well as establishing the general responsibilities and accountability for serving the institution. It is from this official charge to create an archives program that the leaders of the new unit develop initial strategy, a policy statement, a clear mission, and eventually a vision (Maher, 1992).

The Mission Statement

At the heart of an academic archives program is its mission statement. This relatively short statement clearly outlines the principles of the archives program and should be well understood by all involved with the unit (Ramos and Ortega, 2006). The official institutional charge to create the program may have a clear mandate or mission statement, often carefully designed by those who will staff the new unit. Other times the official charge for an archives is vague (i.e., "the archives will collect and preserve evidence of the institution's history"), which makes it necessary to clarify and communicate the purposes of the archival program through a concise and clear mission statement.

For most organizations, developing a mission statement is integral to the process of strategic planning. For businesses, this kind of planning involves identifying how the most precious resources are allocated and how they are used to deliver products and services (Matthews, 2005). For academic libraries, which most academic archives are part of, the process of strategic planning is more about identification of user needs than determining the needs of the library (Jacob, 1990). As new or reenergized academic archives work toward refining their mission statement, the leaders and planners of the unit must not ignore the larger plan set out by the library system.

Academic library leaders regularly engage in strategic planning. Nonprofit organizations, such as libraries, have adapted the strategic planning methods first developed by businesses to focus their resources on planning, organizing, and controlling their programs and services (Zaltman, 1979). The ongoing planning process involves review of the current plan, establishing goals, measurement of outcomes, and adjustment of programmatic priorities for the library. Because of technological shifts and economic downturns, most strategic plans for academic libraries are focused on no more than a five-year period with frequent smaller adjustments to the plan as short-term goals are met (Jacob, 1990). Changes in academic library leadership (i.e., retirements, arrival of a new dean or director) may also result in a reassessment of the strategic plan, if not a complete reorganization of the library. As strategic plans change, the mission of the academic library may also shift to reflect new focus areas.

At any point in the strategic planning process—planning, implementation, or assessment—the mission statement should always address the main purpose of the organization (Pfeiffer, 1991). For academic libraries, a well-written mission statement encompasses the primary user groups, key services and programs, availability of library collections and technology, and benefits to the academic community (Evans and Ward, 2007). Most likely, the library's document includes principles from their institution's mission statement, especially on the points of promoting research, community outreach, diversity, and life-long learning.

The mission statement for any academic archives defines the purpose, audience, and services of the program. Those principles must support the mission of the library and the institution. Underlying the mission statement for academic archives, or for an archives program of any kind, are the archival elements of identifying materials of enduring value, preserving those materials, and then making those materials available for research (Hunter, 2003).

A sample mission statement for an academic archives program at a medium-sized university could be: "The archives program collects official records of the institution, materials related to local and family history, and other collections documenting the history of African American education, for use by students, the academic community, and external researchers. The archives program stores, preserves, and arranges these collections according to standard archival practices, and provides patrons with access to original materials in the reading room and through online digitization, finding aids, and exhibits. As part of the university library system, the archives program supports research, scholarship, learning on campus and throughout the scholarly community."

In addition to large-scale objectives, academic archivists may develop the mission statement to reflect more specific goals. For example, new academic archives could include in their mission statement the goal to begin collecting the official records of the institution through a records management program, or the goal to acquire the files of their alumni association. When such goals are achieved, then it is necessary to adjust the mission statement to reflect the changes.

The Mission Statement for Academic Archives

- Outlines the principles of the archives program
- Defines purpose, audience, and services
- Is understood by all members of the department
- Fits well with the mission of the academic library and institution
- Underscores the principles of archival work
- Lists specific goals and objectives
- Is flexible and can be updated

Expansion or contraction of the archives program marks an important point to reexamine the mission statement. Without qualified staff an archives program cannot operate, which means that the loss or addition of employees directly affects what the unit is capable of accomplishing.

Certainly the strengths of specific individuals should not influence the overall mission of the program, but the loss of positions often results in decreased services. Likewise, the addition of positions for specific purposes, such as a reference coordinator or a processing archivist for a special collections department, will broaden the mission, services, and capabilities of the unit. Other internal developments, such as new series of public lectures about the Civil War on campus launched by a university archivist, affect the overall purposes of the archives and may result in revising the mission statement to reflect a new commitment to public programs.

A mission statement for academic archives can be both broad and specific, but it should reflect the purpose of the program, the practice of archival work, and the relationship to its institution (Wilsted and Nolte, 1991). Determining the specifics of the mission depends on the location, the nature of the school and its academic programs, and the student body. For example, a mission statement for a growing special collections department on a small college campus may specifically state that the primary users are on-campus undergraduates in the liberal arts and the college publicity office. That same mission statement may also say that the archives program collects a wide range of material (i.e., official records, student publications, photographic collections, scrapbooks, and faculty papers) to document and preserve the 100-year history of the college.

The mission statement establishes the principles for any archival program. With a clear mission, new or reinvigorated academic archives can move from the planning stages into implementation. This second stage involves determining what collections are available, establishing operating policies and procedures, and launching the new programs or services.

Conducting a Survey

Collections help define archives programs, its services, its researchers, and its potential. Building collections of research material is a key component of the mission of academic archives. Established archives programs frequently conduct surveys of collections before adding or not adding them to their holdings. This kind of hands-on evaluation, often called a site visit, is common practice for academic archivists, and the results of the survey frequently become the basis for a subsequent processing plan, preliminary inventory, and eventual finding aid (Hunter, 2003). Following the survey, academic archivists should create a report that documents their decisions about collection development, processing priorities, preservation needs, and collection storage.

For new archives programs, the leader of the initiative must conduct a comprehensive survey of available archival collections. Sometimes the survey is completed prior to the launch of the program. The first part of the survey involves locating the records and historical files maintained by the institution, especially materials that are created by the upper administrative offices (i.e., president, treasurer, and board trustees) (Fleckner, 1977). Some academic archives may work with the institution's registrar or admissions office to maintain legacy student records, such as official transcripts. This part of the survey is intended to identity all of the records created by the institution, and often will later serve as the basis for records retention schedules (Hunter, 2003).

The survey may extend beyond official records. Materials already in the library's possession, such as the literal "treasure rooms" where historical collections have been stored for safe keeping, should be documented. Other groups on campus with possible archival collections, such as the alumni office, the faculty senate, student organizations, or the office of the school's historian, must also be contacted and surveyed. Finally, the survey must account for archival materials outside of the institution, such as collections held by alumni, other institutions and repositories, or still in private hands.

Surveys provide archivists with useful information about collections and that data can be used for a variety of purposes in a new or expanding archival program. It is more important to conduct an effective survey than an efficient survey. The detailed information found in initial survey benefits staff, who will process the material, and patrons, who will use the collections for research (Hunter, 2003). Further, detailed surveys serve as a roadmap for the next steps in the archival process of acquisition, processing, and provision of access.

The end result of an archival survey is a detailed report that guides the growth of the collection and the archival program. The survey document describes the historical range of the available materials, the formats (i.e., documents,

Importance of Archival Surveys

- Locates the official, historical, and other records of the parent institution
- Serves as basis for records management retention schedules
- Forms the basis of a collection development policy
- Results in a final report noting collection strengths, realities, and areas for growth

images, audiovisual, and electronic files), the physical condition of the material, their current storage location and any environmental concerns, the existence of access tools such as finding aids or indices, and an estimate of the size of the collection (Purcell, 2009). For official and student records, the report may include suggestions about retention scheduling and possible restrictions due to privacy concerns. The report addresses future possibilities for collection development, such as historical materials in private hands or still in campus departments that may eventually be donated. Although the results are preliminary, the survey should include cost estimates for managing and storing the expected archival resources. This data must be easily translated into the actual needs for staff, space, supplies, and other necessary program support.

Opening the Archives

With a strong mission statement and a completed survey in hand (or in progress), the first leaders of an academic archives program must establish the procedural details for the operation of the archival program (Kurtz, 2004). Documenting practices, decisions, and policies is a necessary part of archival management. Having standard policies and operating procedures in place and available is essential for all archives programs. The program's visible public activities (i.e., reference services and exhibits) and the more behind-the-scenes work (i.e., processing and preservation of materials) are equally important. Implementation and adjustment of standard practices over time is a critical component of maintaining a successful archives program.

Operating academic archives involves balancing several target areas common for all archives. At the foundation of archives are the following components: staffing; public services and programs; selection and appraisal; physical spaces and collection management; campus and community outreach; preservation; donor relations and collection development; acquisitions and processing; managing records; and digital initiatives (Yakel, 1994). These key elements are the bedrock for archival programs and are evident in daily operations.

While these archival components are covered more thoroughly in other chapters, it is important to remember that these critical areas of operation have direct ties to the mission of the department. For example, a small academic archives program is focused on collecting official school records. When they are approached by the alumni association about a donor with early twentieth-century scrapbooks, the leader of the program should consider the mission, purpose, and available resources before accepting the donation and thus expanding their program. As a possible solution, perhaps another nearby archives, museum, or library would be a better home for the scrapbooks.

Similarly, academic archives cannot effectively serve all potential audiences. Some larger programs may have the collections, staff experts, and other resources to serve many groups (i.e., students, faculty, genealogists, documentary filmmakers, and international scholars), while other academic archives target the campus and scholarly community. As a general principle, academic archives are not museums for storing historical material for the institution, nor should they be designed to support all possible research uses. Instead, academic archives are focused campus units, designed to serve the research needs of specific audiences with selected historical materials.

Academic archives resemble other archival programs in their structure, operations, and procedures. The most effective academic archives programs have clear policies that support and enhance their mission. Academic archives programs must establish clear targets for collecting material, processing collections, providing access to materials, and reaching the intended user groups (Dearstyne, 2001). Building services, staff expertise, and collections around the core mission of the program will lead to developing even larger goals, or the vision, for the academic archives.

CHARTING A VISION FOR ACADEMIC ARCHIVES

Charting a direction for any organization is challenging, but it is a necessary step to make measurable progress toward larger goals (Matthews, 2005). Articulating the purposes of the organization is best expressed in a clear mission statement. From the mission statement and the actual experiences of operating an archives program, a more philosophical vision for the archives should develop. The vision should set realistic goals and expectations for the future of the archives program. It should be based on current and expected resources available to the program. Developing a shared vision for academic archives is integral to the success of the program. The vision begins with the leader of the program, who develops, implements, and adapts the long-term goals and aspirations of the archives program (Figure 4.1). That vision then grows and adapts with input from stakeholders.

Figure 4.1
Charting a Vision for Academic Archives

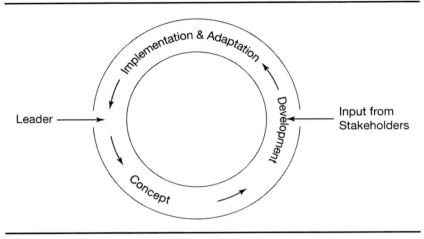

Source: Graphic by Marc Brodsky.

What Is the Origin of Visionary Leaders?

The vision for archives primarily comes from the leader of the program. In addition to operating the department, the leader serves as the visionary for the archives. Finding a person who possesses the skills of an archivist, a manager, and a visionary leader is a difficult task. The search for a program director position is usually more complicated than position searches for an entry-level or mid-level academic archivist.

Locating candidates to lead an archival program is a lengthy process. Even if accomplished internal candidates exist, it is necessary to do a national search. Internal candidates have the advantage of being familiar with the program, the employees, and the current challenges more than outside applicants. However, internal candidates are at a disadvantage when their experiences are too focused on the immediate issues and when their perspective of the larger archival profession is limited.

During the search process—telephone interviews, on-campus interviews, and calling references—the committee should make careful note of each candidate's potential for developing a vision for their archives department. Strong academic credentials, job history, and professional connections are important and expected for candidates at this level, which makes candidates with leadership skills and the ability to articulate a larger vision stand apart from the pool (Dearstyne, 2001). Sometimes, candidates in the pool with the least archives experience may demonstrate the most potential for building an archives program. The committee must look at each candidate for indications of the ability to lead, motivate, and inspire. Search committees narrowly focused on the candidates' years of experience, academic credentials, or association with prestigious institutions are likely to miss an opportunity to recruit a budding or quietly proven leader to build their archives. They may instead fill the position with an archivist who can manage the status quo and keep

Searching for Visionary Leaders

- National search preferable to limiting to internal candidates
- Looking for an archivist to serve as a leader, a manager, a mentor, a colleague, and a visionary for the department
- Qualified candidates with advanced academic credentials and several years of relevant work experience
- Importance of leadership skills and potential for building a program
- Indication of the ability to inspire, lead, and develop a vision
- Perspective on the archival profession and larger challenges
- Managerial skills and the ability to work within the institution's framework

the program afloat—important skills, but only one component needed to create a vibrant archives program.

The successful candidate should approach the position the same way he or she approaches archival work—looking toward the future, planning for new directions, and finding creative ways to solve old issues (Dearstyne, 2008). To be an academic archives visionary does not mean that the person operates in an unpredictable, unrealistic, or revolutionary fashion. Rather, a visionary leader is someone who can motivate the department to follow a clearly articulated path, which in turn provides a great deal of stability and continuity for the program. A strong leader should also have a transformative effect on their department, which is part of the process of achieving a shared mission and vision (Dearstyne, 2008).

Leaders of academic archives face the basic challenges of operating their departments. Limited resources, disappearing shelf space for burgeoning collections, patron demands, and supervision of employees are just a few of the daily challenges that take up large amounts of time. Most directors of academic archives are reasonable managers and improve with experience. However, some leaders—too focused on achieving a vision for their archives—may in fact be poor managers. Both management scenarios can be alleviated if the leader shares, or delegates, certain daily responsibilities to the other employees, and defines clear responsibilities for each member of the program (Evans and Ward, 2007). If the employees are willing and qualified, a leader builds trust and shares important experience with others in the department. As part of the process, the leader demonstrates a nonadversarial approach even in the face of possible adversity. The best leaders find ways to allow employees to capitalize on their strengths, address weaknesses that affect their work, follow their interests, and be empowered to make decisions (Stueart and Sullivan, 2010).

Developing the Vision

The leader of an academic archives program is the visionary. In addition to managing the daily operations of the archives, the designated leader plans for the future of the program, both for individuals in the department and the group as a whole (Kurtz, 2004). Developing a vision for an archives program is part long-range planning and part adapting to changing needs. Numerous internal and external factors influence the vision of an academic archives program, with the larger mission and vision of the institution and the academic library being the most significant.

The program's leader is the originator and chief promoter of the vision for the department. He or she considers variables such as expected or emerging demands, available resources, pre-existing strengths, and sources of support to develop a vision for the archives (Dearstyne, 2008). Having a vision for academic archives is not limited to a specific program or place. Sometimes the leader of a program comes from within the organization and has developed a vision over many years of observation, while other times a new director coming from a different institution brings to the program a larger perspective and vision.

While the vision begins with the leader of the program, the process of developing a vision statement should include multiple voices and perspectives. The most successful programs develop their vision statement with input from others. To begin, the leader of the program should work with existing archives staff to refine a vision. Their understanding of current conditions, attitudes, operations, and challenges are important to the process of charting a direction for the archives program. Other members of the academic library, such as the dean or director, the coordinator of reference services, and catalogers for special formats, are important colleagues with a vested interest in the future of the archives or special collections department. Another factor in vision development is the understanding of the institution's history, culture, traditions, and accomplishments (Kurtz, 2004). Greater awareness of why and how past decisions were made may help the new leader capitalize on past successes and avoid similar missteps.

Discussions and contemplation about the future of an academic archives program leads to the creation of a written vision statement. Similar to a mission statement, the vision for academic archives should be brief, list measurable goals, and define the overall purpose of the program. But what sets the vision apart from the mission is that the vision should inspire and motivate the members of the department to define and achieve goals that lead the program into an exciting future. Archivists who believe in the mission and vision for their program are more focused, efficient, and intent on achieving the goals that ultimately will transform their archives.

There are important practical differences between the mission and the vision. The mission defines the overall purpose for the program, while the vision is a set of much longer-term goals for the program. For example, a college archives may have the general mission to collect material about the school's history for use by students and faculty, but the vision may be that the college archives will develop into a nationally known archives program through innovative use of technology to deliver online access to its materials. Another example, a special collections department at a medium-sized university may have the mission to provide the campus community with access to original materials about the school's history and the surrounding region. The vision for this program may be focused on establishing

> **Factors in Building a Vision for Academic Archives**
>
> - Begins with the leader of the program
> - Refines with shared input from those already in the department
> - Supports the mission and vision for the academic library and the institution
> - Considers current and future demands, available resources, and sources of support
> - Outlines an achievable future
> - Defines the purposes of the program
> - Lists goals, objectives, and outcomes
> - Is fluid and adaptable
> - Is shared with supporters, constituents, colleagues, and others in the academic community
> - Reviews and updates as necessary

the department as a research center on its campus and for the region. Quite simply, a vision creates a sense of purpose, while the mission is the purpose only.

Making the Vision Tangible

Specific goals and expected outcomes should accompany the vision statement. In collaboration with others in the department, the leader of the program should identify specific courses of action that move the department toward the future. As an example, an academic archives desiring to become identified as a center for scholarly events in its medium-sized city might want to establish goals such as renovation of library spaces for public events, host several lectures and exhibits, prioritize successful grant submissions, and focus existing staff and expected new employees on these objectives—all realistic goals, which could be altered to achieve the larger purpose.

In the face of limited resources, it is important that goals be directly connected to the mission and vision statement, link to the overall strategic plan of the institution and the library, and capitalize on existing strengths and resources. Building a vision only on anticipated resources weakens the faith in the plan, especially if linchpin goals do not materialize.

Once the vision statement and goals are defined, the leader of the archives program should share the plans for the future with a wide audience. Sharing a broad outline of the possible future for the archives program with others throughout the campus community—academic faculty, administrators, library friends organizations, scholars, and local groups—may yield significant partnerships and opportunities to keep the department moving toward its goals (Dearstyne, 2008). Sharing the vision even further afield with archival and library colleagues at other institutions may also result in collaborative projects that will benefit the goals of all of those involved. Contributors and proponents of the vision become allies and stakeholders for the program. Their "buy-in" for the vision creates positive energy, publicity, and support for the academic archives program.

It may take several years to fully realize the expectations set forth in the vision statement, or the vision may be redefined as conditions and realities change. Vision statements are most successful when the preliminary goals are achievable and the right combination of resources (i.e., funding, staff, spaces, and collections) exists. A vision statement inspires archivists to work toward larger shared goals, serves as an important ingredient for change, positively affects the staff's behaviors and interactions, and becomes an integral part of all departmental decisions and initiatives (Matthews, 2005).

Maintaining and Adapting the Vision

Charting a vision for academic archives is an organic and gradual process. A part of that evolution is building on strengths and sustaining the programs that support the vision. The leader of the archives program sets the tone for the department, frequently adjusting the mission and vision according to the changing demands and environment. Other contributors to the vision—employees in the department, stakeholders, and supporters—are integral to the success of the program. The vision must remain fluid, manageable, possible, and, most of all, relevant to what is developing in archives, libraries, and the scholarly community (Dearstyne, 2001). Over time, the vision takes on new directions and the program develops.

The vision for academic archives programs may change because of internal factors. As departmental goals are achieved, the vision may become even more forward-thinking. For example, a special collections department at a large college began with the initial vision to be the anchor program in an emerging campus humanities center. Within a few years, the department relocated to a new humanities building and launched a successful instruction program for humanities majors. After revisiting their goals and accomplishments, the leader announced that the new vision for special collections was to become a nationally known digital humanities center, serving both the campus and the broader scholarly community. Other times, new developments, such as a large donation of materials and funding, creates new priorities for the archives, which directly influence the mission and vision.

External pressures from the institution may also affect the purposes and direction of an academic archives program. For example, the president's office at a land-grant university decides to make record keeping a priority and reassigns a pre-existing records management unit to the university archivist, who works in the special collections department. In addition to the new duties for the university archivist, this decision results in a mission and vision change for the special collections. While taking on more responsibilities for collecting and managing records for the institution, the department's vision now includes the expectation to become a centralized clearinghouse for digital and textual information produced by the institution and all of its satellite campuses. Thus, many times a vision change for academic archives is unintended and unpredictable.

The most common change to the vision and mission occurs with the arrival or departure of the program's leader. The departure of a visionary from the program does not mean an end to the vision, rather the new leader or leaders can adapt to new realities. The arrival of a new department head represents an opportunity for the archives program to try new directions or to maintain the current path. Most commonly, new leaders favor initial strategies that build on pre-existing strengths and available resources. Adapting the existing vision, rather than taking a completely new direction, has the advantage of maintaining connections with past contributors, stakeholders, and supporters. Over time, of course, a new vision for the department will emerge from those who work daily toward achieving goals that support and enhance the mission of their academic archives program.

> **Factors in Maintaining a Vision for Academic Archives**
>
> - Achievable and realistic
> - Flexible to meet emerging demands
> - Connects to the daily operations of the program
> - Adapts to changing internal demands, such as increased interest in specific collections
> - Considers new institutional demands from the program
> - May change with the departure and arrival of the program's leader
> - Shares awareness of the vision with staff, colleagues, and supporters

Keeping the vision active depends on all of those involved with the program. The staff of the archives unit, the other academic librarians, and those directly associated with the functions of the program should be well aware of the vision, and in their role as stakeholders they understand the methods needed to achieve those aspirations (Matthews, 2005). Campus supporters, which may include the provost's office, teaching faculty in specific academic departments, and the editors of the student newspaper, are valuable allies in promoting the purposes and long-range plans for the special collections or archives department. Library friends organizations and regional archives associations are also important groups who can affect the direction of archives programs.

The leader of the archival program is the key player in the vision building process and has the most responsibility for maintaining the vision. However, achieving the vision requires involvement from multiple contributors, who genuinely believe in the program. Connecting that vision to the daily operations and mission of an academic archives program is a complex task. Academic archivists, both program leaders and contributors, have the shared duty to enhance the mission and vision of their department. In the process, academic archivists have become leaders in not only their departments, but also in their academic library system and on their campus.

ACADEMIC ARCHIVISTS' ROLE IN THE MISSION AND VISION

The leaders of academic archives play an important role in the development of their department's purpose and future. Creating a vision for an archives department is a gradual process, which takes time, experience, training, and observation. Charting a realistic and achievable direction for an archives program also depends on understanding multiple perspectives and factors (i.e., institutional settings, personality types, past history of the department, and administrative structure) (Dearstyne, 2008).

Much like developing a vision for an archives program, the process of becoming a leader in the archives profession is difficult to quantify and can be elusive or amorphous. Leadership in academic archives includes the ability to build a program with a clear mission and a realistic and inspirational vision. A demonstrated understanding of the archivist's task—acquisition, arrangement, description, preservation, and access to historical records, archives, and manuscripts—is imperative for emerging archival leaders (O'Toole and Cox, 2006). The ability to attract solid archivists, with a combination of education, experience, and expertise, to their program and to work well with current staff is yet another sign of an effective archival leader (Dearstyne, 2001).

At the heart of the most successful academic archives is a visionary leader who both manages the daily activities of the department and leads the program toward the future, with foresight, perspective, and patience. These archival leaders are an important part of the academic library and campus administration, and contributing members of the campus community.

Leaders Not Managers

Archivists are educated and trained to be practicing archivists, often with little focus on the theories of management. Whether based in a large or small organization, archivists quickly assume managerial responsibilities.

Training students to process collections, evaluating and supervising entry-level archivists, or coordinating a grant project, academic archivists in any sized program are by default managers. Training programs, professional development, and practical experience are the most common paths for archivists to learn methods for management of their departments, staff, students, and their own time (Kurtz, 2004).

For many years, archivists in supervisory positions described their work as archival management. Keeping the doors of the "shop" open, filling the seats of the reading room with researchers, adding collections to the stacks, and supervising employees were largely thought of as "managing archives." During the past few decades, the work of archivists has become more complicated, user-centric, digital, and affected by decreasing resources. These shifts and other factors have resulted in archivists taking more of a leadership role than a managerial role in building and maintaining their programs (Dearstyne, 1993).

Managing people, spaces, and collections is a significant part of the work of academic archivists. These daily activities appear on official job descriptions and these duties take up the bulk of each work day. Whether focused on reference services, donor relations, digital work, or processing collections, academic archivists of all types also serve as leaders. Having a skilled leader (who looks outward) instead of just a competent manager (who looks inward) at the helm of an academic

---

Common Traits of an Archival Leader

- Ability to build a dynamic program with a clear mission and a realistic and inspirational vision
- Solid understanding and proven application of archival skills
- Ability to build a solid team of archivists
- Serves as a coach, mentor, and collaborator with staff
- Competent, effective, and an equitable manager
- Willing to delegate and share responsibilities
- Communicates effectively to a broad community through a variety of formats
- A good listener, who appreciates feedback
- Respected in the profession, institution, library, and academic community
- Current on the trends that affect information professionals, archivists, scholars, and others in higher education
- Able to build meaningful partnerships and consortia at all levels
- Builds excitement for their program through publicity, outreach, and service
- Politically savvy

archives often results in the most successful and innovative programs (Dearstyne, 2001). These leaders not only look toward the big-picture goals, but utilize consistent and proven managerial skills to take their programs toward the vision.

Leaders, more than managers, connect the objectives of their program with the larger goals of the academic library and institution (Dearstyne, 1993). As an example, most colleges and universities stress the importance of diversity on campus. Academic libraries have long been proponents of diversity initiatives in hiring, training, and within the workplace. Special collections and academic archives have identified a commitment to diversity by expanding their collection development policies to include material related to historically neglected groups such as African Americans, Native Americans, women, and other minorities. Documenting the experiences of minorities on campus and in the community and then providing access to those important collections, is just one example of how academic archivists have aligned their programs with the broader principles of inclusion and diversity.

Archival leaders come from all ranks and levels of the profession. Directors of academic archives are the most obvious leaders in their departments, because of their responsibility to fulfill the mission and chart a vision. However, other members of the department may also emerge as leaders in the library, on campus, and the archives profession. Contributing archivists with recognized skills, expertise, and commitment to service become departmental leaders. Entry-level positions in academic archives are proving grounds for emerging leaders. Beginning archivists with initiative and willingness to create or take advantage of the right opportunities can quickly transform from a manager of their collections into an archival and departmental leader.

Leading Archives and Leading Archivists

Leaders are not born; they are made. Leaders and their leadership styles develop through years of practical experience, trial-and-error, observation, training, and often guidance from a mentor or supervisor. Archival leaders emerge from a variety of environments, backgrounds, and influences. While archival leadership can be an elusive concept, there are common approaches to leading people and programs. In academic archives, the leader of the program guides the department toward the vision using several proven tactics.

Within their units, archival leaders build their departments on the formative pillars of clear communication, cooperation, and respect. They recruit motivated archivists and focus all members of the department on sharing the responsibilities of satisfying the mission and achieving the vision. Leaders build trust and earn respect by serving as a coach, mentor, and collaborator with their staff. They involve all employees in decision making, seeking input from contributors and stakeholders at each step in the process. Leaders of archives programs encourage professional development, are committed to research and scholarship, and encourage continuing education and training for all members of the department. This kind of support inspires, motivates, and builds a strong team of archival professionals with shared goals (Dearstyne, 2001).

In addition to building a strong department, the leader of an archives program plays a crucial role in the academic library. The recent interest in unique and hidden collections by library deans and directors has created leadership opportunities for academic archivists. Whether as directors of special collections, university or college archivists, or processing archivists, the demand for archivists to lead these initiatives in academic libraries has never been higher. Many archives leaders find that their path leads to increasingly more responsible administrative positions within the academic library, such as an associate dean for special collections or dean of libraries. In the short term, these professional jumps take academic archivists further away from the people, collections, and users of their archives. However, these library leaders have unparalleled long-term opportunities to build the archives component of their college or university library program. Having an archivist within the top levels of the academic library's administration is an excellent indication that the special collections or archives department is a valued part of the library's programs, services, and priorities.

A trusted and well-known academic archives leader is connected to his or her campus. Archives leaders serve on campus committees, work closely with administrators, communicate with department heads and deans, talk with students, and cultivate support from related groups (Kurtz, 2004). Even at a large institution with thousands of students, staff, and faculty, it only takes a few years to build a reputation (both good and bad) for the archives program. The best archival leaders can quickly and accurately explain to other nonarchivists the purposes of their program, including the mission and vision, without becoming frustrated or condescending. It takes practice to effectively work with administrators and academic faculty, who are often unsure of what archivists do or have little concept about the purposes of a campus archives program. The best archives leaders can bridge these gaps of understanding by explaining how the archives program benefits departments, colleges, and the institution as a whole. In the process, these archival leaders are demonstrating the usefulness of archives and generating positive energy for the profession at multiple levels (Dearstyne, 2001).

Academic archives leaders build successful programs through advocacy, outreach, and partnerships. Promoting the archives program to the campus and the public involves working with the press within the parameters and guidelines of the institution. The acquisition of a significant collection, the arrival of a traveling exhibit in special collections, and a sponsored lecture by a well-known historian are just a few examples of reasons for archives to promote themselves. Successful programs have strong relationships with their media outlets (i.e., campus newspapers, radio and television stations, and webmasters) and the institution's public relations office to develop articles, press releases, and announcements about their archives (Wilsted and Nolte, 1991). Some programs work closely with related organizations such as a library friends group, a local board, or student group to promote the archives through other channels.

An academic archives program with a strong donor base means access to funding sources, and sometimes beneficial political connections. Interacting with elected and appointed officials, as well as local citizen groups, is an ideal opportunity. Speaking about the importance of documenting campus activities with alumni who happen to work in the state's capital or in Washington, DC, may result in new support. The chance to make a case for the archives program outside of the boundaries of the academic institution may result in unexpected resources and attention. Having community and political connections may lead to possible donations of material and greater interest from the citizenry (Dearstyne, 2001).

The most successful academic archives are dynamic. These programs are built on balanced expansion or growth, necessary services, high visibility, strong leadership, and a commitment to their users (Dearstyne, 2001). The employees in these archives have skills that reflect the blended nature of academic archives, which means that academic archivists interact with a variety of materials, not just archival records, and work with a wide range of researchers, not just on-campus users. All the functions of the unit relate to the mission of the program, and the leader of the program works with others to chart and achieve the vision.

Leaders of strong archives programs lead by example. Their actions and communications reflect a high sense of professionalism, an understanding of the needs of others, and accessibility. Much like their programs, archival leaders are dynamic, willing to take risks, and forge new partnerships to achieve their goals. They value the skills and needs of their employees and advocate for their departments as necessary. As leaders in their academic libraries they promote their program and seek out opportunities within the library and on campus to make it a vital and integral part of the community. As contributors to the archival profession they produce scholarship, develop best practices for others to follow, and represent their program before peers. In response, archival leaders gain respect and recognition from their colleagues, peers, and supporters.

CONCLUSION

Colleges and universities establish academic archives programs for a variety of reasons. Whether to serve the administration, students, faculty, or scholarly community, academic archives are most commonly based within the academic library, often as a special collections department. Academic archives programs may manage the institution's official records, historical manuscripts, rare books, audiovisual collections, or some combination of unique primary sources. The initial purpose or charge for the program dictates specific goals for the academic archives to accomplish. A clear charge, which should be updated as the program matures, serves as a roadmap for the archives program.

A strong academic archives program is based on a clear mission, which considers the needs and expectations of users, the library, and the institution. With the mission in place, leaders of the program must survey available collections, develop policies and practices, and plan for the basics of operating an archives program. Having the right mix of services, projects, and initiatives requires careful planning, vision, and strong leadership.

Leaders of academic archives manage their units while creating an achievable vision. Crafting a vision involves developing specific goals that motivate the department and its employees while aiming for a more challenging future for the program. The leader of the archives makes the vision tangible, possible, believable, relevant, and dynamic. While maintaining the mission and charting a vision, the leader of the program oversees the smooth operation of the department and maintains connections to other initiatives. As part of building a successful program, leaders of academic archives must exhibit broad leadership skills, promote the archives, manage and share resources, identify stakeholders, and attract users for their collections and services. Successful academic archives programs and their leaders benefit the library, the institution, and the profession.

REFERENCES

Cox, Richard J. 1992. *Managing Institutional Archives: Foundational Principles and Practices.* Westport, CT: Greenwood Press.

Dearstyne, Bruce A. 1993. *The Archival Enterprise: Modern Archival Principles, Practices, and Management Techniques.* Chicago: American Library Association.

———, ed. 2001. *Leadership and Administration of Successful Archival Programs.* Westport, CT: Greenwood Press.

———, ed. 2008. *Leading and Managing Archives and Records Programs: Strategies for Success.* New York: Neal-Schuman.

Evans, G. Edward, and Patricia Layzell Ward. 2007. *Management Basics for Information Professionals.* 2nd ed. New York: Neal-Schuman.

Fleckner, John A. 1977. *Archives and Manuscripts: Surveys.* Chicago: Society of American Archivists.

Hunter, Gregory S. 2003. *Developing and Maintaining Practical Archives.* 2nd ed. New York: Neal-Schuman.

Jacob, M.E.L. 1990. *Strategic Planning: A How-To-Do-It Manual for Librarians.* New York: Neal-Schuman.

Kurtz, Michael J. 2004. *Managing Archival and Manuscript Repositories.* Chicago: Society of American Archivists.

Maher, William J. 1992. *The Management of College and University Archives.* Chicago: Society of American Archivists.

Matthews, Joseph R. 2005. *Strategic Planning and Management for Library Managers.* Westport, CT: Libraries Unlimited.

O'Toole, James M., and Richard J. Cox. 2006. *Understanding Archives and Manuscripts.* Chicago: Society of American Archivists.

Pfeiffer, J. William. 1991. *Strategic Planning: Selected Readings.* San Diego: Pfeiffer and Company.

Purcell, Aaron D. 2009. "Making the Most of Your Historical Assets." *The Information Management Journal* 43, no. 1 (January/February): 46–48.

Ramos, Marisol, and Alma C. Ortega. 2006. *Building a Successful Archival Programme: A Practical Approach.* Oxford, England: Chandos Publishing.

Stueart, Robert D., and Maureen Sullivan. 2010. *Developing Library Leaders.* New York: Neal-Schuman.

Wilsted, Thomas, and William Nolte. 1991. *Managing Archival and Manuscript Repositories.* Chicago: Society of American Archivists.

Yakel, Elizabeth. 1994. *Starting an Archives*. Chicago: Society of American Archivists.

Zaltman, Gerald. 1979. *Management Principles for Nonprofit Agencies and Organizations*. New York: Amacom.

5

Records Management and Academic Archives

INTRODUCTION

A records management program is a common counterpart to academic archives. These programs help identify the institution's official records and schedule them for either eventual destruction or permanent retention. The retained records eventually become part of the college or university archives. Some records management units are part of the academic archives program, while at other institutions the records management program is connected to an administrative part of the institution, such as the treasurer's office.

Academic archivists must understand their relationship to these records programs if they are to build successful archives programs. Even if an academic archivist interacts with the campus records manager once a year, there should be a clear understanding of their shared roles, tasks, and objectives. Recognizing the principles of records management is even more important for an academic archivist who may be asked to start or assume responsibilities for a campus records program.

This chapter examines how records management programs operate within an academic environment. It reviews the basic work of academic records managers, how to launch or revamp a records program, and the relationship between records management and archives programs. A solid campus records management program is one indication of a successful academic archives program. This chapter seeks answers to the following questions:

1. What is a records management program?
2. How does one start and sustain a campus records management program?

3. What is the relationship between a records management and an academic archives program?

THE PRINCIPLES OF RECORDS MANAGEMENT

Terms and Purposes

The discipline of records management involves the capture, organization, analysis, and control of recorded information. The field developed in the mid-twentieth century, largely for business purposes, in order to help support, protect, and document the organization that created the information. More than just keeping files in order, records management is focused on managing information that is essential for short- and long-term operation of an organization: monitoring transactions, developing and delivering new products and services, long-term planning, legal and regulatory compliance, and managing the daily activities of an organization (Saffady, 2004). Of course, records management practices are not limited to the business environment. Other kinds of organizations such as government agencies, professional groups and societies, clubs, nonprofit groups, and academic institutions rely on records management to achieve their goals and support their mission.

At the heart of records management are the records themselves. From e-mail to internal documents to annual reports, organizations

> **Reasons for Records Management**
>
> • Monitoring of transactions
> • Research and development
> • Short-term and long-term planning
> • Legal and regulatory compliance
> • Management of the institution's daily operations
> • Fiscal obligations

create numerous types of records during their normal operations. Records can be defined as information recorded on nearly any medium, such as paper, slides, electronic files, audiovisual tapes, microfilm, film, or photographic material (Diamond, 1995). The recorded information may include specific kinds of records such as correspondence, financial data, publications, reports, and minutes of proceedings. In contrast, unrecorded information, such as undocumented oral-based communication, cannot be effectively managed.

Central to records management is the information life cycle concept (Figure 5.1.) The first stage of this cycle is the creation of the

---

Figure 5.1
Life Cycle of a Record

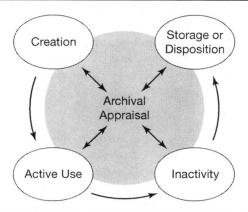

Source: Graphic by Marc Brodsky.

information, whether written, typed, or recorded on film. Next, the records enter a period of active use, which could last for a few hours, a few years, or even decades, depending on how the record relates to the information needs of the organization. The third period occurs when the information is no longer needed for active or daily use. This phase, known as inactive records storage, often means that the records are removed from their primary location (i.e., file cabinets or hard drives) and relocated to an area of more long-term storage for more occasional access. Many records identified as having legal and fiscal characteristics remain in this phase for very specific time periods. As part of this third phase, many historical records are identified as archival, meaning that they will be retained permanently and relocated to an archival repository. The final stage of the information life cycle is the storage of archival records or the destruction of records no longer needed by the organization for long-term or short-term purposes. At each stage, an archivist and records manager should be involved in some kind of evaluation, also known as appraisal, of the material.

While it is a somewhat linear process, each record moves through the stages of the information life cycle at its own pace. The different time is dependent upon the informational value of each record. All records have some kind of value or usefulness. Determining the value of records has much to do with how the records support the various functions of the organization. Records can be administrative, fiscal, legal, or historical, or some combination of these general categories (Sampson, 1992). These attributes help determine the amount of time to retain the records and select which records will become archival. Because the value of these materials changes over time and records may have multiple values, there are short-term and long-term considerations for records.

The Life of a Record

As an example of a record going through the information life cycle, academic library administrators disseminate an internal document discussing upcoming budgets cuts with the recommendation to eliminate some weekend library services. When the document is first created it is considered an active record, possessing primary value for daily activities or transactions. At this point the report has immediate administrative and fiscal value. Librarians want to share the information in this document with others to help develop alternate proposals, such as offering online reference services.

Over time the value of the record changes and it can take on different attributes. As other library policies are initiated in reaction to the document, such as the decision to concentrate on more virtual reference services, the relevance and value of the initial report changes. Further, a new budget report with different financial data and recommendations could possibly render the information in the original document obsolete. Even though the value of the document changes, the information is relevant and the document itself may need to be accessible for daily use. The record may also be duplicated or recreated elsewhere. For example, at the end of the fiscal year the internal document, which has a great deal of information about the reasons for cutbacks, becomes part of an appendix for the library's annual financial report.

The original document remains an active record as long as it is needed by the organization on a regular basis. When the document has become unneeded for planning purposes or is superseded by another document it is then considered an inactive record. These records have informational value and may need to be consulted at a later time. Most inactive records move into the storage or retention phase. During this phase, records leave their offices according the records schedules and become the responsibility of the records manager.

In this same example, after five years of use the original budget document has become part of a set of administrative files from the dean's office of the academic library. Each year, the library sends inactive groups of records to the records manager for storage. According to the records schedule for library records, all financial documents are retained for seven years in case of a state or federal audit, with all annual budget reports and recommendations being retained indefinitely. The original record as a stand-alone document was not scheduled for permanent retention, but the same information as an appendix in the library's annual budget report did become part of the permanent collection of records.

After more than a decade since first created, the information from the original budget cutback document is now considered an archival record. In the next phase, records managers work with their college or university archivists to transfer permanent records to the campus archives, where administrators, librarians, and researchers will have access to these collections. The archivist processes the new boxes of records, adds the materials to the record or archives group for the academic library, and updates the finding aids. At this stage the record is also considered an official record, meaning that it was created by the institution and was retained as evidence of the library's activities. As an archival record, the document takes on secondary values for users. The document could be useful for researchers to understand when and why the library stopped offering weekend reference hours, or helpful in documenting the beginnings of the library's investment in online technologies for user services.

The Role of the Records Manager

An organization's records management program depends heavily on the records manager. The principles of records management and the concept of the information life cycle can support and enhance the activities of any organization, but only with the guidance from a records manager. The records manager works to ensure that all members of an organization understand that records have value and how their records fit within the information life cycle. He or she develops a records management program that affects all components of the organization.

Records managers are strong organizers, with diverse backgrounds and experiences. Some have professional backgrounds in information management, librarianship, or business administration, while others have graduate degrees in archives and records management (Shepherd and Yeo, 2003). Often, an organization selects a records manager from the ranks of the current workforce, instead of doing an external job search. The appointed records manager, who is frequently the only employee for the records program, builds mastery of the field through practice and professional involvement (Brumm, 2008).

The majority of professional records managers are active in ARMA (Association of Records

Profile of a Records Manager
• Skills as an organizer, a leader, and promoter for the program
• Degrees and experience in diverse fields such as business, information technology, archives, or libraries
• ARMA member
• Certified by ICRM
• Electronic records expertise

Managers and Administrators) International, an organization that provides members with professional development opportunities and other resources. ARMA International promotes a set of core competencies for records managers at different professional levels. The measurable competencies include knowledge of business functions, records management practices, understanding of risk management, communications and marketing skills, familiarity with information technology, and leadership (ARMA, 2007). ARMA also promotes the process of becoming certified through the Institute of Certified Records Managers (ICRM). Regardless of credentials, training, and organizational skills, records managers must be effective communicators and promoters of their records programs (Choksy, 2008). More common today is the need for records managers to have strong technological skills to determine electronic records policies for their organization.

A records manager is responsible for launching the records program. For any sized organization, the records manager must complete a survey of existing records, analyze the structure of the organization, and develop retention plans or schedules to capture records (Barritt, 1989). Similar to an archivist starting an archives program, the records manager evaluates existing records and considers all potential sources of records creation. In the process, the records manager becomes familiar with the structure of the organization (i.e., its departments, divisions, top positions, and reporting lines). The records manager for a business with 1,000 employees or for a small college employing 100 staff and faculty must understand how the organization functions, makes decisions, and generates recorded evidence.

Based on the analysis of existing records and the way in which an organization creates records, the records manager either develops records schedules or follows an established state retention schedule to help capture recorded information in a systematic way. These schedules may be based on each individual department, division, or branch of the organization, and offer guidelines on which types of records should be kept, how long they should be kept, which ones become archival, and which ones are disposed of (Gold, 1995). When analyzed together, all of the records schedules for an organization provide a comprehensive approach to capturing, managing, and preserving an institution's records. With records schedules in place, records managers work with their organization to manage incoming records.

Unless their work is solely with electronic records, records managers have responsibility for operating or working with an independent records center. This space contains ranges of shelving capable of holding numerous boxes of paper records. Many records centers are in warehouses, where forklifts, boom lifts, microfilming or imaging equipment, and industrial-sized paper shredders are available for use by the records manager. Even for smaller institutions, records managers work with a high volume of incoming records, often hundreds of boxes in a single shipment. Records managers electronically track these boxes using barcodes, targets, or other tools. At the records center a majority of the incoming records are retained for a certain period and then destroyed, with only a small fraction of records either permanently retained on the shelves or sent to the archives (Diamond, 1995). Managing the activities of a records center, however, is largely limited to paper records.

Challenges and Opportunities for Records Management

The greatest challenge for today's records managers is electronic records, including those born digitally and those reformatted into electronic files. The umbrella term of electronic records includes a variety of formats including e-mail, instant messaging, databases, webpages, Twitter updates, spreadsheets, PDF documents, videoconference files, and geospatial data (Mims, 2006). These records are created using a wide range of hardware and software programs, which are often required to access the record itself. Some electronic records may in fact be digital reproductions of paper records. To further complicate the picture, electronic records are stored on a variety of magnetic and optical formats, including tapes, disks, and hard drives, all of which can be fickle, unpredictable, and unreliable (Hunter, 2000).

Digital records are more fluid, changeable, and less secure than paper-based records. To meet these basic challenges, records managers must consider security, preservation, access, and the effects of data migration when developing schedules for electronic records (Stephens and Wallace, 2003). At the same time, records managers must monitor how electronic records are created, stored, deleted, and accessed.

As much of our communication has become electronic, organizations have turned to electronic mechanisms to conduct their business. Automation brings efficiency, faster service, and expansion of services to all kinds of organizations. The resulting electronic records created through more automated processes are important because they support mission-critical operations and may contain unique information not available elsewhere (Saffady, 2002). In comparison, electronic records are more voluminous and have more associated information than paper-based records. Electronic records can also be disseminated faster and perhaps more widely than paper records, making privacy of records more difficult.

While electronic records can be valuable assets to organizations, without careful oversight they can create numerous problems for records managers. Collecting, organizing, and providing access to electronic records requires a clear knowledge of information storage and retrieval systems, hardware and software, and the information needs of the organization (Saffady, 2007). Support from the organization is crucial in developing schedules for retaining electronic records. In particular, the records manager must work closely with the organization's information technology department to understand how active electronic records are stored, backed-up, and accessed (Langemo, 2002). Managing electronic records is further complicated when organizations upgrade or change their computer systems. Records created and housed using legacy systems may lose some if not all data during the migration process to new platforms.

Records management is a profession in transition, largely because of the influence of electronic records and new technology (Bantin, 2008). Greater volume of records, complexity of recorded information, technical obsolescence, and electronic access to important inactive records are just a few of the challenges for the managers of electronic records (Stephens, 2007). These global shifts greatly affect records management practices and call into question the very definition of a record. However, records managers who are adept with technology and familiar with the issues of electronic record keeping are devising new methods to effectively capture, contain, preserve, access, and select digital forms of communication for their organization.

The overall purpose of having a records management program, for both paper and digital records, is to support and enhance the activities of the organization. A strong records management program effectively and efficiently manages the active and inactive records of an organization, while retaining the most valuable records. Records schedules provide a basis for much of the decision making on what to keep, how long to keep it, and what to dispose. Making those selections depends on institutional practices, legal obligations, storage space, and cooperation from the units within the organization (Langemo, 2002).

Records management practices make information more accessible and retrievable, make the institution accountable, identify informational assets for the organization, and ensure compliance with federal, state, and institutional regulations. Benefits of an effective records management program include legal protection, identification of important evidence, elimination of noncritical information, greater access to vital records, more efficient information storage and retrieval, and preservation of historical materials (Bantin, 2002). Much like an archives program, an effective records management initiative is based on a clear mission, vision, goals, and a common understanding of its place and authority within its organization.

RECORDS MANAGEMENT IN AN ACADEMIC SETTING

Background and Development

Record managers have long played important roles in the academic environment, especially at larger colleges and universities. Much like the growth of college and university archives, the proliferation of campus records management programs occurred after World War II (Skemer and Williams, 1990). As the structure and administration of academic institutions became more complex, records management programs started or grew to meet those new needs. Some programs began within the academic library, often with a college or university archivist also serving as the records manager, while other records initiatives emerged from administrative departments to help supply information to the key decision makers of the institution.

Colleges and universities founded their campus records programs for practical reasons. The first studies of academic records management programs revealed that most campus programs developed because of the institution's need for compliance with public records laws, greater efficiency in locating information, and demonstrating accountability for the expenditure of public funds (Kunde, 2008). The ability to be more efficient with information, to legally dispose of nonvital records, and to establish near-automatic procedures for record keeping made records management programs attractive to higher education, especially for larger institutions.

Campus records programs have strong connections to campus archives programs. Early studies demonstrated that a majority of academic records management programs emerged from campus archives programs and were led by academic archivists, most commonly the college or university archivist (Burckel and Cook, 1982). The organizational skills and the ability to arrange and describe collections, made archivists qualified candidates to develop records programs. In the role as records manager, these archivists made first contact with campus departments and offices, provided input to the institution before or at the time of record creation, supported their institution by locating information, and ultimately built strong archival holdings (Maher, 1992).

Characteristics of Campus Records Programs

- Programs developed in second half of twentieth century
- Compliance with public records laws led to creation
- Strong connections to academic archives
- Many programs led by archivists
- Either based in academic library or an administrative unit
- Limited resources resulting in selective, not comprehensive, records programs that target high-level and cooperative units on campus

However, these same studies indicate that the "archivist as records manager" approach had limitations for carrying out campus-wide records initiatives. First, most archivists did not have the training or were not fully prepared for managing the disposal of such large amounts of inactive and nonvital records. More important, archivists leading records management initiatives were not solely focused on managing records, and that lack of full attention often resulted in limited records scheduling for campus offices and departments (Kunde, 2008). With limited time and resources, academic archivists serving as records managers could most often offer their institution only partial records management strategies and programs. Quite simply, very few colleges or universities can boast comprehensive records management programs; instead most academic records programs are focused on developing records schedules for the most important or cooperative segments of their campus, or they respond to records needs when requested (Barritt, 1989).

Electronic Records on Campus

The largest shift in campus records management practices in the past few decades has been the ability to identify, schedule, dispose of, and retain electronic records. Past studies indicate that a majority of academic records programs are still focused on "traditional" records management practices (i.e., managing and disposing of large quantities of inactive paper records) and do not have the resources, policies, and procedures in place to maintain an electronic records management program for their institution (Kunde, 2008). But in a time of increasing litigation and heightened accountability, colleges and university cannot ignore the importance of having an electronic records management program. Top administrators and chief information officers at many colleges and universities understand that properly managed and documented records are vital assets that can protect, promote, and preserve the mission of their institution (Bantin, 2002).

Colleges and universities create millions of electronic records during the regular course of business. For students, processes such as registering for classes, paying tuition, receiving a dormitory assignment, activating a library card, applying for campus jobs, and ordering transcripts have become electronic. For faculty, processes such as accessing class rosters, receiving assignments from students, communicating readings and notes to students, and applying for grants are also largely electronic. For campus administrators, processes such as updating budgets, paying employees and contractors, submitting data to accreditation officers, and reporting to agencies have also become somewhat paperless. The transition from paper records to electronic records is far from complete; however, higher education is at the forefront of using technology to make many campus processes electronic (Bantin, 2002).

Academic records managers with strong technological skills have a great opportunity to participate in electronic record keeping on their campus. Records managers, some also college or university archivists, must make clear connections between the value of properly managed electronic records and the fundamental objectives of their academic institution (Kunde, 2008).

Many times, colleges and universities are disinterested in monitoring their electronic records until a problem (i.e., lawsuit, security breach, or compliance with new requirements) occurs. This unfortunate scenario results in records management functions, for both paper and electronic, becoming relegated to risk management activities. Instead, proactive academic records managers should promote their electronic records programs as a way to use technology to better manage, preserve, and access electronic content (Kunde, 2008).

Successful academic records programs have clear electronic records policies. These policies include how to schedule e-mail from different departments, how to capture and preserve digital images, which kinds of electronic files need to be retained for legal and operational purposes, what kind of metadata elements are present

> **Challenges of Electronic Records Management on Campus**
>
> - Most records programs focused on managing paper records
> - Lack of resources, policies, and procedures
> - Millions of records being created, modified, and deleted without oversight
> - Obsolete equipment and formats
> - Administration's view of electronic records as potential risks and not potential assets
> - Scheduling that anticipates the value of electronic records before creation
> - Expanding the reach of existing records schedules
> - Partnering with information technology and other campus groups

with records, the length of retention for records based on department of origin, purpose, and document format, and finally how to transfer and preserve permanent records for the archives (Bantin, 2002). Developing a strong electronic records policy requires expanding the reach of existing records schedules, surveying all departments on campus about the kinds of electronic records being created, and collaborating with information technology departments to develop mechanisms to capture, maintain, schedule, and provide access to electronic records.

Electronic records programs based in academic libraries have the potential to include archival electronic records in a library-based digital repository or dark archives initiative. Many academic libraries manage an institutional repository with various levels of access and storage. These repositories provide the campus community (i.e., faculty, students, and affiliated users) a place to access a wide range of content needed for teaching, research, and publishing. Including scheduled electronic records in such a campus repository encourages preservation and access and avoids creating duplicate systems. However, there are preservation advantages to having duplicate copies of electronic records on multiple servers across campus and institutions, as long as the original version of the file is secure.

Perhaps the most effective way to begin a campus electronic records initiative is through a phased approach. Many colleges and universities began their electronic record-keeping initiatives through pilot-projects, often based on specific electronic formats, such as campus publications, promotion and tenure documentation, committee reports, and podcasts (SAA, 2011). Often the lessons learned during such a pilot-project will lead to a fuller implementation of an electronic records program on campus. Sometimes, however, campus records managers face the even larger challenge of starting or restarting a comprehensive records management program, with electronic records only accounting for a portion of the initiative.

STARTING OR RESTARTING A CAMPUS RECORDS MANAGEMENT PROGRAM

Founding Principles and Resources

Beginning a campus records management program is similar to launching a campus archives program. In both situations, the demonstrated needs of the institution, potential users, stakeholders, and participants coalesce to bring the program to fruition. Formalizing records practices to conform to legal, technical, and institutional requirements are often the impetus for a records management unit. Creating a records program may in fact be in reaction to a recognized weakness in campus record keeping, such as the necessity to keep financial data for a certain period in case of an audit.

The reasons for beginning methodical record keeping must be defined by the program's sponsors and then articulated in a founding document. Academic records programs begin with some kind of official charge, which articulates the mission, includes tangible objectives, and specifies where the unit fits within the administrative structure of the institution. The leaders of the new program are most often the authors of the official charge. This document or memorandum is approved by the institution's upper administration and put into action by the new program's leaders. The charge should address the program's records policies, including how to approach managing paper and electronic documents, as well as how retention and disposition schedules will be structured and implemented (Bantin, 2002).

The mission, vision, and structure of academic records programs vary by institution. Most records programs are designed to provide campus departments, offices, and units with inactive records storage and disposition services, but numerous variables and influences affect that broad mission. For example, the scope of the records program is most often limited to certain parts of campus, such as the top administrative, financial, and academic offices. The costs of storage, retrieval, and disposition may make it necessary for the records program to charge departments for their services. The records program's relationship to the academic library and archives also shapes how records are scheduled, stored, accessed, transferred, or disposed.

> **Foundations of a Campus Records Management Program**
>
> - Official charge or founding document
> - Clear delineation of reporting lines and responsibilities
> - Strong mission statement with goals and objectives
> - A vision for the program
> - A visionary leader to coordinate the program

The mission statement for a records management program may also include specific goals. For example, a new campus records program at a large university could include in their mission statement the goal to eventually collect administrative records from all ten colleges on their main campus. When such goals are achieved, then it is necessary to adjust the mission statement to reflect the changes. A mission statement for a records program can be both broad and specific, but it should reflect the purpose of the program and how record keeping supports the larger mission of the institution.

Having a vision for campus records management is a sign of a successful program. Just like the leader for an academic archives program, the leader of a campus records program must develop an overall vision for what records management can do for their campus (Dearstyne, 2008). The vision can emerge from input with records staff, feedback from departments served by the program, or from prior records management experience. A common vision for academic records management is to schedule all parts of campus records creation, to provide efficient service to departments, and to work closely with the academic archives to identify historical records for transfer to the archives for permanent storage. Articulating the vision to departments, administrators, and other campus groups is a significant part of promoting the academic records program (Kunde, 2008).

While having a clear mission and vision is important, a records program is only as good as the people who manage the records. The key to operating a successful records program is to have a leading records manager who can effectively oversee records services, serve their constituents, and promote their program across campus. Although records management departments tend to be small, it is common for the leading records manager to hire full-time employees, such as records analysts or technicians. Those employees will complete the daily tasks of records management—pickup of materials from offices, storage and retrieval of records, imaging vital records, transferring permanent records to the campus archives, and most frequently, disposing of records. A successful records manager must effectively coordinate the daily operation of a records center, while being a campuswide advocate for their program (Dearstyne, 2008).

For pre-existing records programs, the addition of new staff or a leading records manager often means a new interest in record keeping on campus. Adding new members to a records program may allow expanded records services to campus, such as the scheduling of a dozen new offices or units. A larger staff may result in greater awareness for the program, and more opportunities to promote the principles of record keeping to the scheduled and the unscheduled segments of campus. Staff may be able to promote the program through workshops, training, and closer collaboration with campus units. Academic records management programs are traditionally small operations, which makes it imperative that all members of the unit (records managers, analysts, and technicians) are committed to the mission of efficient and effective campuswide record keeping (Kunde, 2008).

All members of the records management team should be fully aware of relevant legal and institutional requirements for record keeping and also aware that such rules change over time. Each state has public records laws, often called "sunshine laws," to allow public access to certain records. Public academic institutions are more likely to be affected by state public records laws. Both public and private schools are required to keep financial records for a certain time, most often seven years. Academic records managers must also consider federal-level records regulations, most frequently the Health Insurance Portability and Accountability Act (HIPAA) for medical records, and the Family Educational Rights and Privacy Act (FERPA) for student records (Kunde, 2008). Other federal records mandates such as the Freedom of Information Act (FOIA) and requirements for reporting data on federal grants affect the work of academic records managers. Clear institutional requirements and policies, such as retaining all financial records for 20 years instead of the standard seven years, are also important details needed for effective campus record keeping.

As part of effective long-term record keeping, records management programs are often responsible for disaster prevention planning. Although disaster planning is a much larger campus-wide process, records managers articulate to the administration the challenges of recovering and preserving vital paper and electronic records (Wellheiser and Scott, 2002). These very practical concerns about protecting physical and digital records play a large role in developing the institution's disaster policies and procedures, which is discussed in Chapter 7.

Records programs require other resources to remain relevant and effective. Campus records management units have designated spaces for their operations, either in the form of a records center, off-site storage, or a large footprint within a campus building. Records programs need physical spaces to store large volumes of inactive records, to operate equipment (i.e., shredders, computer backup systems, and imaging hardware and software), to provide work space and offices for staff, and to have a tangible location on campus where potential records contributors can visit (Gold, 1995). Records management programs also benefit from a loading dock close to their stacks storage area, vehicles for transferring records, and an electronic tracking system (often a barcode-based system) that can help staff quickly locate boxes in the collection (Diamond, 1995). Just like an academic archives program, a successful records management department has well-documented policies and procedures that directly connect with the overall mission of the program and the institution.

Legal Considerations for Campus Records

- State public records laws, including "sunshine laws"
- Legal proceedings
- Internal Revenue Service (IRS) for financial records
- Family Educational Rights and Privacy Act (FERPA) for student records
- Health Insurance Portability and Accountability Act (HIPAA) for medical records
- Freedom of Information Act (FOIA) requests

Common Structures for Campus Records Programs

The mission, vision, and purpose of a campus records programs depends on where the program fits within the administrative structure of the institution. For example, a records management program situated within an academic library will have a different mission than a program reporting to the treasurer's office. In the former case, the program may be intimately connected with the college archives and focused on access to inactive records, while in the latter case the program may be focused on storing and disposing of records from departments who pay storage and retrieval fees.

Generally, academic records programs are either based in an administrative unit of their campus or part of the library system. In both scenarios, academic archivists are involved in the transfer of inactive historical files to the academic archives. Whatever the administrative location and mission of the program, few academic records programs are truly comprehensive in their work to manage all of the records created by their academic institution (Barritt, 1989).

Records management units situated in departments outside of the academic library are focused on scheduling and disposing of inactive campus records. For example, a records program could start in a university's provost office to keep better records of campus administration. These records programs can either offer campus units free service for inactive records storage, or they may be dependent on charging fees to departments. Certified records managers, not archivists, are more likely to be leading records programs based outside of an academic library system. However, the leaders of these records programs work closely with academic archivists to transfer permanent records from the records center to the archives.

For many schools, campus records management is a subunit within the academic library, most often as part of the special collections or archives department of the library. The college or university archivist serves a dual role as the records manager, attempting to identify, schedule, and follow school records from the time of creation through either disposition or permanent retention (Barritt, 1989). As one advantage of this model, archivists serving as records manager develop close relationship with departments before records are even created and may be involved with records throughout the entire information life cycle.

Further, archivists who create schedules and work with departments before records are created are able to better manage electronic records. But one disadvantage for archivists as records managers is that too often the focus is on locating archival materials for the archives instead of managing and disposing of inactive records in an efficient manner (Skemer and Williams, 1990). As one result, many records management programs based in academic archives have hundreds if not thousands of feet of inactive records slated for reappraisal instead of disposition.

The nature of the academic institution is another factor in the practices of a records management program. For example, a land-grant university has a great deal of accountability to the federal and state government, and must adopt records management practices that match those standards used by other similar institutions. Likewise, a privately funded school has fiscal responsibilities to the federal government and must keep financial records for a certain time. Since most of the oversight for the operations of a private school comes from a private board and not a state legislature or public govern-

> **Structural Questions for Academic Records Programs**
>
> - Will the program charge for storage and retrieval of records?
> - How will the program connect with the academic library and archives unit?
> - What is the role for the college or university archivist in the program?
> - How comprehensive will the program be?
> - What legal record-keeping requirements exist for the institution?
> - How do the institution's policies and procedures affect record keeping?

ing body, the private institution may establish its own rules for the retention or disposition of its records. Each state has different public records laws, some of which are applicable to private colleges and schools.

The structure of an academic records management program varies by institution. However, the most common approaches involve either an administrative unit on campus or the academic library hosting the records program. Successful records management programs involve both records managers and academic archivists in the process of identifying, scheduling, retaining, and disposing of campus records (Dearstyne, 2008). With a clear mission, clarification of the unit's administrative placement within the institution, and key personnel identified to lead the initiative, the records program can move forward to begin the complicated process of scheduling and managing the institution's records.

Surveying the Academic Landscape

The leader of a new or revitalized campus records management program must always understand the structure and operations of his or her academic institution. While each college and university is a unique institution with its own history and practices, there are identifiable academic, financial, and administrative functions present in every school. A review of the school's website, course catalogs, and publications, followed by in-person discussions with students, staff, faculty, and administrators to elaborate on the details, are the best first places to consult for this information.

Although records managers may not directly work with students or even student organizations, the academic component of their school is essential to the other operations. For example, a records manager should determine what kind of academic programs exist at the institution, how subdivisions of departments, schools, and colleges affect the curriculum, how courses are taught, and how oversight and accreditation is handled by the administration (Samuels, 1992). Understanding how degrees are conferred, grades are kept, and how students advance through academic programs is important contextual information especially if a records manager is required to store and retrieve student records (i.e., transcripts and applications) as part of the records program.

Records managers should also know the financial structure of their institution. Private schools rely primarily on donations, endowments, and tuition to fund their programs. Historically, public colleges and universities rely on state and federal funding and tuition for their support. However, public schools have become much more focused on building endowments through private donations as government funding has decreased. All funds received by an academic institution trigger financial accountability, a budgeting process, and approval from several levels on how to use the funding. Records managers need to know the basic financial patterns of their institution, the sources of funding, how financial decisions are made, and how funding is allocated to individual programs, department, or campus units.

The overall administrative structure of the school (i.e., governance, reporting lines, and employee classifications) is highly relevant for the work of campus records managers. An organizational chart or map reveals the relationships between the external governing body, top administrative offices, schools, colleges, departments, and other units on campus. Records managers need to understand how their program fits into this bureaucratic structure. It is also important to consider the numerous layers in the ranks of campus employees. From the top administrative officers, to the faculty and the staff, and to those who maintain the grounds, the employees perform the functions that operate the campus (Samuels, 1992).

Developing Records Groups, Surveys, and Schedules

Understanding the administrative structure (i.e., who reports to whom, how decisions are made, and delineation of responsibilities) of a college or university is the key to developing records schedules for specific units. Records managers develop records schedules by first identifying record groups (RG) based on the structure of their academic institution. Records managers should first designate the largest components of the campus with a record group system and later add subgroups. The groups should be flexible to allow changes in the organization's structure. For example, a records manager at a medium-sized teaching university might create a record group to represent all of the programs in the college of education (RG 3), with subgroups for each department or program (i.e., RG 3.2 is the designation for the college of education's educational leadership department). Even if no records are available for record groups and their subgroups, it is important to create an initial map of how the records for each segment of campus could be represented. This map and the schedules change over time, especially following campus reorganizations and changes to the administrative structure.

With a clear administrative map and list of designated record groups, the records manager must conduct an initial survey of departments and existing records. That

> **Building the Structure of a Campus Records Management Program**
>
> - Review the academic, financial, and administrative structure of the institution.
> - Create an administrative map or chart of the institution's structure.
> - Establish records groups with subcategories based on the structure.
> - Conduct an initial survey of departments and existing records.
> - Create records schedules for each record group or participating unit.
> - Implement, follow, and honor the records schedules.
> - Expand the records program as resources become available.

survey involves talking with many administrators, department heads, administrative assistants, and other record keepers. During these conversations, the records manager should determine what kinds of records the unit creates, how they have been stored, how inactive records have been disposed, and whether any records are transferred to the archives. The most common answer to these questions is that departments either hoard all of their files or routinely dispose of everything. At the very least, the in-person survey introduces the records manager and the program to the record keepers on campus. At the most, the data from the survey allows records managers to construct records schedules and begin the task of managing the records of their academic institution.

Records schedules are simple documents outlining the kinds of records created by campus offices or departments, which inactive records need to be stored and for how long, and finally which inactive records will be destroyed or sent to the archives for long-term retention (Saffady, 2004). Schedules contain some detail about the different classes of records (i.e., financial, student files, faculty materials, or tenure documentation) found in each department, office, or unit. The schedules may also contain information about the formats of the records, especially if there are born-digital records (Stephens, 2007). Once finalized, the records manager and the person responsible for the transfer of the inactive records both sign the document. The specific instructions on transfer, storage, and disposition of inactive records in the document will be followed until the schedule is adjusted or a new schedule is created.

As an example, the records schedule for a university's office of the assistant provost for academic affairs (RG 4.3) may include all official correspondence, annual reports from each college under the office's supervision, accreditation files, and final reports from all committees chaired by the assistant provost, both in paper and electronic format. This schedule could specify that all inactive records will be stored for seven years for legal and financial purposes. Following the schedule for these records, the records manager will dispose of all seven-year-old inactive records from 4.3, except for official correspondence files relating to specific individuals or organizations which will be retained and sent to the archives.

While records schedules can have some degree of flexibility, records managers should follow their schedules and avoid conducting unnecessary reappraisal on their inactive records (Langemo, 2002). Sometimes political pressures emerge to place records management programs in a difficult or perhaps opportune position. For example, if the assistant provost for academic affairs is accused of academic misconduct and all files from 4.3 were scheduled for destruction in the coming month, then it would be necessary for the records manager to provide access to those inactive materials, and possibly revise the retention schedule to make sure those files will be available for a longer period. Access to those records will result in a more comprehensive investigation of the assistant provost and ultimately highlight records management as an important part of campus operations and oversight.

Indications of a Successful Campus Records Program

Records management programs are designed to protect academic institutions, while making the storage, retrieval, and disposition of inactive records an efficient process. Because efficient campus records programs are hidden from public view they are often misunderstood and forgotten by the very people on campus who rely on their services. It is up to the leaders of academic records programs to promote their program across campus as an active, vital, and integral part of their institution. Records managers can build the reputation of their programs by hosting office management and file keeping workshops, arranging site visits to meet the record keepers, and making general presentations to the campus community about records management (Dearstyne, 2008). Online and print newsletters about the services offered by the records management unit are another way to promote the program.

Effective and ethical management of the institution's inactive records is the gold standard for academic records programs. Successful programs develop detailed records schedules for multiple departments, units, and offices. Records managers implement those records schedules accordingly, adjust the schedule only when necessary, and maintain the authenticity of the information. Successful academic records managers make ethical decisions about records retention, do not succumb to political pressures, are responsive to requests and changing standards, and uphold their scheduling decisions (Barry, 2005). As an example, when a records manager receives an inappropriate request related to records (i.e., pressure to destroy, retrieve, or manipulate inactive records) that request should be shared with the campus community before any actions are taken. Keeping records management a transparent operation in light of privacy concerns is challenging, but a requirement for effective programs.

> **Key Indicators of a Successful Campus Records Management Program**
>
> • Efficient and responsive services (i.e., storage, retrieval, and disposition) for campus units
> • Identifiable presence as an integral campus unit
> • Demonstrates ethical practices and follows legal requirements for record keeping
> • Strong relationship with academic archives
> • Records schedules that include electronic records
> • Partnerships with other campus units
> • A visionary leader who effectively manages and promotes the program

The strong relationship between the records manager and the academic archivist is another sign of a successful records program. It is common for archivists to request larger amounts of material from inactive records storage for the archives at the end of the records schedule cycle, even though records schedules have defined what is retained and what is disposed. A better approach is for records managers and archivists to work together to develop records schedules, especially in the case of electronic records (Bantin, 2002). In the case that the records manager and the archivist is the same person, then that person must focus on the entirety of the information life cycle and not just on building interesting collections in the archives.

Strong leadership is a requirement for successful records management programs. Effective leaders cultivate interest in their programs, develop and carry out schedules, work with archivists, manage a records center, and inspire their staff. Academic records managers keep a careful balance between the mission and vision for their program and the realities of operating a records program on their campus. Budding leaders in the field of academic records management are politically and technologically articulate. These skills are imperative for communicating the goals of the records program across campus, to the public, and to the media.

CONCLUSION

Records management has become a frequent counterpart program for academic archives units. Whether located within the academic library or situated in another campus unit, records management activities have wide implications for academic archives. In addition to identifying and scheduling inactive campus records, records managers also make decisions about which records are identified as permanent records and ultimately transferred to the archives. The skills needed by today's records managers—a clear understanding of legal regulations, electronic record keeping, student privacy, and institutional policies—are also valuable for academic archivists.

College and university archivists must understand their relationship to campus records programs if they are to build successful archives programs. Understanding the principles of records management is even more important for an academic archivist who may be asked to start or assume responsibilities for a campus records program. Even if the two units do not work together on a daily or monthly basis, records management and archives programs should have some overlap in their missions, visions, and objectives.

The most effective records management programs have a dynamic leader, provide offices and departments with efficient records services, create and implement detailed records schedules, are well known by the campus community, and work closely with academic archivists. These record units operate with full knowledge of emerging technical challenges of record keeping, along with legal and institutional regulations. Records managers also set realistic and achievable goals for their programs, and uphold ethical practices when working with inactive records. For academic archivists, records management programs are vital to building strong archival collections. Simply put, a solid campus records management program usually indicates the existence of a successful academic archives program.

REFERENCES

ARMA International. 2007. *Records and Information Management: Core Competencies.* Lenexa, KS: ARMA International.

Bantin, Philip C. 2002. "Records Management in a Digital World." *EDUCAUSE Research Bulletin* no. 16 (August 6): 1–14. https://www.educause.edu/ir/library/pdf/ERB0216.pdf.

———. 2008. *Understanding Data and Information Systems for Recordkeeping.* New York: Neal-Schuman.

Barritt, Marjorie Rabe. 1989. "Adopting and Adapting Records Management to College and University Archives." *Midwestern Archivist* 14, no. 1: 5–12.

Barry, Rick. 2005. "Ethical Issues for Creators, Managers, and Users of Records." In *Political Pressure and the Archival Record*, edited by Margaret Procter, Michael Cook, and Caroline Williams, 131–149. Chicago: Society of American Archivists.

Brumm, Eugenia K. 2008. "The Records Management Leader." In *Leading and Managing Archives and Records Programs: Strategies for Success*, edited by Bruce W. Dearstyne, 25–44. New York: Neal-Schuman.

Burckel, Nicholas C., and J. Frank Cook. 1982. "A Profile of College and University Archives in the United States." *American Archivist* 45, no. 4 (Fall): 410–428.

Choksy, Carol E. B. 2008. "Leading a Successful Records Management Program." In *Leading and Managing Archives and Records Programs: Strategies for Success*, edited by Bruce W. Dearstyne, 69–90. New York: Neal-Schuman.

Dearstyne, Bruce W. 2008. "Leading Archives and Records Programs: Perspectives and Insights." In *Leading and Managing Archives and Records Programs: Strategies for Success*, edited by Bruce W. Dearstyne, 291–312. New York: Neal-Schuman.

Diamond, Susan Z. 1995. *Records Management: A Practical Approach.* 3rd ed. New York: AMACOM.

Gold, Gloria. 1995. *How to Set Up and Implement a Records Management System.* New York: AMACOM.

Hunter, Gregory S. 2000. *Preserving Digital Information.* New York: Neal-Schuman.

Kunde, Nancy M. 2008. "Reframing Records Management in Colleges and Universities." In *College and University Archives: Readings in Theory and Practice,* edited by Christopher J. Prom and Ellen D. Swain, 185–208. Chicago: Society of American Archivists.

Langemo, Mark. 2002. *Winning Strategies for Successful Records Management Programs: Proven Strategies for Developing New Programs and Improving Existing Ones!* Denver: Information Requirements Clearinghouse.

Maher, William J. 1992. *The Management of College and University Archives.* Chicago: Society of American Archivists.

Mims, Julian L. III, ed. 2006. *Electronic Records Management.* Washington, DC: International City/County Management Association.

Saffady, William. 2002. *Managing Electronic Records.* Lenexa, KS: ARMA International.

———. 2004. *Records and Information Management: Fundamentals of Professional Practice.* Lenexa, KS: ARMA International.

———. 2007. Digital Document Management. Lenexa, KS: ARMA International.

Sampson, Karen L. 1992. *Value-Added Records Management: Protecting Corporate Assets and Reducing Business Risks.* New York: Quorum Books.

Samuels, Helen Willa. 1992. *Varsity Letters: Documenting Modern Colleges and Universities.* Chicago: Society of American Archivists.

Shepherd, Elizabeth, and Geoffrey Yeo. 2003. *Managing Records: A Handbook of Principles and Practice.* London: Facet Publishing.

Skemer, Don C., and Geoffrey P. Williams. 1990. "Managing the Records of Higher Education: The State of Records Management in American Colleges and Universities." *American Archivist* 62 (Fall): 532–547.

Society of American Archivists. 2011. "Campus Case Studies." Society of American Archivists. Accessed September 20. http://www2.archivists.org/publications/epubs/Campus-Case-Studies.

Stephens, David O. 2007. *Records Management: Making the Transition from Paper to Electronic.* Lenexa, KS: ARMA International.

Stephens, David O., and Roderick C. Wallace. 2003. *Electronic Records Retention: New Strategies for Data Life Cycle Management.* Lenexa, KS: ARMA International.

Wellheiser, Johanna, and Jude Scott. 2002. *An Ounce of Prevention: Integrated Disaster Planning for Archives, Libraries, and Records Centers.* Lanham, MD: Scarecrow Press.

6

Collection Development for Academic Archives

INTRODUCTION

Building strong collections of research materials is an important component of the work of academic archivists. Because there is a large amount of material potentially available for acquisition, academic archivists must clearly define what they collect, how they collect, and why they collect. Merged academic archives programs, frequently defined as special collections departments, collect in many areas and offer services to a variety of researchers. No matter how large or how small the archives program, without clear collecting parameters academic archivists run the risk of overextending their programs and duplicating the efforts of others.

Successful academic archives programs have a clear collection development policy that connects the material to the overall mission and vision for the archives program, while supporting other initiatives within the academic library and the academic programs of the institution. A collection development policy should state what an archives program collects and what it does not collect. A strong collections policy helps build collections and keeps academic archives from becoming storage units for unwanted materials.

The sources of the material found in academic archives are wide ranging. Alumni, donors, auction houses, faculty, students, book dealers, campus department heads, private sellers, families, groups, businesses, and records officers are just a few of the potential sources of collections for campus archives. When working with any of these individuals or groups to build collections, academic archivists must consider available funding, potential research uses, storage space, and accessibility. In the case of a donation, the needs of their repository must also be carefully balanced with the wishes and possible long-term expectations of the donors.

This chapter describes how academic archivists approach collection development for their archives program. It covers the challenges of defining a collections scope, working with donors, collection advisory boards, managing resources, anticipating user needs, and locating sources of potential collections. Collection development practices and policies directly affect the other components and services of academic archives, making it imperative for academic archivists to understand how collections are planned, acquired, and built. This chapter seeks answers to the following questions:

1. How do academic archives create a collection development policy?
2. How do academic archivists build collections and collecting areas?
3. What are the major sources of collections for academic archives?

PRINCIPLES OF COLLECTION DEVELOPMENT FOR ACADEMIC ARCHIVES

Collections and the Mission and Vision

The collections in academic archives support a variety of purposes and users, but most important, the archival holdings must enhance the mission and vision of the program, the academic library, and the institution. The actual collections are often what define new and well-established academic archives programs. As an example, the leaders of a new archives initiative begin their program based on the available collections that were identified during the survey process. The storage unit full of papers from three recent college presidents, campus photographs, and yearbooks become the basis for a college archives program, which is dedicated to collecting, preserving, and providing access to the college's history. Similarly, a decades-old special collections department at a large university may be known for its collections of labor union papers, radical pamphlets, and photographs of campus protests, rather than just its collections on the university's history. In both cases, the collections help define purposes of the archives program and either the expansion or contraction of the collection development policy affects the mission and vision of the department (O'Toole and Cox, 2006).

The holdings of academic archives also have the potential to define the academic library of which they are a part, especially if those collections are unique and historically significant. In the past few decades academic research libraries have built print and electronic resources that are somewhat homogenous. In academic libraries, the past trend of measuring success on the number of total volumes and the current trend of expanding online access to scholarly journals are two reasons for this uniformity. While titles and subscriptions vary, large academic libraries tend to purchase many of the same print sources and access to electronic collections, such as databases and full-text journals, as their peer institutions. As an example, two academic libraries in the Midwest, both serving land-grant institutions, may hold 80 percent of the same print titles in their online catalog and have access to nearly the same number and type of online resources. As a result of this common collection overlap, the unique holdings, such as rare books, manuscripts, archival collections, and official institutional records, are often what define academic libraries (ARL, 2007). It is the responsibility of academic archivists to demonstrate that their collections are not only unique, but to know how their archival holdings enhance the services and programs of the academic library.

> **Larger Context of Collections in Academic Archives**
>
> - Support a wide range of research initiatives
> - Diversify and strengthen the academic library
> - Support mission and vision of the institution

Colleges and universities benefit from having a strong documentary record of their past. Archival holdings can be used by many groups to learn more about events, traditions, athletics, student life, campus buildings, faculty, alumni, and past presidents. These collections can support a variety of campus activities, administrative functions, and external inquiries. Academic archivists must connect institutional records and collections to the larger needs of the academic community (Burckel, 2008). From a political and resource standpoint, the academic archives program has much to gain by cooperating and collaborating with its institution's upper administration and other campus units.

When selecting materials for possible acquisition, it is important to consider how those collections will support the larger goals of the archives program, the library, and the institution. Collecting archival material for the mere sake of collecting does not support the needs of the program or the campus. Instead, the collections in an academic archives program must have the potential to be historically significant, have a wide range of uses by a wide range of users, and relate to the needs of the campus.

Researchers of Today and Tomorrow

Academic librarians and archivists alike emphasize the importance of their users. Library assessment activities, user studies, and focus groups are just a few of the methods that academic librarians use to determine the information needs of their primary users (Wright, 2007). Academic archivists are also concerned with identifying their users and then determining the research needs of those users. In general, the researchers who visit academic archives are either on-campus users (i.e., students, staff, faculty, and affiliates) or off-campus users (i.e., academic scholars, family historians, and members of the local community). Some academic archives place a priority on the on-campus user group, but external scholars are an important part of the research and collection development equation. These two general user groups may conduct their research with an in-person visit to the reading room or through online communication.

The research needs of on-campus and off-campus users of academic archives are different. Students, staff, and faculty in the nearby academic community expect that academic archives will have extended hours, can handle advanced reference questions when they emerge, hold collections and other research materials that relate to their field of study, and can provide in-depth research assistance and bibliographic instruction (Maher, 1992). Teaching faculty who bring their students to academic archives for instruction or require their students to use archival materials in their class research projects are important links to understanding the research needs of students (McCoy, 2010). Not only will the needs of students drive how the academic archives approach instruction, but those same student researchers may point academic archivists to the emerging paths of research. Campus faculty and staff who conduct their own research in the academic archives also have important insights into what should be collected and where those materials might be available (Brichford, 1979).

Similarly, off-campus users of academic archives are more focused on the availability of specific collections and resources that may support their specific project. Generally, off-campus scholars from other institutions are more likely to plan a research visit during the summer or at slow times during the regular academic semester. Other off-campus users, such as genealogists and local historians, often require frequent interaction with the academic archives staff (Yakel and Torres, 2007). This subset and the most interested faculty may form a cadre of "regulars" in the reading room. In terms of collection development activity, the frequent users of the academic archives often have the greatest insights on what to collect, where to find those materials, and how to begin the acquisitions process.

For academic archivists responsible for building collections, the most undefined group of researchers are those who have yet to enter the reading room, either in present day or 100 years from now. In addition to building collections that support current users, academic archivists must consider the future generations of researchers. Predicting future research needs is difficult if not impossible, but the basic principle of targeted collecting across different units, departments, programs, and groups on campus is one method of capturing a documentary record. Academic archivists who are familiar with current scholarship and on-going research projects in their reading rooms have a better sense of what areas are being studied by re-searchers. These observations and predictions about potential uses of material and deciding which collections to acquire should be fully documented and available for the next generation of academic archivists.

Expected Researcher Groups
• On-campus students, faculty, and administrators • Off-campus scholars • Local and family historians • Researchers of the future

Academic archivists should also remain aware of current and emerging research trends. The methodological approaches to research are varied across the academic disciplines and have changed significantly in the past few decades. Humanities scholars have pushed their research boundaries into cultural and social studies that have little resemblance to standard political and economic approaches. Interdisciplinary approaches to research have further blurred the lines between disciplines. As an example, a historian may use methods from anthropology, sociology, and psychology to research how objects from a nineteenth-century household imparted differing social and gender norms in a small New England town. As part of the collection development process, academic archivists should remain aware of the emerging trends in academic scholarship. At the least, academic archivists should familiarize themselves with the new books and articles that relied on research materials from their archives.

Access, Use, and Limitations of Collections

When making collection development decisions, academic archivists should consider how materials might be made accessible and any possible limitations to that access. As a general rule, archivists promote wide access to their original material, either through a reading room setting or online delivery. In the former case, use of material is on a democratic first-come-first-served basis, while in the latter case online access can support a nearly unlimited number of users. The trend of greater access to archival materials is a recent development in the profession. Greater use of academic archives has resulted in a stronger awareness for academic archives and has demonstrated to many new researchers the power of original materials (Robyns, 2001).

However, the standard archival principle to preserve and protect materials sometimes adversely intersects the push for greater use of and access to original items. Archivists are charged with the responsibility of ensuring that their collections are protected from harm. Archivists guard the collections under their care through basic preservation techniques and creating a stable environment for collections storage. All archival collections (paper and electronic formats) experience some level of normal deterioration, but it is up to the archivist to consider additional factors that may accelerate deterioration, such as storage location, type of archival container, environmental conditions, and, perhaps most important, aggressive or frequent use by patrons (Ritzenthaler, 2010). Scanning materials for online delivery is one possible solution for protecting the physical materials from these external factors. However, many items are either too fragile or inappropriately sized for digitization to be an effective alternative. Access to archival materials through scanning projects is discussed more fully in Chapter 9.

The ease of use of the material greatly influences collection development decisions for academic archives. Whether scanned or available for in-house use only, archival material offers unique challenges to researchers. Handwritten documents with difficult to decipher handwriting, foreign language material, undated and unidentified photographs, and documents offering little contextual clues are common components of archival collections. Archivists often overestimate the expertise of their users and their understanding of how collections are arranged, described, and accessed (Yakel, 2002). However, these kinds of challenges offer all researchers a level of difficulty, and in fact can form the basis for department-led instructional sessions on how to use primary sources.

The challenges of research may create strong reasons not to acquire specific collections. For example, if a professor in the foreign languages department encourages special collections to purchase a large collection of an obscure eighteenth-century German poet, written in several languages on rapidly deteriorating paper, the academic archivists must consider the resources (i.e., funding, staff time, archival enclosures, and preservation costs) needed to make the collection accessible. The projected research uses for this collection may in fact be limited to less than a dozen seasoned scholars and have little appeal to students and other users. Undergraduate students walking into a reading room for their first experience may not warm to some of the challenges of using original sources, especially if the collections they are confronted with are seen as impenetrable. If the challenges of using the physical collection would adversely affect the potential research activity in a collection, then acquiring the collection may not be the best use of resources for the institution.

Many collections in academic archives contain material of a private or sensitive nature. Personal data is the first layer of this kind of information, which includes Social Security numbers, personal details such as addresses and names of children, and financial records. Many types of documents contain personal data including grant applications, tax returns and investment reports, medical records, curriculum vitae, retirement forms, student records, and personnel files (Pyatt, 2008). While this information may be useful for some types of research, it is standard archival practice to limit or even eliminate this information from collections. Depending on the donor and the data, archivists may choose to dispose, return, or redact material containing this information. Archivists must protect the privacy of individuals whose materials are represented in their collections by limiting access to their personal information without limiting access to other useful information in the collection. Limiting the occurrence of and access to this personal data deters identity theft and other nefarious activities, while decreasing institutional liability.

Personal content is the second layer of personal information that often appears in archival collections. More detailed than simple personal data, personal content includes specific content about family and non-professional matters. Some examples of personal content include love letters, frank recollections, correspondence with children, details about specific family members, compromising or family photographs, and

> **Challenges of Providing Access to Archival Materials**
>
> - Fragility and preservation of original materials
> - Creating online versions that are searchable and discoverable
> - Legibility and lack of contextual information with archival materials
> - Collections containing private, personal, and sensitive information
> - Restrictions in donor agreements

diaries. While this kind of information adds context to the individuals represented in the collection, some may need to be withheld for a time to protect living members of the family (Boles, 2005). Unlike personal data, the decision to limit access is largely on a case-by-case basis. Often collections that contain large amounts of personal content are restricted for a time or until the passing of the donor or certain family members.

Academic archives contain collections with large amounts of private and personal information. When making collection development decisions, academic archivists must consider how to protect the privacy of the individuals while maintaining the integrity of the collection for researchers. Academic archivists must decide how personal information is removed or restricted, and whether researchers will find value in the resulting publicly available collection. Acquiring collections that contain large amounts of personal content and are expected to be closed for a number of years may not be the best use of resources for academic archives. On the contrary, collections with large amounts of personal content (such as a prominent politician's set of diaries covering 30 years) might be a treasure trove of information for scholars when the collection is made fully available.

Donor Obligations

A large part of collection development depends on the generosity of donors. Potential donors may be alumni, local residents, business owners, or other supporters of the institution. Working with donors is a necessity for academic archivists and having an active donor program is an indication of a successful academic archives program. Donors may be generally classified as individuals, families, organizations, boards, or other groups. They have the potential to donate a wide range of material, such as yearbooks, historic manuscripts, family papers, first editions of rare or significant books, photograph collections, audiovisual recordings, posters, or ephemera. These possible donations may relate to the history of the institution or to the academic archives' specific collecting area. The most common reason that donors place material in academic archives is to ensure that their collections will be preserved and available for researchers.

In addition to offering collections, donors may also offer direct financial donations to support the archives program. Monetary donations may be designated for the purchase of new materials from the rare book and manuscript marketplace. Financial support can assist with the costs of processing, preserving, and storing collections. Some donors specify the uses for the funding, whereas others make financial gifts that are unrestricted. Larger donations may form the basis of endowment accounts, which are designed to be ongoing gifts that generate income from the principal donation. Endowments can financially support positions, assistantships, publications, equipment purchase and upkeep, archival supplies, and purchase of original material, such as books and manuscripts.

Determining donor expectations is a significant part of donor relations. Even before the donation of material or funding is made, archivists must determine how the gift will support the program and what the donor expects as a result of the contribution. In some cases the wishes of the donors affect how the collections are processed, promoted, and accessed. Some donors incorrectly assume that their collection will be available for use within a short time, that only selected scholars will have access to their papers, that the entire collection will be digitized or photocopied for their use, or that they may be able to take back part of their collection for a short-term or permanent loan. Archivists need to clarify these expectations and implicit assumptions early in the acquisitions process and avoid agreeing to impossible or difficult to manage demands. Unrealistic expectations from the donor or from the archivist will only result in disappointment.

Since most donors are not archivists and are unfamiliar with procedures, academic archivists must make a point to explain the steps that occur following the donation. The archives' mission to provide access to material, through methods such as digitization, finding aids, and in-house researchers, must be explained fully and clearly. Some potential donors may conceptualize archives as only as a safe place to store valuable material, or they may not want unrestricted access to their papers. Academic archivists should be clear with the donor that their collection will support the program, will be accessible to all interested users, and will remain with the repository in perpetuity. Once the archivist and the donor have determined their shared expectations, all agreements between the donor and the archives should be listed in the deed of gift, and not just depend on oral agreements that are often forgotten and not passed forward to the next generation (Browar, 1991).

As general principles of collection development and management, archivists should avoid accepting collections that feature significant limitations and long-term obligations that may be difficult to meet. When negotiating with donors, academic archivists should avoid entering complicated legal agreements between the archives and donors, deposits or bailments of materials, and promises of future financial dividends to the donor's heirs. Sometimes, however, negotiations with donors begin with library or the institution's administration, meaning that agreements and expectations are set before the archivist becomes involved in the process. Thus, it is imperative that archivists become an active part of the acquisitions process by working with development officers, library administration, advisory boards, and alumni groups to explain the realities and limitations of managing and processing archival collections.

CREATING A COLLECTION DEVELOPMENT POLICY FOR ACADEMIC ARCHIVES

Collections Survey

A collections survey is the first step toward creating a realistic collection development policy. This survey should include information about existing or forthcoming material. With the realities of shrinking spaces, budgets, and staff it is important to know what has been collected, what should continue to be collected, and what collecting areas should be limited or even discontinued (Hunter, 2003).

The leader of the archives program begins the survey process by assembling a team to gather detailed information about the processed and unprocessed materials held by the archives. The team discusses the repository's known collection strengths, the weak areas, and segments with the greatest potential for growth, and then methodically gathers collection-level information (Fleckner, 1977). For processed collections with electronic finding aids, much of that information is easily compiled. Repositories with strong accessioning processes may be able to quickly compile collection data about material in the backlog. Collections with use restrictions, joint ownership, preservation concerns, and digitization potential should be noted. The raw data about each collection should in a searchable format, such as a spreadsheet or a database, so that information can be sorted, resorted, and queried.

Once the data is collected, the survey team creates a collections report with general recommendations about the program's future collection development initiatives (Hunter, 2003). The survey should note any kind of consistent patterns in processed and unprocessed collections such as frequently occurring subjects, individuals, formats, time periods, and types of media. The report should also note whether that information relates to other holdings in academic archives, such as rare books and printed pieces, historical newspapers, institutional publications, and subject files.

Identifying Strengths, Constituents, and Resources

The collections report points to strengths in the program's collection development approaches. However, collections reports commonly discover the absence of archival and manuscript material covering topics in social history (especially documenting women and minorities), institutional records and collections from the latter decades of the twentieth century, and uneven coverage of born-digital content. This information provides a solid basis for future collection development decision making.

The collections report should also identify research areas with the greatest demand, potential for expansion, and possible limitations. It is important to determine whether a strong research interest exists for both the campus and the scholarly community. Obvious collection areas emerge when collection strengths match research strengths of the archives program. The collections report may also identify wonderful resources that have been underutilized or even ignored by researchers. Underutilized collections offer archives programs opportunities to promote hidden research treasures, which may result in new research interest and new donations of similar material. Gauging future research interest in preexisting collections is an ongoing process.

> **Steps to Formulating a Collection Development Policy**
>
> - Conduct a collection survey.
> - Draft a survey report that identifies collection strengths and weaknesses.
> - Identify collaborators and resources.
> - Seek input from external experts, researchers, and other supporters.
> - Create a clear collections policy describing what is and is not collected and why.

While fundraising to help purchase materials and supplies is important, academic archivists must consider other departmental resources that are needed to support collections. Taking in new collections or focusing in new areas represents a large commitment from the academic archives program, including staff time, storage space, and provisions for supporting ongoing access (Hunter, 2003). The need for resources to support collections should be factored into all discussions and considerations of a collection development policy.

Clarifying a Policy

A collection policy is based on the findings of the collections report, past experience, known resources, and some assumptions about the future. Much like a mission or vision statement, a collections policy is a brief summary of what the repository primarily collects. The policy includes a simple listing of the subjects, topics, or genres of material that connect with the larger aims of the department (Maher, 1992). It may also specifically list what an archives program does not collect, especially if the repository had previously collected in areas that are no longer practical or possible. Other members of the library, the academic community, and especially potential donors want to know what an archives is willing to accept. Most important, the collection development policy should give the academic archivist the ability to say no to potential donors and their collections. A collections development policy should be flexible and adaptable as new resources, collections, and research interests emerge.

A collection development policy should also acknowledge that other archives programs exist and collect in related or unrelated areas. When another repository also collects in a similar area (i.e., Civil War in the South) there may be a possibility for both archives to collect in a collaborative and noncompetitive fashion (Pyatt, 1999). Other times a written collections policy makes it clear that two archives in the same town are collecting different kinds of material for different purposes.

Working with Collection Advisory Boards

Many academic archivists have responsibilities for serving on advisory boards. These groups are often the result of collaborative projects to support campus or community initiatives (Hunter, 2003). Membership on a board could in fact be part of the duties of an academic archivist. Working with boards frequently involves collection development and working with nonarchivists to understand the details and realities of acquiring new collections.

Collection advisory boards are most successful when the academic archivist is in full command of the group. The academic archivist should chair the committee, lead the discussions, rely on the subject experts on the board for their advice about collections and possible usage, be prepared to explain the larger mission and vision of the department, and reserve the right to make the final decision on matters of collection development. If possible, academic archivists should make both practical and political appointments to their collection advisory boards (Krizack,

2007). Collection boards should focus on how the archives program relates to campus instruction, scholarly research, public programming, possible grant opportunities, and other relationships.

Advisory boards may also discuss the possibilities of adding new collections, either through donation or purchase. Inviting potential donors to these meetings may be advantageous. However, advisory boards can become mired in the details of collection development, sometimes resulting in lasting disagreements that may harm the archives program. The academic archivist should avoid bringing every acquisitions decision to the advisory board and should focus the group on the larger shared goals of the program.

COLLECTION STRATEGIES FOR ACADEMIC ARCHIVES

Documenting Campus Activities

The majority of academic archives programs have a collecting focus on their own institutions and campus. Whether serving as the official or unofficial repository for their institution, academic archives regularly document the activities and history of their college or university. Those activities may include components of student life, teaching and instruction, research, community outreach, or administrative decision making (Maher, 1992). The resulting collections serve as the sources that will be available for current and future researchers.

College or university archives programs are most often part of an academic archives department, such as a special collections unit. In this common scenario, collection development for institutional history is folded into the larger collection approach for the department. It is important to build overlapping collections that document the institution's history while supporting other areas of collection strength (Boles, 2005). For example, a special collections department for a medium-sized university in a small town could collect material documenting the history of the town and the university, by seeking both official records and materials about the school created in more unofficial ways.

Other times, academic archives function outside of a library environment and have the distinct collecting area of institutional history. If other areas of the school's past, such as the town's history, are being documented through a manuscripts department in the academic library, then the leaders of both programs should decide how to avoid overlap and competition for collections. Whether functioning within a library or operating as an independent unit, academic archives programs must resolve any collecting conflicts with other units, create a clear collection development policy that avoids overlap with other programs, and build complimentary collections that support their mission and the needs of researchers.

Collecting material to document the institution's history is a complex task. The constant pace of change on a college or university campus is evident in student life, the courses being offered, research activities of faculty, and teaching methods. While perhaps less glamorous, the inter-workings of a campus, such as the activities of administration, support staff, facilities services personnel, and part-time employees, are a vital part of a college or university. Documenting diversity and underrepresented groups on campus is also a key component of collection development for academic archives (Neal, 2008). All members of the campus community create some kind of documentary record; it is up to the academic archivist to decide what to collect and how to collect it.

Academic archivists must consider collecting both the official records and the other material that documents the campus experience. The institution itself generates a massive amount of material, which can be captured through comprehensive records management schedules. However, most campus records management programs are limited and only collect a small portion of official records from the highest administrative offices. The process of scheduling departmental disposition records and operating a campus records management unit is fully covered in Chapter 5.

Developing a documentation strategy is perhaps the best way to attempt to capture the unofficial material that documents what happens on a college campus. A functional approach to collecting material about the institution is the most common campus documentation strategy. This approach emphasizes the importance of context, how college or universities are structured, how individual campus units operate and connect with other units, institutional culture, selection of material rather than comprehensive efforts, and the importance of all parts of a campus, not just collecting material from the top-level administrative offices (Samuels, 1992).

Taking a functional approach to documenting life on-campus begins with examining and studying the different units, and developing an institutional documentation plan. This plan examines college and universities through the following themes: conferring credentials through attracting, selecting, advising, and graduating students; conveying knowledge through teaching, learning, and assessment; fostering socialization through regulations, services, and extracurricular activities; conducting research; sustaining the institution through operations, governance, personnel management, and financial oversight; providing public service; and promoting culture (Samuels, 1992). Such an approach could also incorporate a traditional records management program into the collections strategy.

Casting the collections net to capture a wide range of perspectives on campus life is challenging. As one caveat, efforts to expand campus collecting areas may lead to unwanted items, collections, expectations, and backlog. To avoid such misunderstandings and consequences, academic archivists must communicate clear aims, methods, and goals for documenting their campus (Maher, 1992). Academic archives are repositories containing research materials with historical value and wide-ranging uses. Academic archives are not museums, are not an attic for people and departments to store materials, and are not collecting material about the campus merely for the sake of collecting it. Efforts to document the campus should be determined by academic archivists and not from other constituents, administrators, or the creators of the material. While taking realistic and flexible approaches to documenting campus life and activities, academic archivists should connect this collecting area to the department's larger collection development policy.

Documenting Other Areas

In addition to documenting institutional history, academic archives collect material to support other areas of research. The kind of research areas supported by academic archives may be subject based, geographically focused, centered on specific groups or populations, or limited by time period. Areas of research may also develop in academic archives because of external factors such as strong partnerships with academic units or as a result of decades of specific kinds of donations. Some academic archives also serve other roles in the community or region such as being the unofficial historical society with information about local topics, a place for genealogists and family historians to conduct research, or even as a facility for displaying art, objects, or museum pieces.

Humanities scholars, especially historians, have long-standing connections and relationships with their campus archives. In many cases, professors in humanities departments, such as history and English, took early and active roles in building academic archives programs on their campuses. In turn, academic archives collected material to support the research of humanities and social science scholars. This relationship helped shape the collection development priorities for many academic archives, resulting in a large number of special collections departments collecting in areas such as the American Civil War, the Civil Rights Movement, topics in American political history, and British literature. In the past few decades, academic archives have continued to support humanities scholars and interdisciplinary research by expanding their collecting areas to include the African American experience, topics in social and cultural history, women's and minority history, and grassroots activist movements.

While many of the established collecting areas have remained a constant part of collection development for academic archives, the collections have become more diverse and overlapping in content. A trend of a merged or blended department, which often includes the official records, manuscripts, and rare books, has resulted in a broader and more integrated approach to collection development. For example, an academic archives program that collects official records and local history may make special efforts to acquire the papers of town officials who also worked for the institution. As another example, the acquisition of nineteenth-century correspondence from the school's first president, years before assuming that position, supports multiple purposes of the academic archives. The correlations between different formats and collecting areas makes collection development a much broader process in academic archives, especially when a college or university archives program is part of a special collections unit within an academic library.

In addition to collecting in specific subject areas that support research and scholarship, there are affiliated types of materials that academic archives should consider for their collection development policy. Faculty papers are one type of material that may accentuate the repository's holdings. The papers include classroom and teaching material, research files, and collections related to professional organizations and activities. Many college and university archives do not actively seek faculty papers, simply because of space constraints

---

Types of Documentation Strategies

- Functional approaches
- Collecting official records and selected unofficial materials
- Collecting a variety of formats (i.e., textual, oral histories, and images)
- Targeting diverse voices and perspectives to achieve a more complete picture
- Finding parallels and overlap between collecting areas

and such tangential and unofficial materials may not support the mission of the archives (Hyry, Kaplan, and Weideman, 2008). However, many merged academic archives programs, such as a special collections department, have the resources to pick selected faculty papers for their holdings or work with faculty to accept specific materials.

Documenting other areas besides the college campus requires a clear plan with defined collection boundaries. For example, if an academic archives program collects in the area of eighteenth-century Dutch poetry to support a specific interdisciplinary humanities program, leaders of the repository should be prepared to work with a donor who has a large number of printed books and manuscripts of European poetry. However, the archivists should focus their attention on only the materials related to Dutch poetry for possible acquisition and identify other repositories for the donor. Also it is important to consider how the acquisition of these materials fits into the department's larger documentation strategy for the department and if there is overlap between collecting areas (Cox, 1996).

Oral Histories

One of the most common ways to expand collection development in specific areas of study is to include an oral history component. While there are only a handful of archives focused only on collecting oral histories, almost all academic archives have some oral history collections (Stielow, 1986). Oral histories allow academic archivists to fill important gaps in the documentary record of their institution's history or in other collecting areas. Further, oral history projects are a tremendous development tool for acquiring new collections, supporters, and monetary donations.

Gathering oral histories is a common expectation of donors or groups interested in a specific area of study. There are limitless possibilities of what to document, whom to interview, and how to expand an oral history collecting program. Likewise, a multitude of research uses exist for oral history collections by scholars, especially those in the humanities and social sciences (Yow, 2005). Oral histories accentuate collections and collecting areas by adding personal perspective, highlighting the importance of memory (both shared and collective) in studying past events, and revealing conflicting opinions and accounts (Perks and Thomson, 1998).

The practice of oral history is taught in academic departments in the humanities, mostly as upper-level history courses (Ritchie, 2003).

Advanced courses in English departments may also include an oral history component of the class. The Collecting and managing audiovisual projects is also taught in some library and information sciences departments, especially those programs focused in archives and records management.

The context and reasons for creating oral histories is also very important when using the materials for research. The choice of interview questions, how the conversations were recorded, and the dynamics between the interviewer and the interviewee have direct affect on the usefulness of the final product for researchers (Dunaway and Baum, 1984). Unlike handwritten or printed documents, oral histories are more complicated to collect, authenticate, access, and use. Simply put, oral histories may have exceedingly valuable historical material, but a focus on building oral history resources requires a great deal of time, resources, and institutional commitment (Maher, 1992).

The process of interviewing participants is the first consideration for any oral history project. In addition to conducting background research on the selected individuals and the topics that will most likely be discussed in the session, the interviewer must follow a standard protocol for oral history recordings (Ritchie, 2003). If possible, the interviewer should share a list of questions with the interviewee before the session. As a baseline for conceptualizing oral history interviews, the sessions should be conducted in a professional manner, the interviewer should assume a neutral position and avoid taking an adversarial stance, and the interviewer must respect the preferences and requests of the interviewee (Charleton, Myers, and Sharpless, 2006). It is common for answers to oral history interview questions to go in unexpected directions or tangents. The interviewer should allow extra time and flexibility with the questions, while still keeping the session focused on the planned topics.

How to record the session is an important factor in the oral history interview process. Professional recording equipment is preferred when conducting quality oral history interviews. If the interviewee is willing to visit the campus and conduct the session in a professional recording space, then sessions may be video recorded, resulting in a much richer experience for researchers (Ritchie, 2003). But in reality, most oral history interviews take place at the interviewee's residence with handheld tape recorders. Practitioners of oral history also encourage that the multiple interviews be conducted within a short time span, which helps deepen the quality of the content. However, the results of many of these limited-budget and fast-paced oral history projects are boxes of unmarked cassette tapes stuck in the backlog of many academic archives.

Part of the oral history interview process and building strong oral history collections for academic archives is to ensure that the recorded information will be accessible for researchers. The interviewees are in fact donors of information and the resulting collection is technically their personal property. To provide access to these collections, or donations, interviewers should obtain written permission to release the information from all interviewees at the time of the oral history sessions and also at the time a written transcript has been compiled (Ritchie, 2003). The release forms are nearly identical to standard deed of gift forms used by archivists when acquiring collections. Without permission to release the information, the oral history tapes and transcripts remain inaccessible for researchers. It is common for interviewees to request redactions, corrections, and limited restrictions on their oral history sessions. Just like other areas of collection development, academic archivists should push for open access to information without compromising personal information.

Once an oral history session is complete the recorded information must be reviewed and transcribed. This process is time-consuming and requires careful attention to detail. The resulting transcript should be shared with and approved by the interviewee before it can be made available to researchers (Ritchie, 2003). While online access policies to oral history collections vary by institution, some repositories post full-text transcripts to their websites and a select number of academic archives provide online streamed access to the audio recordings. The ongoing management of the oral history collections often includes frequent transfer of recordings to new media, especially when the original recordings were captured on low-quality cassette tapes, which rapidly deteriorate.

Beginning or expanding an oral history program in academic archives requires realistic planning, attention to detail, and an ongoing commitment of resources. Like any other area of collection development, the academic archivist must define the scope and purposes of an oral history collection (Maher, 1992). One of the most practical ways to support oral history collections in academic archives is to partner with other campus departments. Academic programs that are active in collecting oral histories may be able to deposit the results of their work—recordings, transcripts, and release forms—in the academic archives. Managing oral history collections depends on having staff expertise and the right equipment to record and transfer the information to a reliable format. Academic archivists may also expand their oral history program by pursuing grant funding with other archival repositories. If carefully managed and expanded, oral history collections have the potential to greatly enhance the quality of research resources in an academic archives program. A well-organized oral history program will result in new acquisitions from supporters and interviewees, with the potential for financial donations.

SOURCES OF COLLECTIONS FOR ACADEMIC ARCHIVES

Collections for academic archives come from a variety of sources (Figure 6.1). It is common for archives programs to both receive donations and purchase material to build their collections. A strong development program increases awareness, resources, donations, and direct funding to support building new collections in an academic archives program.

Donors and Donations

A successful development program is the key to obtaining new donors, collections, and resources for academic archives. Development is broadly defined as fundraising, building endowment accounts, and securing

---

Figure 6.1
Sources of Collections for Academic Archives

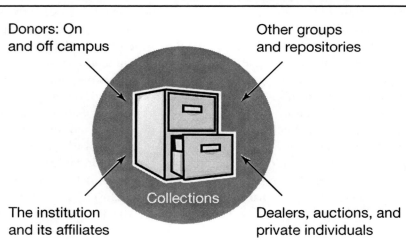

Donors: On
and off campus

Other groups
and repositories

Collections

The institution
and its affiliates

Dealers, auctions, and
private individuals

Source: Graphic by Marc Brodsky.

promises of resources for the archives program. This ongoing work is an integral part of working with the various sources of collections for academic archives. Even donated collections require resources to make them accessible and usable for patrons.

Academic archivists rely on donors to keep their collections growing. The majority of collections found in academic archives were donated by a person, a group, or by the institution itself. Donors from on campus may include a faculty member, a student, an administrator, or a campus department. Donors from off campus may include regular researchers in the academic archives, local residents, historical or genealogical organizations, or alumni.

A donation is defined as a gift made to the academic archives without any obligation of financial payment. Donations to academic archives are most commonly in the form of documents, photographs, records, printed publications, and objects. A simple deed of gift document, described more fully in Chapter 7, legally transfers the physical property of materials to the academic archives. In addition to donating collections, many donors make financial contributions to academic archives to help cover the costs of archival supplies, wages, or special events. Donations of funding to the archives most often triggers involvement from the institution's development office. In an era of unprecedented fundraising campaigns, colleges and universities have centralized their development efforts. As a result, academic archivists often work with a development officer assigned to them or to the academic library when working with potential donors (Dewey, 1991).

Friends groups may also connect donors with academic archives. Many academic libraries have friends groups to help raise awareness and funding for the library (Dolnick, 1990). Because academic archives and special collections units have great potential for fundraising, there are often separate friends groups for just the archives program. Friends groups reach a wide range of potential donors through events, conferences, publications, and direct solicitations (Steele and Elder, 1992). Because most friends groups are tax exempt and separate from the institution enormous possibilities exist for enhancement of archival work through these groups. At the very least, friends groups for academic archives can attract potential donors to their ranks.

At the campus level there are frequent sources of donated material. Campus departments, offices, and administrative units offer academic archives a large amount of donated material. Colleges and universities with records management programs (either within the archives program or as a stand-alone unit) supply academic archives with official records from specific campus departments through a records scheduling process (see Chapter 5). Many schools, however, lack a records management component, which makes collecting official records problematic. Instead, academic archives work with campus departments to manage their office files, to identify material with historical value in those files, and to transfer appropriate materials to the academic archives for researcher use (Maher, 1992). Other unofficial materials, such as research files from significant faculty members, draft reports, or images from the department's holiday parties, may also be acquired for the academic archives.

The senior administrative assistant in each department is often the only person with access to and comprehensive knowledge of the files. Academic archivists should communicate frequently with administrative assistants while also keeping clear lines of communication with the department head or chair. Because of the large number of campus departments and offices, academic archivists could easily spend all of their time sorting through office files. Offering workshops on managing office files is one way for academic archivists to educate campus units about the academic archives program and to encourage departments to manage their own files. Another time-saving strategy is for academic archivists to encourage departments to transfer infrequently used files to the archives every five years, instead of every year. A change in departmental leadership, such as the arrival of a new chair or a new provost, is also a good opportunity for the academic archivist to plan for the transfer of material and cultivate a new relationship. With or without a records management component, the donor relationship between academic archivists and their campus units is crucial and an ongoing process.

Faculty and other employees of the institution are frequent donors to academic archives, and relationships between academic archivists and these on-campus donors can last for decades. During the course of a sometimes lengthy career, academic faculty collect research materials, rare volumes, original sources, and documents to support their scholarship and teaching. In fact, the earliest and most significant donations of books and manuscripts to countless academic libraries have originated from faculty members. There is still a strong tradition of faculty members donating their libraries, office files, and class notes to the academic archives (Maher, 1992). Other employees of the institution, such as administrative officials, deans, architects, and public relations staff, may also have amassed significant research collections that might accentuate the holdings of an academic archives program. In addition to placing their research material in the academic archives, some of these on-campus donors make significant financial contributions to support processing, wages, and other archival needs.

With such a wealth of on-campus material available, academic archivists must make consistent decisions about which collections to accept. Taking in random collections from faculty and administrators for political or strategic reasons should be avoided. Instead, academic archivists should take a methodical approach to building collections of official and unofficial material from on-campus sources. To make such decisions easier, the program should have a clear collection development policy, which addresses the more unofficial materials such as faculty papers, teaching materials, and files from departments not covered by record schedules. For example, the following collection development policy describes the types of materials collected by a fictitious archives program at a small university: "The university archives documents the history of the institution by collecting official records and publications produced by the institution, materials generated by student groups, and files from the alumni organization. The archives does not collect objects, personal or faculty papers, student work, or material related to local history."

Common Donor Groups

- Campus offices and departments scheduled by a records management program
- Faculty and employees of the institution
- Alumni
- Unaffiliated supporters
- Internal and external organizations

Beyond campus, academic archivists work with a wide range of donors and donor groups to build collections. For most academic institutions, off-campus donors are managed by an institution's development office through assigned development officers. It has become common for academic libraries to have at least one development officer, who works in the library to promote the library. Sometimes the development officer is in fact employed by the development office and not the library.

Alumni are one of the largest groups of off-campus donors for academic archives. Generally speaking, these donors come from a variety of backgrounds, represent a wide range of ages, have both positive and negative opinions about their alma mater, possess both collections and financial resources in need of a good home, and have different motivations for donating to the archives (Steele and Elder, 1992). Working with alumni donors can be a long-term or a brief process, depending on the needs and expectations of the donor. Many of these donors are active in an alumni association, which may also coordinate development activities for the institution's development office. This reality can sometimes make working with alumni donors with potential collections a one-way-street: donors may initially contact the archivist on their own, but archivists may not be "allowed" to make cold calls to alumni donors without permission from the development office or the alumni association.

A wide range of archival materials come from alumni. Most commonly, alumni have institutional publications (such as yearbooks and newspapers), personal items from their collegiate experience (such as scrapbooks and programs from sporting events), and photographs of campus, important events, or themselves. These materials document collegiate life and sometimes significant moments in the school's history. For example, a student from the late 1960s who participated in antiwar protests at a large university may have kept dozens of broadsides that document the number and location of student meetings related to organizing on-campus demonstrations. Such underground student movements may have had little documentation in the official records of the university. Other more notable alumni donors may include former sports stars, with

Common Types of Donations

- Official records
- Material related to school history
- Material related to other collecting areas
- Ephemera and memorabilia
- Funding to support the program

significant material from their collegiate athletic career. If the campus does not have an athletic-related museum then the academic archives is often the repository for these collections.

Working with alumni donors requires patience and careful attention. Their love for the institution is often the primary motivation for donating their material. These donors frequently share their recollections, making a strong working history of the institution necessary for academic archivists. Alumni donors may also have strong opinions (both positive and negative) about the institution, which makes for awkward conversations. Because their material to be donated holds such a personal connection, some donors want to take an active role in processing their collections (i.e., advising the processing archivist and reviewing the finding aids). This kind of arrangement can be problematic for efficient processing. The leader of the archives program should make clear to donors that archivists are trained professionals who will ask for help from the donor if needed. On the other hand, some alumni donors take little interest in their donation after placing it in the archives. Their gift of material and funding may be their final communication with the academic archives.

Other major off-campus donors include organizations and unaffiliated individuals. Both groups have the potential to contribute new collections to the holdings and financial support for the program. Organizations such as a local fire department, a regional nonprofit agency, a chapter of the Daughters of the American Revolution, a nearby Presbyterian church, a family-owned business, an energy company headquartered in the region, and a professional society with strong ties to the college or university, all represent potential donors to academic archives programs. These various groups may have wonderful collections of original material that could significantly enhance the repository's holdings on local and regional history. Furthermore, many of these organizations have financial resources that could accompany their donation and support multiple components of the archives program (Steele and Elder, 1992).

Unaffiliated individuals often "stumble" into an academic archives program offering potential donations. Most are motivated by wanting to place original material in their possession in the right location for researchers to use. For example, an individual in Seattle purchases a box of letters at a flea market and soon discovers a handwritten document from the first president of a large university in the South. Eventually the donor decides to donate the item to the institution and contacts the university archivist explaining that he or she wants to make a donation. The donor has no interest in selling the item; instead, the individual just wants the document to be returned to its appropriate home. These donations occur suddenly and are usually completed in a very short time. Such unexpected donations require academic archivists to make quick decisions about accepting tangential materials. These situations are also excellent opportunities for the academic archives to recognize the significance of the gift by publicizing the donation and the donor through websites, newsletters, blogs, and exhibits.

Other unaffiliated off-campus donors are quite well known by the academic archivists. Local residents, independent researchers, family historians, collectors, and scholars from nearby institutions are frequent donors to academic archives. Their collections of family papers, research files, ephemera, photographs, and local publications have tremendous value for academic archives. Since many of these donors are frequent visitors to the reading rooms of academic archives, the relationship between the donor and the repository may stretch across many decades.

There may in fact be little indication that a donation is expected or impending from this group of donors. In some cases such a donation of material or funding occurs after their passing and the academic archives is listed in the estate plan or will.

When donors are interested in making a large financial donation, often they want to take an active role in shaping new directions for the archives program, such as creating an endowment to support new collecting areas and positions. If indeed a financial donation can affect the mission and vision of the program in a positive way, then the archivist should work with the donor and campus development officers to help set shared realistic goals and expectations. However, archivists should not sacrifice their principles for one large donation. Archivists should rely on clear documentation and open communication with all donors, whether they are receiving from a donor a set of letters, a $1 million unrestricted gift, a much-needed college yearbook, files of an significant nonprofit organization, or an unexpected $20 contribution. The abilities to listen, communicate, negotiate, and empathize with these donors can result in enormous long-term opportunities for the academic archives program.

Purchasing from Dealers, Auctions, and Private Individuals

Traditionally archivists have focused their collection-building efforts on material that may be donated to their repository, either because of a legal mandate to collect certain records or because of the generosity of a donor. What has changed significantly in the past few decades is the reality that archivists purchase material for their archives from book and manuscript dealers, through auction houses, and even from private individuals. For decades this kind of collection development work has been reserved for rare books and special collections librarians; however, it is essential that all archivists understand the basics of purchasing archival material for their repository.

Academic archivists, especially those already working in a special collections environment, are often faced with reality of purchasing material for their archives. Similar to donations, these kinds of acquisitions have to fit well within the repository's collecting areas. An archivist must determine if the material fits with the mission and vision of the unit, how the material will be used by researchers, and available resources for its processing, storage, and access points. But unlike donations, acquiring purchased material requires an understanding of budgets, invoices, standard dealer practices, rules of auctions, and who else might be in competition for the material. Academic archivists, who are now taking on the once-stratified responsibilities of special collections librarians, manuscript curators, and rare books experts for their departments, have an incredible opportunity to build their collections through purchasing historical material.

Many aspects of the rare book and manuscript trade have remained unchanged for decades. For generations, dealers in books and manuscripts have reached their buyers (i.e., collectors, historical societies, and academic institutions) through printed catalogs or direct communication (Rendell, 2001). Potential buyers could then request that specific material be sent to them "on approval" for their review, which allowed them a period to review the items, make a decision on purchasing, and return unwanted items (Carter, 2002). This process could take months to complete, especially because larger institutions like colleges and universities often take several weeks to generate a payment.

The work of a rare book and manuscript dealer is time-consuming. Dealers scour estate sales, auctions, and even obituary notices to uncover leads to new collections. They also work with numerous individuals who have rare items in their possession, who may want to sell the material, or they simply want to know the estimated market value. This latter activity is known as appraisal. Far different from archival appraisal, this kind of appraisal establishes a price range based on the dealer's knowledge of similar items, rarity, desirability, and collectability. The appraisal process results in a detailed description of the item or collection. Some appraisals are requested by individuals who are interested in donating their material to an archival repository. Other times, individuals sell their material to the dealer, who may eventually offer the item or collection in a printed catalog, on a website, or through direct contact with a likely buyer. For the most part, dealers are more concerned with making their buyers happy by matching them with the right items than they are trying to make a fast profit (Rendell, 2001).

Book and manuscript catalogs offer academic archivists a wide range of detail about potential acquisitions. The most basic catalogs include simple bibliographic information (i.e., author, title, publisher,

Common Methods for Purchasing Archival Material

- Catalogs from book and manuscript dealers
- Receiving materials "on approval"
- Bidding in online and live auctions
- Discovery of material on eBay
- Working with private individuals

publication date, and number copies in libraries) about their printed offerings. Likewise basic catalogs may only list limited details about their manuscript materials (i.e., creator, date range, number of pieces or linear footage, and a few notable topics). Depending on past purchases and relationships, academic archivists may receive a dozen dealer catalogs each week. The more ornate catalogs include multiple color images of the items, several paragraphs of descriptions, and excerpted transcriptions of text. Each dealer incorporates his or her own style into a printed catalog, with the larger objective of trying to present the material for what it is, its historical significance, and comparing it to related materials known in the book and manuscript trade. Many dealers have a strong web presence, with links to their traditional print catalogs and additional information about specific items (Holzenberg, 2001).

The relationship between academic archivists and book and manuscript dealers is important for several reasons. First, dealers are often the first people to be aware of "new" collections and items that have just been discovered in attics, basements, and shoeboxes. Reputable dealers see more than profits when they first view these materials. Instead, they recognize the most likely archival repositories for these materials to reside and know who to contact. Second, dealers can provide appraisal services for donors, while academic archivists are ethically unable to provide their donors with market value for their collections. That appraisal value may be used by the donor to claim an income tax deduction. In numerous cases of theft from repositories, dealers have been a first line of defense against stolen material reaching the marketplace. Dealers have a consistent pattern of working with archivists, law enforcement agencies, and lawyers to keep archival robbers at bay. Finally, dealers are quite familiar with the practices and realities of academic institutions. They understand that acquisition budgets are fickle, that payments may take many weeks to arrive, and that academic archivists have multiple responsibilities.

Auction houses offering rare books, manuscripts, and archival materials are another source of purchasable materials for an academic archives program. Academic archivists should focus on the auction houses with established reputations in the rare book and manuscript trade. Traditionally auctions for historical items required actual attendance or a proxy bidder at the auction. However, most auctions now have an online component, thus expanding the range of bidders. Similar to dealers, auction houses produce detailed color catalogs with extensive description of materials, with much of the same content available on the company's website. In an effort to attract bidders, auction houses do a large amount of promotion to potential buyers.

While the material listed by auction houses is similar to the material offered by dealers, several considerations make this kind of acquisition riskier. Unlike working with dealers, auction houses do not send material "on approval" and unless otherwise stated all sales are final. Purchasing material "sight unseen" is a huge consideration for academic archivists. Without review of the material, archivists must rely on the auction house's description for important components such as legibility of the material, its physical condition and other preservation concerns, the accuracy and scope of the historical content, and provenance. Some items such as printed pieces, ephemera, books, images, and short letters can be easily described and displayed through a print or online auction catalog. More complex items such as diaries, collections of letters, business records including ledger books, and historical object are much harder to describe and are the kind of formats that warrant a thorough examination. Some auction houses do allow preliminary questions about specific items, but most times the posted description is the extent of their knowledge of the piece at auction.

Before any bidding takes place, several archivists should review auction listings and share their opinions with the leader of the program's collection development efforts. A team approach to book and manuscript auctions builds consensus on collection development priorities and often results in narrowing the list of potential items for bidding. The group may be able to determine a maximum bid for each item on the basis of desirability of the item and available funding. After compiling a short list, academic archivists must understand the realities of bidding and the process of paying for any items won. Most auction houses allow registered bidders to see current bids and sometimes the bidding history, but never the identity of the bidders. However, it is advisable to bid the predetermined maximum amount for each item and avoid increasing bids during the auction. A significant bidding consideration is that most auction houses also add a buyer's premium to the final "hammer price," often as much as 25 percent of the sale price. When estimating bids, academic archivists should calculate the buyer's premium and additional shipping into the final bottom line.

For items won at auction, most auction houses require fast payment, often a prepayment before the item or collection is shipped to the winner. While most dealers are accustomed to slow payment times from academic institutions, auction houses typically want payment within 30 days of the auction and have little patience for winners slow to respond. If the archives department wins material from an auction, there must be a plan in place to facilitate a speedy payment. Another payment hindrance for academic archivists is the common practice at many academic institutions to require that large purchases (i.e., over $10,000) have some kind of authorization or even preapproval from the institution's financial officers. Further, it is common for auction houses to ship the won items after payment has been received, which may run counter to traditional library acquisitions policies. The entire process is much more efficient when archivists know the rules of auction houses before they bid.

The least regulated and reputed of the online auctions with historical and archival material is through eBay. While amazing offerings are available, bidding on eBay items requires significant research into the item, the seller, and how to make an efficient and secure payment. Some academic archives have made eBay purchasing a regular part of their collection development work, while other archives are either too cautious or unable to develop a payment workflow that works with their institution's financial policies. Academic archivists should carefully consider the risks of purchasing material through eBay and keep in mind the advice that "if it sounds too good to be true, then it probably is." From a traditional archival perspective, purchasing material on eBay is not a sustainable or realistic way to build quality collections, but it may be a suitable avenue to obtain selected items.

Acquiring new material from auctions is an exciting prospect; however, academic archivists should read the fine print when considering working with auction houses and other online auctions. Consulting numerous opinions in the department and in the library is a solid strategy for selecting relevant material from auctions. At the same time, the rules of online auctions require academic archivists to work closely with their institution's treasurer's office to generate a fast payment.

Private individuals with historical or archival material may also be potential sources of new acquisitions. This group consists of people, who are not dealers, with material that they are willing to sell directly to academic archives. Their material is often connected to their own family and for a variety of reasons they have decided to sell the items. Other times these individuals have inadvertently acquired material as gifts from friends, through inexpensive methods such as a yard sale, or by cleaning out the attic of their Victorian home.

Generally speaking, private sellers are limited in their knowledge of the rare book and manuscript trade. Information from Internet sites and television programs such as PBS's *Antiques Roadshow* seem to fuel the idea that handwritten manuscripts and rare books are worth a small fortune. On the other hand, advice from an actual rare book and manuscript dealer, preferably one who is a member of the Antiquarian Booksellers Association of America (ABAA), provides a much more realistic estimate of market value. Private sellers also contact academic archivists in order to find out more about the history and value of their item. However, as an interested party in the material, the archivist is ethically bound to not provide an estimate or name a selling price. The academic archivist should refer the person to a certified appraiser or a list of ABAA members.

Some private sellers contact an academic archivist with a specific price for a specific item. The archivist must then determine the historical value of the item and whether the cost is reasonable and fair. Because most of these sellers are unfamiliar with the practices of the rare book and manuscript trade, academic archivists should request that the material be sent "on approval" before any purchasing decision can be made. If the seller demands advanced payment then it is wise to pass on the opportunity. Despite the dangers of purchasing outside of the traditional manuscript and book trade, acquiring new materials and collections from private individuals can yield impressive results.

Materials from Other Archives

In addition to shrinking budgets and spaces, academic archives face the challenge of maintaining research areas and collections that are no longer central to their mission and researcher base. Academic archives have experienced a recent trend of deaccessioning collections. When deaccessioning materials, repositories attempt to correctly place collections at other archives where research use will occur. The repository receiving the deaccessioned material may in fact be adding a significant collection to their holdings that supports their mission and researchers' needs. Although a controversial practice, some repositories place their deaccessioned collections on the market through online auctions in order to fundraise for their archives program (Doylen, 2001).

Deaccessioning materials, including archival collections, from academic libraries is not a new phenomenon. The largest deaccessioning issue for many library systems is that once any item (book, manuscript, CD, etc.) is accessioned then it becomes property of the institution. The process of ending that ownership can be complicated, especially if the donor of an underutilized manuscript collection targeted for deaccession is still an active donor to the academic library. Another issue with deaccessioning is whether the collection is adequately processed, if processed at all, and if the repository receiving the collection has the resources available to provide appropriate access to the relocated material. However, if these and other issues can be easily resolved, acquiring deaccessioned collections can be a mutually advantageous way to add new material to academic archives.

CONCLUSION

The collections found in academic archives are what define the program. Academic archives may collect nineteenth-century manuscripts, official college records, oral histories of significant women engineers, records of local churches, or ephemera relating to regional fairs and festivals. These collections document a variety of historical topics such as the institution's past, local history, or international movements. Many academic archivists create documentation strategies to approach the difficult work of collecting material in multiple areas. Acquisitions that overlap collecting areas serve numerous research purposes and strengthen the collecting mission of the department.

Evaluating existing collections and collecting areas is the first part of defining or re-defining an effective collection development policy. The collecting areas must support the department's mission and vision, while providing a wide base of research support. Because each collection is unique there may be access restrictions, donor obligations, and research demands to consider before accepting new materials. While gathering information about existing collections, academic archivists uncover trends in past collecting areas, recognize areas of strength and weakness, and identify constituents for future development of the program. These results and observations can be used to help reformulate collection development priorities.

Every academic archives program should have a clear collection development policy that explains what is collected, why it is collected, how it is collected, and what is not collected. Without clear collecting parameters academic archivists can become overwhelmed with available material from donors, sellers, and from the institution itself. Acquiring new material from each group requires special attention, patience, and a clear understanding of institutional policies. Academic archivists who understand how collections are planned, acquired, and built can be more effective in planning for the acquisition, processing, providing access to, and long-term management of those collections.

REFERENCES

Association of Research Libraries. 2007. "Building on Strength: Developing an ARL Agenda for Special Collections." Last modified November 2. http:// www.arl.org/resources/pubs/mmproceedings/139brown.shtml.

Boles, Frank. 2005. *Selecting and Appraising Archives and Manuscripts*. Chicago: Society of American Archivists.

Brichford, Maynard J. 1979. "University Archives: Relationships with Faculty." In *College and University Archives: Selected Readings*, 31-37. Chicago: Society of American Archivists.

Browar, Lisa. 1991. "An Oral Contract Isn't Worth the Paper It's Printed On." *Rare Books and Manuscripts Librarianship* 6, no. 2: 100–107.

Burckel, Nicholas C. 2008. "Academic Archives: Retrospect and Prospect." In *College and University Archives: Readings in Theory and Practice*, edited by Christopher J. Prom and Ellen D. Swain, 3–26. Chicago: Society of American Archivists.

Carter, John. 2002. *ABC for Book Collectors*. New Castle, DE: Oak Knoll Press.

Charlton, Thomas L., Lois Myers, and Rebecca Sharpless. 2006. *Handbook of Oral History*. New York: Altamira Press.

Cox, Richard. 1996. *Documenting Localities: A Practical Model for American Archivists and Manuscript Curators*. Lanham, MD: The Scarecrow Press.

Dewey, Barbara I. 1991. *Raising Money for Academic and Research Libraries*. New York: Neal-Schuman.

Dolnick, Sandy, ed. 1990. *Friends of Libraries Sourcebook*. 2nd ed. Chicago: American Library Association.

Doylen, Michael. 2001. "Experiments in Deaccessioning: Archives and On-line Auctions." *American Archivist* 64 (Fall/Winter): 350–362.

Dunaway, David K., and Willa K. Baum, eds. 1984. *Oral History: An Interdisciplinary Anthology*. Nashville: American Association for State and Local History.

Fleckner, John A. 1977. *Archives and Manuscripts: Surveys*. Chicago: Society of American Archivists.

Holzenberg, Eric. 2001. "Second-Hand and Antiquarian Books on the Internet." *RBM: A Journal of Rare Books, Manuscripts, and Cultural Heritage* 2, no. 1 (March): 35–44.

Hunter, Gregory S. 2003. *Developing and Maintaining Practical Archives*. 2nd ed. New York: Neal-Schuman.

Hyry, Tom, Diane Kaplan, and Christine Weideman. 2008. " Though This Be Madness, Yet There Is Method In't'": Assessing the Value of Faculty Papers and Defining a Collections Policy." In *College and University Archives: Readings in Theory and Practice*, edited by Christopher J. Prom and Ellen D. Swain, 117–133. Chicago: Society of American Archivists.

Krizack, Joan D. 2007. "Preserving the History of Diversity: One University's Efforts to Make Boston's History More Inclusive." *RBM: A Journal of Rare Books, Manuscripts, and Cultural Heritage* 8, no. 1 (September): 125–132.

Maher, William J. 1992. *The Management of College and University Archives*. Chicago: Society of American Archivists.

McCoy, Michelle. 2010. "The Manuscript as Question: Teaching Primary Sources in the Archives—The China Missions Project." *College and Research Libraries* 71, no. 1 (January): 49–62.

Neal, Kathryn M. 2008. "Giving it More Than the Old College Try: Documenting Diverse Populations in College and University Archives." In *College and University Archives: Readings in Theory and Practice*, edited by Christopher J. Prom and Ellen D. Swain, 97–116. Chicago: Society of American Archivists.

O'Toole, James M., and Richard J. Cox. 2006. *Understanding Archives and Manuscripts*. Chicago: Society of American Archivists.

Perks, Robert, and Alistair Thomson, eds. 1998. *The Oral History Reader*. New York: Routledge.

Pyatt, Tim. 1999. "Cooperative Collecting of Manuscripts in the 'Old South.'" *Rare Books and Manuscripts Librarianship* 14, no. 1 (September): 19–25.

———. 2008. "Balancing Issues of Privacy and Confidentiality in College and University Archives." In *College and University Archives: Readings in Theory and Practice*, edited by Christopher J. Prom and Ellen D. Swain, 212–225. Chicago: Society of American Archivists.

Rendell, Kenneth W. 2001. "The Future of the Manuscript and Rare Book Business." *RBM: A Journal of Rare Books, Manuscripts, and Cultural Heritage* 2, no. 1 (March): 13–30.

Ritchie, Donald A. 2003. *Doing Oral History: A Practical Guide*. 2nd ed. New York: Oxford University Press.

Ritzenthaler, Mary Lynn. 2010. *Preserving Archives and Manuscripts*. 2nd ed. Chicago: Society of American Archivists.

Robyns, Marcus C. 2001. "The Archivist as Educator: Integrating Critical Thinking Skills into Historical Research Methods Instruction." *American Archivist* 64 (Fall/Winter): 363–384.

Samuels, Helen Willa. 1992. *Varsity Letters: Documenting Modern Colleges and Universities*. Chicago: Society of American Archivists.

Steele, Victoria, and Stephen D. Elder. 1992. *Becoming a Fundraiser: The Principles and Practices of Library Development*. Chicago: American Library Association.

Stielow, Frederick J. 1986. *The Management of Oral History Sound Archives*. New York: Greenwood Press.

Wright, Stephanie. 2007. *Library Assessment*. Washington, DC: Association of Research Libraries.

Yakel, Elizabeth. 2002. "Listening to Users." *Archival Issues* 26, no. 2: 111–127.

Yakel, Elizabeth, and Deborah A. Torres. 2007. "Genealogists as a 'Community of Record.'" *American Archivist* 70 (Spring/Summer): 93–113.

Yow, Valerie Raleigh. 2005. *Recording Oral History: A Guide for the Humanities and Social Sciences.* 2nd ed. New York: Altamira Press.

7

Acquiring, Processing, and Managing Collections in Academic Archives

INTRODUCTION

Archivists who are responsible for acquisitions and processing are often unsung heroes of the research world and the information profession. Their jobs involve literally making order out of chaos, or homogenizing a raw product into something consumable. They must be detail oriented, be well organized, have knowledge of their collections, and be able to contextualize collections within the scope of the repository's holdings. As a common occurrence, after months of negotiations with donors, a dozen or more boxes of random materials unexpectedly arrive at the repository's loading dock. The archivist responsible for acquisitions and processing takes physical control of the collection by accessioning, storing, and tracking the collection. Then, the archivist creates intellectual control of the collection by surveying, processing, and creating a finding aid for the material.

Processing collections, also known as arrangement and description, is a core skill for archivists. Learning to process collections takes study, observation, and practice, usually over the course of many years. Processing collections takes time, even for the most experienced archivists. The amount of time to process a collection depends on the complexity of the material, its original order, size, and research potential. Further, many approaches, technological tools, best practices, and descriptive standards are available for archivists who process collections. Processing involves the logical organization of documents and other formats into folders, boxes, enclosures, and other types of archival containers. Archivists create finding aids or inventories to describe the intellectual arrangement and content of the processed collection. Finding aids are the road maps for archival collections.

Once collections are processed, archivists must manage those collections in a deliberate and efficient manner. The oversight of storage space for archival collections involves monitoring environmental conditions (climate and humidity control), creating a system to locate processed collections and material in the unprocessed backlog, effective use of shelving units (movable and stationary), security of all spaces, and disaster and emergency planning. When making acquisitions decisions, academic archivists must be aware of how much empty storage space, if any, is available, where backlog collections are stored, and where to store the most frequently and infrequently requested collections for rapid retrieval.

Different from academic librarians, academic archivists are trained to acquire, accession, survey, appraise, arrange, describe, preserve, store, protect, and provide access to original materials. This chapter is focused on the technical aspects of what happens behind-the-scenes in an academic archives. It describes the basic steps of archival acquisitions and accessions, archival processing, creating finding aids, and collection management in academic archives. This chapter seeks to answer the following questions:

1. How do academic archivists acquire and establish physical control over their collections?
2. What are the common procedures for the arrangement and description of archival collections?
3. How do academic archivists manage and protect their collections?

ACQUIRING AND ACCESSIONING COLLECTIONS
IN ACADEMIC ARCHIVES

Principles of Acquisitions

The best academic archives build their collections in an intentional and pragmatic fashion. The first principle of building collections for academic archives is to take only the materials that fit the collections policy and that can be made available, processed, and housed appropriately. By accepting collections, the archives program is pledging responsibility for the permanent maintenance of the material. Taking collections that are only tangential to the purposes of the program will result in a growing backlog and disappointed donors. Academic archivists should take a noncompetitive approach to collection building and refer the donor to a repository where their collections will receive the most use from researchers (Pyatt, 1999). While a good number of archival and manuscript collections are unique and generally interesting, many of them have little real research value and do not belong in academic archives. Again there may be a different kind of archival repository (i.e., government, community, private, or corporate archives) that would better serve the needs of the collection, donor, and potential researchers.

Determining the resources needed to process and maintain a collection is another basic acquisitions consideration. To process a large closet full of material will require the archivist to order archival supplies, perhaps dozens of boxes and hundreds of folders. Other more specialized collections, such as 50 boxes of photographic images, will require the purchase of thousands of photographic enclosure sleeves. Storing the collection, both as an unprocessed backlog collection and as a fully processed collection, requires knowledge of available shelf spaces (Kurtz, 2004). Literally, academic archives may not have enough room to house and manage a 300-box collection, even if the material fits perfectly with the department's mission and collection policy. Storing materials and preserving those collections in archival containers requires both initial and ongoing resources.

The actual processing of the collections requires the most important resource in any archival repository: full-time, part-time, and student employees devoted to the project. Unless the repository has designated processing archivists, most full-time faculty and staff have a limited amount of time each week to devote to processing. In reality the majority of archival processing is completed by trained students, part-time hires, or other

---

Practical Considerations When Acquiring Collections

- Only take in collections that fit the policy.
- Only take in collections that have a current or potential research use.
- Consider the physical spaces needed for storage.
- Consider the amount of archival supplies (i.e., boxes, folders, custom-made containers) that will be needed during the processing.
- Consider if a financial donation is being made to support the collection or program.
- Take collections that can be processed within a reasonable time.
- Avoid taking photocopies; always insist on having the originals for the archives.
- Avoid complicated deeds of gift, joint copyright, and onerous restrictions.
- Avoid deposits, bailments, or other agreements that do not entirely transfer the collection to the repository.
- Consider the long-term obligations for storage, maintenance, and access.

assistants. This group is often the most vulnerable to limited or fickle budget allocations. The value of this group as a resource makes it imperative for archivists to ask donors for financial support to enable the processing of collections, or more minimally, enough funding to cover student wages.

Archivists should acquire only collections that can be processed within a reasonable time. For example, a small department of three full-time archivists and funding to support two students might pass on a 500-box collection in favor of working on their already large backlog of unprocessed collections. Archives struggling with large backlogs may want to make progress by taking a minimal processing approach, which is described more fully later in this chapter.

A final consideration of archival acquisitions is having clear title and ownership of the original material. Unrestricted collections fully under the purview of the archives program offer a variety of options for promotion, research, digitization, and future uses. Archivists should also avoid accepting photocopies of material, even if the donor's intention is to eventually donate the originals. The archives must have a signed deed of gift on file for each of their collections. Complicated agreements, loans or bailments of material, shared copyright, and other arrangements should be avoided by academic archives. Instead, each collection in the archives should be fully owned and part of the program.

The Acquisitions Process

Contact is the first step of the acquisition process. Academic archivists may either contact or be contacted by potential donors, dealers, campus units, or auction houses when relevant material is available (Hunter, 2003). Over the following days, weeks, months, or even years, discussions continue between the archivist and person or organization with the material. It is helpful for the academic archivist to document these conversations and record the details of the discussions in a pending accessions folder (either a paper-based file or in an electronic accessions system such as Archivists' Toolkit or Archon). That information about pending collections can be invaluable, especially when a new program leader arrives and wants to reinvigorate efforts to contact potential donors. Likewise, archivists should retain dealer catalogs that have a large amount of relevant material for their own future reference, especially since many items in catalogs are never actually sold by dealers. Keeping files on potential purchases from dealers, auction houses, and private individuals also results in more efficient accessioning and processing of that material. It is also important to keep documentation on collections that were not accepted, including the rationale for the decision and the key players in the discussions, in case the collection is offered at a later time.

The amount of conversation and contact with potential donors varies according to the situation. For example, when a person cleans out the basement and discovers family letters, he or she may want to enjoy the find for a few months or years before donating the letters to the archives. On the other hand, when a faculty member passes away, there is often an urgency to clean out the campus office and make immediate decisions on what to do with historical treasures. Without being pushy in either situation, academic archivists should be accessible, offer to examine the material according to the donor's schedule and preferences, and make contact when appropriate. Some donors expect a large amount of attention before, during, and after the donation, so academic archivists must find a balance of time between their various potential donors and their other responsibilities.

During conversations with potential donors, the academic archivist begins to determine the range, size, and significance of the donor's material. There may in fact be numerous meetings with the donor during the acquisitions processes. During these conversations and meetings, the academic archivist must articulate the purpose of the archives, and more specifically what the archivists will do with the material (i.e., arrange, describe, preserve, store, promote, and provide access to) in terms that the donor understands. Clear discussion about the deed of gift document, physical and intellectual ownership of the material, and any ongoing obligation to the family should occur during these meetings and be agreed upon by all parties (Hunter, 2003). In-person conversations with potential donors are also prime opportunities to ask for a financial donation to support the processing of the collection and the archives program in general.

Many times, donors ask the archivist to provide a market value for their collection. This kind of appraisal is not within the purview of academic archives, and in fact is a conflict of interest since the program is an interested party. The archivists should refer the donor to a list of certified appraisers rather than providing inaccurate or inappropriate information.

The next step in the acquisitions process is the site visit. Unless the donor is hundreds or thousands of miles away, the academic archivist should offer to conduct an in-person visit with the person and examine the collection. On-campus visits are the easiest to complete, but a significant potential donation may require an archivist to take a lengthy trip to meet the person and his or her family. If a site visit by the archivist cannot be conducted, then the donor may choose to ship the material or bring the collection to the archives. It is common for unexpected donors to arrive in the reading room with boxes of material to be given to the archives that they expect will be accepted.

A primary objective of an archival site visit is to survey the material. During one or many visits to survey the collection, the academic archivists should note the variety of formats, historical range of material, size of the collection, preservation issues, privacy concerns, and discuss options for transporting the collection back to the archives (Fleckner, 1977). During this stage of the process, the archivist may be able to decide that certain portions or series of the collection are not of interest to the archives program (Maher, 1992). For example, research files kept by the sociology department may contain interesting material, but possess limited research value to the users of the academic archives.

Evaluation of material for its historical value is also known as archival appraisal. There is a rich history of archival theory about appraisal, with discussions about selecting official records the most relevant for academic archivists (Boles, 2005). Deciding which official records to add to the archives involves evaluating the "value" of the material. Traditionally, archivists evaluated records for evidential and informational value, but now archivists have expanded their criteria to include the operating, administrative, fiscal, legal, and archival value of records (Hunter, 2003). When visiting donors in their campus offices or private homes, archivists must also apply appraisal principles to collections. Academic archivists utilize appraisal techniques in conjunction with possible research uses of the material and how the material fits within the collection development policy and mission of the program to support the decision to accept or reject a collection.

Following the site visit, the academic archivist creates a collection report to share with others in the academic library and with the donor. This brief report may also include an inventory of significant items, a container listing, or even an item-level inventory. The document will also mention which segments of the collection would be most valuable for researchers and specific materials that do not fit the mission or purpose of the archives program (Hunter, 2003). In the former category, the archivist may want to list the kinds of archival supplies needed and the number of hours needed to best process the collection. In the latter case, a collections report may recommend that certain parts of the collection would be well suited in another archives program focused in that collecting area. A good collection report with a detailed inventory can easily transition into a finding aid, especially if the collection is targeted for minimal processing.

A deed of gift document, signed by the donor and the archivist or an institutional official, officially transfers the collection or item from the donor to the archives (Hunter, 2003). Donors of official records (i.e., department heads, a dean, or the records manager) sign a transfer document rather than a deed of gift. However, less official institutional material such as faculty papers should be accompanied with a deed of gift. The actual signing of the document may take place before, during, or even after the transfer of the material to the archives. The ownership policy at many colleges and universities is that the donor is technically donating the material to the institution or to the external tax-exempt fundraising foundation, with the understanding that it will be placed in the academic archives. When archivists are negotiating with donors about why they should place their prized collections with an academic institution, a very effective argument is to explain that as long as the institution exists their collection will be in good hands. While there are exceptions, such as deaccessioning projects or changes in policy, the basic principle is that once an academic archives program receives a collection from a donor it is the archives' property and responsibility in perpetuity, or, in a more convincing statement, "until the day after forever." Most donors want this kind of reassurance and are motivated by the desire to place their collection in a safe place.

Steps in the Acquisition Process

- Contact donor contact, begin negotiations, and have clear discussions of expectations.
- Create a donor file.
- Visit site, if possible.
- If unable to view the collection, request an inventory from the donor including the approximate number of boxes and size of boxes.
- Discuss the deed of gift document and any stipulations.
- On matters of the market value of the collections, refer the donor to certified appraisers.
- Always ask for a financial donation to support the collection.
- Sign deed of gift and distribute copies to all involved parties.
- Arrange for pickup and transfer of the material to the archives.
- Write thank-you note to the donor.
- Provide updates on processing, promotion, and use, as necessary.

Once the donor and the archivist have agreed to terms of the donation, the next step is the transfer of the material. Shipping collections
through the mail or by a delivery service is common. Academic archivists
should also be prepared to gather material and pack it into their own
vehicle or use a vehicle from the institution's motor-pool. In the case
of direct pickup of material, archivists should bring archival boxes and
other people to help load the collection.

Transferring all of the collection in one large shipment or in a series
of closely occurring shipments is preferred. Many times donors want to
review every document or item before sending it to the archives, which
could take months if not years to complete. Archivists should insist on
a fast-moving transfer of material to avoid partial collections waiting to
be fully accessioned. Some donors may also want to organize their collections in their own way before transferring everything to the archives.
Archivists have the duty to remind the donor that archivists are trained
to evaluate, research, describe, and organize material using standard
archival methods. Of course, processing archivists often work closely with
donors to answer questions about family connections, historical details,
and other topics that need to be addressed during processing of the collection and the creation of the finding aid (Hunter, 2003).

Following the transfer of material to the archives, communication with
the donor continues. The leader of the academic archives and possibly
the dean or director of the academic library should write the donor a letter to acknowledge and thank the donor for the contribution. Providing
the donors with updates on the processing of their collection is a good
way to encourage future donations of material and funding. After large
or historically significant donations are fully processed, the academic
archives may sponsor an event or exhibit to mark the "opening" of the
collection. It is wise to continue communicating with past donors either
through direct contact or by mailing them announcements of activities
at the academic library and archives (Dewey, 1991). The archivist should
take the opportunity to inform donors about the results of their donation, such as the publication of a book that relied heavily on their collection. However, it is unwise to maintain high levels of communication
with past donors, especially with donors who require significant attention
and take large chunks of time from academic archivists.

Accessioning Collections

When new collections arrive, the archivist with responsibility for coordinating processing has to "check-in" or accession the material. Accession-

ing collections establishes physical and initial intellectual control over collections that have yet to be fully processed (Maher, 1992). At this point, the pending accession file for the new collection, which contains information about the donor and the material, becomes a permanent collection file. Electronic accessioning tools, such as Archivists' Toolkit and Archon, allow archivists to create, ingest, and manage inventories, donor information, bibliographic records, metadata, and other descriptive collection information about each collection (Weideman, 2006).

Accessioning involves physical examination of the material. As Figure 7.1 illustrates, incoming collections may have a mix of organization, formats, and containers. If a collection arrived in inappropriate housing or no housing at all, then the materials should be moved into more stable boxes without disturbing the original order (Roe, 2005). When necessary, archivists examine the contents of the collection and either create a survey or add more detail to the on-site survey. Using standard guides, such as Describing Archives: A Content Standard (DACS; Society of American Archivists, 2007), academic archivists broadly describe the basic elements

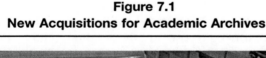

Figure 7.1
New Acquisitions for Academic Archives

Source: Photograph by Marc Brodsky.

of each collection. First, the archivist gives the collection a title, according to whom or what created or collected the material. In the case of university records, the files transferred by the college of agriculture would be named records of the college of agriculture or placed in the appropriate record group for that college. In cases of unofficial tangential materials the archivist must describe the collection using standard practices. For example, a collection of personal papers donated by a humanities scholar named John W. English, the person who created and assembled the material, would be named the John W. English Collection.

Basic accession information for incoming archival collections includes the approximate inclusive dates of material, the scope of the contents that may include historical topics including any significant individuals or subjects, and the size or extent of the collection. Detailed accession information for the above example would be: The John W. English Collection, 1952–1984, personal manuscripts relating to family matters, and professional correspondence documenting English's leadership in the American Philosophical Society with particular focus on promoting the field of Native American research, 16 boxes with three containers of oversize awards, which translates to 25 linear feet of shelf space.

The archivist responsible for processing uses the information gathered during the accessions process to create a basic accession record for the collection. This basic record will form the foundation for an expanded library catalog record and the resulting finding aid. The initial record should include an accession or tracking number for the collection and a temporary location.

Accessioning is used to gain initial control over a collection before more complete processing takes place. Most archives struggle with overwhelming backlogs, and therefore it is difficult to immediately process all new incoming collections. The archivist determines a level of processing priority to the collection. For example, academic archives may devise a rubric for evaluating the importance of backlog collections. A numbering system can be used to designate priority for each collection (e.g., number one as the highest priority and number four as the lowest priority). The collections with the highest priority are kept at the top of the list for processing, while other collections are placed further down the list. Processing priorities are influenced by factors such as the availability of people to process collections, new initiatives or focus areas in the department, the actual size of the collection, available funding for archival supplies, and even having enough shelf space to properly store the collection (Roe, 2005).

For academic archivists, the last part of the accessioning process is designating a physical location for the collection. Whether the collection remains in the backlog for a few days, months, or even years, each collection has some kind of documentary record about where the collection came from, its contents, its expected research uses, and possible approaches to arrangement. Tools such as Archivists' Toolkit and Archon have streamlined many of the common acquisitions and accessions processes to make a more efficient use of data gathered. One distinct advantage of storing this information in an electronic form is that multiple archivists can access and update accessions information, and that the information can be sorted and compiled for multiple uses. Some of this information will become part of an EAD finding aid, which is discussed later in this chapter.

PROCESSING COLLECTIONS IN ACADEMIC ARCHIVES

Processing Principles

Processing collections is at the core of archival work. Also known as arrangement and description, processing collections is a method of grouping individual documents, folders, and formats into similar units and then organizing those units into meaningful relationships (Schellenberg, 1956). More simply, archival processing is taking a stack of seemingly random pieces of paper, creating folders to include similar topics or formats (i.e., correspondence, photographs, or publications), and then sequencing those folders in an order that reflects larger intellectual groupings or series. The purpose of archival processing is to create order, organize information, and establish intellectual control of archival and manuscript material (O'Toole and Cox, 2006).

The principle of provenance (also known as *respect des fonds*) is at the heart of archival processing, and emphasizes the relationship between the creator and the collection (Schellenberg, 1956). The provenance of a collection is the source of manuscript or archival material, such as a person, a family, an organization, or an academic institution. The collection may include materials both generated by and collected by the creator. The creator of the material may or may not be the donor of the collection. The creator of the collection has a unique relationship to the materials themselves. For example, a best-selling author may have collected a room full of documents, manuscripts, correspondence, and notes throughout his or her literary career. How the author arranged, used, and managed the materials is vital to understanding the resulting manuscript collection.

Maintaining original order of collections is a component of the principle of provenance. Original order literally means that processing archivists keep files in the same order in which they were kept by the creator, unless of course, the collection has no perceived logical order whatsoever (Schellenberg, 1956). Local business and official institutional records are good examples of collections that should be kept in their original order, while a box of student memorabilia and boxes of unidentified campus images would need to have some kind of organizational structure imposed to be usable. Preserving the original order of materials reveals much about the creator, the context, the relationships between the materials, and the function of the collection (Schellenberg, 1956). Further, collections with an original order worth preserving allow the archivist to focus more on the physical processing and spend less time developing new organizational schemes and access point. Generally, collections with a pre-existing file structure are processed by students, while the more complex and disorganized collections are processed by full-time archivists. All of these processing decisions could be documented and described in the finding aid.

In addition to evaluating the relationship between the creator and the collection, the principle of provenance also refers to the archival concept of not combining collections, files, or items with those of a different provenance or source. Keeping similar materials separate according to their provenance allows archivists and

> **Core Elements of Archival Processing**
>
> - Establish physical and intellectual control of archival material.
> - Recognize and document provenance, or the relationship between the creator and the collection.
> - Maintain original order when it exists.
> - Maintain integrity of provenance by not mixing collections.
> - Develop logical levels of organization when no organization exists.

researchers to discover the contextual reasons associated with the creation or collecting of the material (Schellenberg, 1956). For example, two collections related to the 1934 Southern Textile Strike may both have broadsides, correspondence, and images of picket lines. Leaders of a labor union branch in Charlotte, North Carolina, donated the first collection, and the second collection came from a donor in Danville,

Virginia, whose parents participated in several mill strikes. While the material overlaps and tells similar stories about the 1934 strikes, the principle of provenance affirms that the collections remain as separate units: the first collection as records of a labor union branch; the second collection as a set of personal papers. As another facet of provenance, the purposes and functions of these materials to the labor union and strikers during 1934 is valuable contextual information that archivists must consider and document during the arrangement and description of these two collections.

Processing archivists must establish or reaffirm some level of intellectual control over their collections. If original order exists and it is clear who or what created the collection then the processor should have enough information to develop a very simple processing plan. However, if a collection has little organization or comes from an unknown source (i.e., anonymous donation with no paperwork) the processing archivist must create some kind of organizational structure to assist researchers in accessing the material. Because of the variety of material in academic archives, academic archivists process collections using standard archival approaches and methods used by manuscript librarians and archivists.

When processing collections, academic archivists arrange materials in hierarchies, according to relationships and similarities of material (Roe, 2005). Arrangement and description of collections in academic archives begins with the highest or collection-level (i.e., the records of the office of student affairs in record group ten, the John Smith Civil War Diaries, or the Burt Johnson Faculty Papers Collection). Archivists use the DACS standards to describe a collection as personal papers, records, family papers, diaries, manuscripts, or other common designations (DACS, 2007). The collection level represents and describes the provenance of the material.

Archivists look for patterns in the unprocessed collection and rely on experience and professional judgment to determine how researchers might want to access the material (Roe, 2005). These patterns or groupings are called series, which can be further organized into subseries. Similar formats, topics, and types of materials are common approaches to developing series for collections. Defining series and descending levels establishes intellectual control over collections. For example, a collection of papers from John Einstein, a renowned scientist on campus, may have large amounts of correspondence, publications, grants, and research notes. If there is no real original order to the collection, those general categories serve as reasonable organizational units and therefore series. Further subdivisions within the series, usually for clarification purposes to enhance access, follow the general series level, and even more specific intellectual breakdowns. Using the previous example, the correspondence series may have three subseries: personal, professional, and institutional. Many collections have even further levels of series-level subcategories. Following on the same example collection, underneath the grants series there is a National Science Foundation (NSF)-funded subseries, followed by a sub-subseries focused on a particular grant.

The next stage of categorization is the file or folder level. These files or folders consist of individual folders that contain related documents, images, or other formats. For example, a folder from the above sub-subseries on a specific NSF grant may include draft copies of the grant narrative and numerous revisions. The sequence of these documents and the presentation of folders may be chronological, alphabetical, or based on what the creator had originally developed as part of the creation of the collection. The listed folder title serves as an important guide to the kind of documents contained within that folder. The most recognizable and valuable level of collection organization is at the folder or file level, simply because the folder title provides the researcher strong clues about the documents in the folder and keeps the archivist from the labor-intensive task of describing every document.

Example of a Multilevel Arrangement for an Archival Collection

John Einstein Collection

Series 1: Correspondence
  Subseries: Personal
  Subseries: Professional
  Subseries: Institutional

Series 2: Publications

Series 3: Grants
  Subseries: NSF-Funded
      Sub-subseries: Protons and Electrons, 1983–1985
          Folder: Grant Narratives
              Item: Final submitted draft, 4/1/1983
          Folder: Budgets and Financial Reports
              Item: Final Report to NSF, 1/12/1983
          Folder: Letters of Support
              Item: Senator James Buchanan, 3/25/83
      Sub-subseries: Neutrons and Electrons, 1985–1987

Series 4: Research notes

The final stage of collection organization is at the item level. Collections that are small, historically significant, have large amounts of unrelated material, or have great digitization potential often deserve descriptions of specific items. Collections such as a set of diaries from a Nobel Prize–winning scientist, a half dozen Civil War letters, or two folders of unpublished poetry from an eighteenth-century Spanish writer may justify item-level descriptions. However, it is very uncommon for large complex collections to be arranged and described at the item level.

The ability to group materials into logical categories is the first step in establishing intellectual control over collections in academic archives (Hunter, 2003). Once archivists have developed further organizational patterns for the collection then they can proceed with the actual processing of the material. During the processing, the series, subseries, and other categories may need refinement to better reflect the content of the collection and the intent of the creator. The resulting series and subseries then become the framework for the finding aid and other access points to the collection.

Processing Practices

Processing a collection involves sorting, grouping, addressing basic preservation issues, and weeding duplicate material according to the processing plan. Subject knowledge and experience helps archivists recognize historical context and overlap with other materials. One of the most useful tools for processing archivists is an updated processing manual, detailing the department's practices, procedures, and approaches to processing collections. There are numerous processing manuals available online and most established programs have some kind of introductory guide for new employees with details about processing collections.

Once a backlog collection has been selected for processing, the archivist reviews the accession file and drafts a processing plan and a timeline. Before collections can be processed, academic archivists do a review of the material. Examining one-folder collections may take only a few minutes, while a 30-box collection could take several days or weeks to fully review. During this survey the archivist notes preservation concerns, separates nonarchival materials such as books and objects, and considers how best to arrange the collection (Hunter, 2003). For larger collections, archivists may want to complete a detailed processing plan, which may include recommendations about major series and subseries, how to house oversize material, how to redact personal information from a large number of files, the expected amount of necessary background research, the amount of archival supplies needed, and special storage considerations for unstable media such as nitrate film (Roe, 2005). This plan will serve as the "road map" during the actual processing and can be a useful approach when students are completing the majority of the archival processing. Even if a processing plan is not used, the archivist reviewing incoming collections must document all of the decisions, discoveries, and actions taken.

Before processing begins, the person leading the effort should research the subjects, people, places, and provenance of the collection. If the collection is largely family papers amassed by an individual, then the archivist should gather biographical and family information. Online and print resources in the academic library (i.e., newspaper databases, *Who's Who in America,* and "Biography and Genealogical Master Index") provide access to a wide range of local and national biographical information. The collections themselves may have this kind of relevant information, contained in curriculum vitae, genealogical information, newspaper clippings, and obituaries. Printed books and other manuscript collections held by the academic archives may also have information about topics and individuals mentioned in a new collection. For example, a published history of the college may be useful when researching a set of student scrapbooks from the 1920s. Further, an unpublished typescript history of the college of engineering already held by the archives may be crucial reading before processing ten boxes of official records from the college of engineering during the 1950s. Because processing a collection results in new subjects and names, collection research is ongoing.

> **Common Steps of Archival Processing**
>
> - When in doubt, consult the repository's processing manual.
> - Research the collection, its creator, its subjects, and its significance.
> - Rely on the processing plan for each collection.
> - Order/check status of archival supplies after first review.
> - Decide which level of processing is most appropriate.
> - Adjust the arrangement as needed.
> - Note and address preservation concerns.

While much of the background research may not be included or referenced in the finding aid it is important to retain detailed processing notes for each collection.

Processing collections requires sufficient supplies, adequate working spaces, and other relevant resources. Academic archives should always have on hand a steady supply of folders, archival boxes, and containers. Special boxes for oversize items, enclosures for photographic images, and any other custom-built containers should be ordered in advance of the planned processing. Large tables or counters allow archivists

Criteria for Organizing Archival Collections

- Chronological
- Alphabetical
- Subject based
- By individual name
- Format
- Function of the material

to work and sort materials while processing proceeds. A secure, shared, and flexible space for processing collections is preferred to having archivists processing collections in their offices or while working at the reference desk. Students or full-time employees who process collections need access to computer workstations, archival supplies, reference sources, and other archivists.

When collections arrive with a clear original order (i.e., official records) the work of the archivist is largely to transfer material into new acid-free boxes and folders, while recording the titles of folders and other descriptive data (Figure 7.2). However, many new collections arrive

Figure 7.2
Processing University Records

Source: Photograph by the author.

in academic archives with little or no structure and need some level of archival organization. Establishing logical series and possible subseries for the material provides researchers greater intellectual access.

A Traditional Approach to Processing

The size and complexity of the collection helps determines the extent of the processing (i.e., deciding whether to process at the series, folder, or item level). There are different philosophies on how much processing is necessary to provide adequate access to collections. In principle, all archival collections should receive item-level analysis by the archivist, which ensures that every item will be reviewed for content, authorship, and any preservation concerns (i.e., rusty staples or adhesive tape). Thorough processing of archival collections results in detailed finding aids and extensive description of the material, but it is a very time-consuming and costly approach. Many academic archives reserve thorough processing for smaller and only the most historically significant collections and rarely at the item level.

For example, a collection of 50 documents (handwritten letters and partially printed pieces such as military certificates and muster roles) from a soldier in the Mexican War would be an excellent candidate for folder-level arrangement and item-level description. First, the archivist removes the collection from its shoebox, examines each item, looking for a logical arrangement pattern, notes any significant preservation issues, and rehouses the collection in acid-free archival folders that fit within one box. The archivist creates a series for correspondence and a series for military documents. Beneath the series are the folders that contain the actual letters and documents. If the letters in the first series are dated then they would be best arranged by the ascending date of the letters, with any undated letters placed in a folder at the end or the beginning of the series. The military documents are also arranged in folders according to chronology or by type of document. Each folder will have a title representing the content of the enclosed material and how it relates to the series that it is part of. For example, a folder containing two letters from March 1847 might be titled "Series I, Correspondence; March 1847." If the collection were fully or partially digitized then the archivist would create item-level descriptions for the scanned pieces, and those descriptions would be added to the finding aid. The final step in processing this collection is to number the folders in the box, create a label for the box, and record the storage location for the material (Figure 7.3).

Figure 7.3
A Processed Collection

Source: Photograph by the author.

A Minimal Approach to Processing

A minimal approach to processing is at the opposite end of the arrangement and description spectrum. Minimal processing, also known as "More Product, Less Process" (MPLP), is an approach derived from the research and work of archivists Mark Greene and Dennis Meissner (2005). The MPLP method addresses the problem of uncontrollable backlogs, resulting from decades of archival backlog growth while staff numbers and other resources to process them declined (Weideman, 2006). Minimal processing emphasizes the concept that some access to an archival collection is better than no access at all. The level of arrangement and description is often limited to the basic steps of accessioning—rehousing the collection only if necessary and creating a bibliographic record with a brief collection summary or a box-level inventory (Greene and Meissner, 2005). Minimal processing is designed to streamline and minimize arrangement and description, with the intention that eventually the collection will be fully processed, based on research demand. Many academic archives have embraced a minimal processing approach when dealing with official records and other large backlog collections.

For example, a 50-box collection of faculty papers with some original order might be a good candidate for minimal processing at the folder-level. Because the boxes and folders are relatively stable, show no evidence of deterioration, and are the same size as standard archival boxes that will fit well on the shelves, the archivist does not rehouse the collection. The archivist does note that there are a large number of paperclips and staples in the collection. The processing archivist creates a series based on how the creator labeled the boxes. The four broad series of correspondence, publications, class notes, and personal files capture the essence of the collection and the order imposed by the faculty member. Boxes that belong to the first three series contain folders already in either alphabetical or chronological order, so the archivist reviews the folder titles and examines the contents of just a few folders. The three boxes that make up the personal series, however, have no arrangement whatsoever. The processing archivist spends a few hours developing folder titles and discarding irrelevant material for this last series. The resulting finding aid contains very basic collection-level information and an inventory of boxes with folder titles. Although the collection is processed and accessible, the archivist adds a note to the collection folder explaining that more thorough processing and removal of fasteners should occur in the next few years. The last step in physically processing this collection is to number folders, label the boxes, and designate a storage location.

Training and Processing

Archivists learn how to process collections by hands-on experience, informal instruction, and formal education. Frequently their first exposure to processing collections occurs when they are students, volunteers, or interns working for an archives program (Bastian and Webber, 2008). Even the largest archival repositories rely on student assistants or other part-time employees to process collections. These first experiences lead many students to the field of archives and the practices that they learn inform later processing decisions. As part of the cycle, new professional archivists, who are often led into the field because of their interest in processing collections, take on the responsibility of training students and others in the department to process archival materials.

The academic environment offers a unique opportunity for academic archives programs to recruit student employees and to train the next generation of archivists. Nearly all college and university libraries have a student employment program, which allows academic archives programs to hire students for a variety of work in their departments (Sweetman, 2006). Commonly, students work reference desk shifts and learn how to process collections, while some programs customize student positions for more specific duties.

Academic archivists have a responsibility to be trainers and teachers for their student employees, especially in the area of processing. Working with students requires patience and committing large amounts of time, especially during the initial training period. It also requires academic archivists to maintain some level of processing activity or at the least remain current on developing trends and practices in arranging and describing collections. The investment of time and resources into training students, who may only work in the department for a semester or two, has enormous benefits. First, it creates a strong training and teaching program for basic and advanced archival skills, which benefits all members of the department. Second, it allows academic archivists to develop management skills, while expanding into other areas of their position, such as campus outreach, teaching and instruction, donor relations, and electronic records management. Finally, student assistants represent the next group of professional archivists, who during this initial stage of their careers need direction, advice, support, and practical experience.

Preserving While Processing

The variety of formats in collections creates preservation challenges for archivists. Few collections contain only one format, which makes it important for archivists to understand basic preservation practices and the repository's preferences on how to handle certain processing situations. A medium-sized backlog collection may include paper documents, oral history tapes, publications in print and electronic format, photo albums, two handmade quilts, and a large collection of framed awards and plaques. The processing manual for each academic archives program should address preservation approaches for a wide range of formats. While preservation practices vary by institution, there is standard agreement on preserving paper and photographic material, the two most common types of formats found in archival and manuscript collections.

For textual documents, the paper itself is a fragile and very acidic medium. Many documents are soiled (e.g., covered with coal dust) and need to be carefully cleaned with a cleaning pad in order to make it safe to handle them. Other documents may have tape or other adhesives, which require careful removal or professional conservation attention. When possible archivists should unfold and flatten all documents, even if it means that special oversize boxes or map cases will be needed (Ritzenthaler, 2010). It is also important to isolate highly acidic paper from the rest of the collection, by using a high-quality photocopy as a replacement, inserting acid-free paper in front of and behind the item to protect surrounding documents, or placing the material in its own folder (Ritzenthaler, 2010). Fasteners, clips, staples, rubber bands, and pins are common in paper-based archival collections because they connect material into a unit. However, all fasteners deteriorate and cause damage to the paper. If time and resources are available, the archivist may remove these fasteners permanently or replace them with stainless steel or plastic clips.

Photographic materials offer processing archivists an even more unstable medium. Generally speaking, photographs consist of a layer of chemicals designed to capture light, bonded to a background such as paper (Ritzenthaler and Vogt-O'Conner, 2006). Likewise, photographic negatives (the reverse of the image which does not have a paper background) suffer from rapid natural deterioration. Even with the best of storage conditions, photographs and negatives curl, flake, and fade. As a consequence of their different chemical compositions, photographs and negatives should be individually stored in a sleeve or envelope, and stored in appropriate climatic conditions.

Basic preservation approaches can prolong the life of archival and manuscript materials, but no kind of preservation treatment can stop the natural deterioration of the format (Ritzenthaler, 2010). The general principle of preservation is to only make changes that can be reversed, to do no harm to the original, and to carefully document all decisions for future reference. For example, decades ago many archives embraced the preservation tactic of laminating important documents in order to permanently preserve the paper and the recorded information. However, lamination is a chemical process that cannot be reversed and subsequently replaces the original format with a new type of material. Archivists now recognize the danger of irreversible preservation practices.

Some academic archivists have strong backgrounds in preservation and many academic libraries have a preservation department with an in-house preservation laboratory. When in doubt about a preservation approach, academic archivists should rely on their colleagues in the library and the profession. Commonly, a difficult preservation decision or when a valuable item is in nearly unusable condition leads the archivist to work with or consult a professional conservator. Although conservation of textual or photographic material by an external source is expensive and time-consuming, archivists should rely on experts in the field to prolong the life of their original materials (Balloffet and Hille, 2005).

Creating Finding Aids

Once a collection is processed an archivist finishes writing the finding aid. The finding aid represents the "gold-standard" access tool for archival and manuscript collections. The content of a finding aid is much like the information found in the table of contents and the index of a standard book. However, instead of referring to page numbers, the finding aid leads users to specific boxes and folders that may contain material relevant to their search.

The finding aid summarizes the significance, context, historical value, and actual arrangement of the collection, by including descriptive information about the content of the collection, its provenance, and possible areas of research interest (Pearce-Moses, 2005). While finding aids do mention specific topics and documents worthy of possible study, a finding aid should not provide historical interpretation of the material contained in the collection. The finding aid addresses the arrangement of the collection, by listing series, subseries, folder titles, and sometimes specific items. It includes a container listing or an inventory with a listing of the boxes in the collection and folder titles. Each finding aid also has general information about the processing of the collection, conditions of use or restrictions, provenance, the existence of related or supplemental materials, and repository information (Roe, 2005).

> **Creating Finding Aids**
>
> - Follow professionally established archival standards.
> - Use technology to multipurpose data.
> - Include descriptive information that is jargon-free and clear for researchers.
> - Provide factual information, not interpretations.
> - Let the intellectual arrangement supersede the physical arrangement (i.e., box and folders number can always change, but series and folder title should not change).
> - Seek input from other archivists and knowledgeable scholars.

FINDING AID STANDARDS

While each repository customizes its finding aids, there are standard components to archival finding aids. The first part of a finding aid focuses on the content and context of the collection. A descriptive summary provides basic collection information such as the title, dates, size, creator, name of the repository, and a brief abstract (Roe, 2005). Each finding aid has a scope and content note, which is a detailed summary of the contents of the collection, including the materials, topics, and individuals of significance. The first major section of a finding aid contains biographical or historical information about the primary individuals or organizations connected to the collection. One caveat for researchers is that the biographical note is strictly biographical and does not guarantee that the collection contains material on all of the details mentioned.

For example, the finding aid for a fictitious collection of letters from World War II soldier Jim Stephens would begin with a descriptive summary: James Arnold Sr., Papers, 1942–1945, 1.25 cubic feet, Cumberland State College Special Collections, donated by James Arnold Jr. in 2009. The abstract for the collection might state: "The James Arnold Papers consist of correspondence between Arnold, a private in the U.S. Army, and his family in Iowa during his military service in the North African and Italian theatres of World War II." A scope and content note for this collection would add more details about the contents of the letters, such as frequently occurring places, battles, names, and personal information. The scope and content note may also mention the number and frequency of the letters, and the breakdown of authorship. The biographical note for Arnold would mention his day of birth, the names of his parents, his education, war service, postwar career, and any other significant known personal information.

Another major part of the finding aid is the list of contents and containers. This section combines the intellectual arrangement (i.e., the titles of series, subseries, folders, and items) with the physical arrangement (i.e., the box and folder numbers). The intellectual arrangement dictates the container listing and the order of the boxes and folders (Roe, 2005). For example, the folder in James Arnold's papers that include his earliest correspondence would go at the beginning of the first series, Wartime Correspondence and would become folder number 1, box 1. The folder number is important for guiding the user to the material, but it is really the content of the material as expressed in the folder title and the various levels that is most valuable to the researcher.

Oversize material and objects found in collections are common challenges for traditional arrangement patterns. However, finding aids do not need to be linear and should be focused on the intellectual rather than the physical arrangement. For example, a collection of personal papers from an architect begins with a personal and biographical series, followed by other series. In addition to several folders containing curriculum vitae, biographical statements, and an obituary, the collection also includes a framed 11 × 16 family portrait that fits in an oversize box. A traditional approach to arrangement would be to create an oversize series for the framed portrait or create a subseries within a later photographic materials series. However, since the portrait is clearly related to the personal and biographical series, it could be listed in the finding aid underneath the first series, and the number of the oversize box listed as the physical location (see sidebar).

> **Example of Oversize Material in a Finding Aid**
>
> *Jane Evans Architectural Collection, 1943–1979*
>
> **Series I:** Personal and Biographical
> Biographical statements, various dates (box, folders 1–2)
> Curriculum vitae, 1955–1975, (box 1, folder 3)
> Family portrait, 11 × 16, 1994 (box 28, oversize)
> Obituaries, 1995 (box 1, folder 4)

ELECTRONIC FINDING AIDS

A few decades ago, archivists wrote the finding aid after processing the collection. However, the development of electronic accession software such as Archivists' Toolkit and Archon has combined the work of processing a collection and writing a finding aid. In fact, the basic information in the finding aid begins when an accession record for a new collection is created. Software such as Archivists' Toolkit can generate elements of a finding aid from the preliminary collection inventory, the processing plan, and the collection record. Archivists' Toolkit also effectively transfers collection information into other electronic tools used to create a searchable encoded finding aid, bibliographic records, and similar access resources.

Encoded Archival Description (EAD) is the most recognized standard used to create an electronically searchable finding aid. First developed by archivists in the mid-1990s, EAD represents a departure from traditional cataloging methods of manuscript collections. For several decades, archivists relied on using an expanded version of a Machine Readable Cataloging (MARC) record known as MARC-AMC to describe the scope and content of their collections (Pitti, 1997). The inventors of EAD wanted to improve intellectual access to archival material by creating a standard online finding aid structure that allowed better searching, display, and the representation of hierarchies in archival arrangement and description

(Pitti, 1997). EAD is essentially a set of Extensible Markup Language (XML) and Standard Generalized Markup Language (SGML)–based encoding rules designed to structure and automate archival finding aids (Roth, 2001). It supports up to a dozen levels of collection hierarchy, which means that even the most complicated collections can be fully represented in EAD. While most academic archives repositories have adopted EAD for their online finding aids, some repositories have relied on simple HTML-based finding aids or developed their own mechanisms for online display and searching.

One distinct advantage of using EAD is that other supporting cataloging standards have emerged from the archival community. Perhaps the most significant is Describing Archives: A Content Standard (DACS; Society of American Archivists, 2007). Developed in the mid-2000s, DACS serves as a guide to accurately present collection information in online finding aids. As a replacement for earlier cataloging standards, DACS integrates rules for describing archival and manuscript materials found in the collections of academic archives (Society of American Archivists, 2007). The DACS standards mesh well with the EAD finding aid structure. Another recent development is the standard known as Encoded Archival Context (EAC). As a counterpart to EAD, EAC is a mark-up language that adds contextual information to the finding aid. EAC allows a finding aid to reveal more information about the creation and creator of the material. Further, EAC provides identification, characteristics, and interrelationships of the organizations, persons, and families who created, used, or were the subject of the material (Pearce-Moses, 2005).

Access to Finding Aids

Archival researchers rely on finding aids to identify collections and specific material for their research. Many reading rooms still retain and update print versions of findings aids, especially for frequently requested collections. However, print copies of finding aids are only accessible to in-person researchers. In the past two decades, online access to finding aids has revolutionized the research process. Academic archivists also depend on finding aids for locating material for their researchers and for better understanding the content of their collections. Having online access to finding aids has expanded the ability to search across many collections and repositories.

The process of inputting finding aid information into an electronic form is called encoding. Software such as Archivists' Toolkit or Archon can generate EAD finding aids automatically. However, many repositories use text editing software (i.e., NoteTab, Oxygen) to add EAD tags to finding aid content. For example, the information in a finding aid's scope and content note would be set within the scope and content EAD tag. Within the scope and content field other subjects, proper names, and words or phrases can be tagged. EAD allows archivists to display the hierarchical nature of archival collections (i.e., series, subseries, folder, and item) by designating descending levels of arrangement. Once EAD tags have been added to the finding aid, then the software matches the document with the EAD Document Type Definition (DTD). If there are no encoding errors, the software generates an electronic version that can be viewed on a computer screen.

When these files are part of a database of finding aids or other electronic documents the files can be searched and browsed for keywords, subjects, proper titles, dates, and even specific documents. Encoding and EAD rules can be tedious, but EAD finding aids have much greater uniformity, searchability, and expandability than HTML or unencoded electronic finding aids.

The advantage of creating finding aids with archival standards such as EAD, DACS, and EAC is that the resulting finding aids can be included in multiple digital repositories. EAD finding aids can be posted to websites, included in national or state databases of finding aids, or other online projects where they can be discovered by researchers. While repositories may customize their finding aids to display in certain ways or present unique fields of information, all EAD finding aids have the same backbone structure of tags, fields, and standards.

> **Primary Components of an EAD Finding Aid**
>
> - Front matter includes collection title, dates, and repository.
> - Collection information includes an abstract, access restrictions, acquisitions and processing information, biographical note, scope and content note, and subjects.
> - Contents or container listing includes all series, subseries, and all descending levels of arrangement, box and folder numbers, folder titles, and any specific items.

Regardless of how a finding aid is written and presented, academic archivists spend considerable time refining and promoting their finding aids. When students are the chief processors, full-time archivists review drafts of their finding aids and oversee the release of the final version. The completion and dissemination of the finding aid occurs subsequent to the numbering of the boxes and folders, which marks the end of the physical and intellectual aspects of processing a collection. With the initial work of processing complete, it is then time for the archivist to store the collection in a secure and accessible location.

COLLECTION MANAGEMENT FOR ACADEMIC ARCHIVES

Spaces for Archival Collections

Once collections are processed and the finding aids are complete, academic archivists must shift their attention to where each collection will be stored. Managing the physical spaces for processed and backlog materials is just as important as managing the collections themselves. Storage space for collections is one of the most important resources for academic archives. There must be ample room to receive new materials, space for backlog collections, work areas for arrangement and description, and finally long-term storage for processed collections (Kurtz, 2004). Because successful academic archives are constantly acquiring new collections, it is important to have growth space in all of the above categories.

Whether based in the main campus library or in a building on their own, academic archives have historically had limited collection storage spaces. In the past two decades, the reutilization of spaces in academic libraries for information commons, study spaces, and high-density storage units has a direct influence on space for academic archives. In an effort to create new public and information spaces for patrons, academic libraries have moved portions of their print collections to offsite or invested in compact shelving. Another factor in this shift of spaces is that academic libraries are not buying the same quantity of print journals, in favor of purchasing online subscriptions through propriety databases. These trends have resulted in spaces being repurposed for general library uses and many of the "historic" journals and books being transferred from the vanishing open stacks to the archives. For academic archives, these patterns mean that space for collections will decrease or remain stable while the amount of new collections will only increase.

Some repositories, however, have benefitted from renovation or new building projects sponsored by their academic libraries. Massive fundraising campaigns on many campuses have resulted in new main library buildings, off-site storage units, and high-density and movable shelving. As a result, many academic archives have received new storage spaces, often times in an off-site location rather than expanding their footprint.

Generally speaking, donors to academic archives are more interested in supporting public services and collection development than building new storage spaces. For example, many special collections departments and their reading rooms are named for specific donors, while few donors have taken the opportunity to endow an offsite storage unit. This reality has made it difficult for academic archives to expand their collections because there simply is not enough collection storage space available.

In the past decade a few academic archives programs have moved into new facilities, with ample storage and growth space for collections. However, most repositories are in need of additional collection storage space, shelving, and other resources to manage their collections. With space in academic libraries at a premium, many special collections have only enough collections space to house the most frequently consulted materials. The bulk of the collections in academic archives may be stored many miles from the reading room, sometimes in facilities shared with other departments and campus units. The retrieval of these materials often requires close cooperation with the library's courier service or the managers of the off-site facilities. One concern with off-site storage is monitoring who has access to the archival collections, especially if the presence of academic archives staff at the facility is limited (Hunter, 2003).

Designing and Monitoring Collection Spaces

Control of storage spaces for academic archives is imperative for the safety, preservation, longevity, and management of the collections. Whether collections spaces are new, remodeled, or inherited from a vacating department, academic archivists should consider how to design and monitor their storage areas. Space management involves knowing how much open space is available for collections, who has access to the space, and the environmental conditions of all storage areas (Hunter, 2003).

The practicality of archival work is most evident in the area of collection storage. Literally, archivists must become experts on the size and weight of boxes, shelves, and their equipment (Kurtz, 2004) (Figure 7.4). In the case of new construction or remodeling archival facilities, archivists must have a clear idea of what spaces will be needed to adequately house their existing and future collections. Compact and high-density shelving allows much greater storage capacity in a set footprint; however, these units are exceedingly heavy and may be limited to ground or basement floors of academic libraries (Forde, 2007). The height of the shelving is also an important consideration. For example, if the stacks rise 50 feet high to take advantage of vaulted ceilings, then standard ladders may not be sufficient to provide access to the top shelves. Instead, archivists may need to purchase and then operate a lift device or a crane. Shelving and retrieving archival material should be a practical, not a tedious or dangerous, process for academic archivists.

Security of collection storage spaces is crucial. In addition to limiting access to spaces by keys, many academic archives use some kind of card-identification or fingerprint-scan system to limit access to certain areas (Trinkaus-Randall, 1995). Spaces under the purview of the academic archives are much easier to regulate, but even during regular operating hours security mechanisms, such as locked doors and cameras, should remain active. Shared locations, such as an off-site storage building, raise issues of who has access to the collections (Hunter, 2003). Keeping the stacks as a place to store and retrieve material and not an active workspace improves security. Regardless of the location,

Figure 7.4
Archival Storage Space

Source: Photograph by the author.

all collections belonging to academic archives should have accession records if not full finding aids, each collection should have a designated storage location, and all archival materials should be housed in standard archival boxes with clear labeling and, if possible, barcodes (Trinkaus-Randall, 1995).

Historically, many special collections departments placed their most rare and valuable items in a vault or high-security location. Building such high-security locations in new and remodeled facilities may in fact be counterproductive to limiting theft and efficient retrieval of the material for patrons. Archivists should know where to find the most "valuable" collections and items in their archives, but segregating those materials into special locations is problematic. First, theft of material by a staff or student employee is more likely than pilfering by a patron, which makes the "treasure room" an obvious target for nefarious deeds. Second, frequently used materials often go missing because they are incorrectly shelved and not because they are targeted by thieves. Having numerous shelving locations for archival collections increases the chances that materials become misplaced. As a general rule, the most valuable and most requested materials (which are often the same) should be housed in an obvious location, close to the reading room.

> **Protecting Collections in Storage**
>
> • Limit access to stacks with security measures.
> • Store collections in a fashion understandable by staff.
> • Store collections in a cool, dry, and dark environment.
> • Monitor temperature and relative humidity.
> • When possible, adjust temperature and relative humidity.

Monitoring and adjusting the environmental conditions of storage spaces is one of the most significant forms of preservation for archival collections (Pacifico and Wilsted, 2009). The temperature, relative humidity, and presence of airborne gases have a direct effect on the deterioration of archival materials, even if the items are correctly housed in acid-free folders and archival boxes (Ritzenthaler, 2010). Fluctuations in temperature and humidity are perhaps more dangerous for archival materials than a constant "bad" environment. With simple data monitoring devices, academic archivists can monitor the temperature and relative humidity in their collection spaces. If possible, archivists should adjust the environmental conditions according to the patterns in the data in order to maintain optimum and consistent conditions.

Collection spaces should be cool, dry, and dark. Generally speaking, paper-based archival records are the most stable when stored in minimally lighted spaces that are between 55 and 65 degrees Fahrenheit, with a 30 to 50 percent relative humidity (Pacifico and Wilsted, 2009). Some formats found in academic archives require more specialized environments. For example, film, negatives, and other photographic materials are best stored in a colder environment, with a temperature between 45 and 55 degrees Fahrenheit and approximately 30 percent relative humidity (Pacifico and Wilsted, 2009). While collections storage areas are not designed to support workspaces for employees, there are spaces in academic archives where collections and people are close by. For example, an accessions room, a backlog space, or a processing area is a shared space for people and collections. The climate for such mixed use spaces should be approximately 70 degrees Fahrenheit and have a relative humidity between 30 and 50 percent (Wilsted, 2007).

Maintaining the optimum environmental conditions for archival materials is challenging if not impossible. A new or updated heating, ventilation, and air conditioning (HVAC) system that can be adjusted for different zones in the archives is the key to regulating the environment. However, academic library buildings are commonly served by antiquated or complicated HVAC systems, which make it difficult to regulate temperatures and humidity in specific areas. Adjusting environmental conditions at off-site storage facilities is just as problematic, especially since those spaces are more open, are less insulated, and are greatly affected by temperature fluctuations. At the very least, collections spaces with limited environmental controls should be monitored and fragile materials frequently inspected. Dehumidifiers and fans are common accessories used by archivists to adjust the climate. Optimally, collections should be stored in stable environments that can be easily monitored and adjusted through multiple HVAC systems (Wilsted, 2007).

In the case of new construction or remodeling archival facilities, archivists must play an active role in the design of spaces (Swartzburg and Bussey, 1991). At the planning stage, archivists need to clarify the storage needs for archival collections. Collection spaces should be designed with specific temperature and humidity controls, security mechanisms that limit access accordingly, a fire suppression system, a timed lighting system, manageable shelving units, and adequate drainage (Wilsted, 2007). Protecting the collections from the sometimes "unseen" harm in the stacks is an imperative part of managing academic archives.

Locating and Tracking Collections

During the accession process, an archivist assigns each collection a number and a storage location. Those designations remain with the collection until they are processed, and then the collection receives a more permanent shelf location and collection number before it is stored (Roe, 2005). Repositories develop corresponding numbering systems and location information for their collections to ensure efficient retrieval. Understanding the general patterns of these systems is the key to managing stored archival collections.

Academic archives have a mix of archival and manuscript materials, and there are different designations and locations according to the kind of collection. Institutional practice and the types of collections often determine what kind of classification system is used. For example, official records of a college may be classified as part of a record group (abbreviated as RG), while unofficial materials related to the school's history, such as a scrapbook, may be considered an archival collection (abbreviated as AR or AC). Collections that support the mission of the academic archives but are not directly related to the history of the institution, such as a collection of eighteenth-century diaries of early Midwest pioneers, may be defined as manuscripts (abbreviated as MS or MSS). An academic archives program with RG, MS, and AR collections might designate three distinct areas to shelve each type of collection in numerical or sequential order. While these are some of the most common systems, such designations and classification schemes vary by institution. Whatever system is used, these and other classifications help archivists track and locate the material in the stacks and assign an intellectual designation for the researchers using the collections.

> **Common Types of Archival Classification Systems**
>
> - Archival Collection (abbreviated as AR or AC)
> - Record Group (abbreviated as RG)
> - Manuscripts (abbreviated as MS or MSS)

When archivists access new material, they assign the collection a number, most often based on the date received. That number may help determine a shelf location. For example, the Jean Francis Collection, 1945–1976, might be assigned a collection number MS 2010-16, meaning that it was the sixteenth manuscript accession during the year. Once processed, MS 2010-16 will be shelved following MS 2010-15. Other repositories simply give their processed collections a numerical number representing the total number of collections in the archives. For example, a new collection might become AR 1786 and would be shelved at the end of the processed archives collections following AR 1785.

For official records, the collection number may be predetermined by the record group number. A set of three boxes from the physics department would go in record group nine, the physics department, college of science. However, new additions to record groups often result in new series and subseries, which are often expressed in additional numbers. In the above example, the new accession is related to the physics department's participation in distance education programs, which falls under the record group's third series, academic programs (expressed as RG 9.3). The three boxes represent a new subseries, distance education programs. The boxes should be labeled as RG 9.3.2 and shelved within the third series of record group nine. There are numerous shelving and arrangement patterns for college and university records, largely because the record group concept (originally devised for federal records) must be adapted to best represent the organizational and structural changes that mark the history of each institution.

Whatever system is used, the retrieval of collections should be an efficient and seamless process. Nearly all academic archives pull materials on-demand for their patrons and try to accommodate researchers by quickly locating and retrieving material. However, researchers are dismayed when the collections they want are housed in a remote location and they must wait hours if not a few days for delivery of their material. When archival materials are housed off site, academic archivists should make clear notes in the library catalog records and finding aids that certain boxes are in a remote location and must be requested. The efficient retrieval of material for patrons depends on having a clear shelving system that all library employees can understand and use.

Disaster and Emergency Planning

Preparing for a disaster is another component of collection management. Nearly all academic libraries have a disaster plan and a committee that updates the plan (Kahn, 1998). For academic archives, however, there are much different concerns for protecting and saving collections. The wide range of formats under the care of academic archivists, such as boxes stuffed with textual files, electronic media, film and photographic material, oversize pieces, and printed books, make developing a disaster plan even more complicated (Fortson, 1992). The basics of such emergency planning for academic archivists involve being prepared, knowing how to respond when a disaster strikes, and working with others to implement a recovery strategy.

There are numerous kinds of natural and human-made disasters for academic archivists to consider. The threat of fire, flooding, earthquakes, snowstorms, and tornadoes are common disasters for all archives, with more unique disasters such as hurricanes, volcanic eruptions, and tsunamis affecting archives in largely coastal or island regions (Fortson, 1992). More deliberate disasters such as terrorist attacks, bombings, and vandalism have resulted in damage to archives and libraries across the world. Other less obvious disasters for libraries and archives include mold outbreaks and water leaks, both of which can quickly spread across thousands of books and into archival boxes. The lessons learned from responding to a disaster are extremely helpful to academic archivists. While it may seem that an academic archives program is immune to a large-scale disaster, such as a massive flood caused by a hurricane, there are many repositories with first-hand disaster experience.

The most important part of emergency and disaster planning is being prepared. In addition to being part of a library disaster planning team, the leader of the academic archives program should form an internal group of archivists to develop emergency preparedness measures. The group should first survey the environmental conditions of the department—all public, collection, work, and staff spaces (Wilkinson, Lewis, and Dennis, 2010). During this survey it may be helpful to identify specific possible emergencies, such as fire, water, or mold damage, and how those disasters might affect the collections (Fortson, 1992).

Reviewing scenarios makes it easier for the committee to consider which disaster supplies and equipment might be needed. For

Emergency Preparedness Planning

- Form a team to survey the spaces and identify possible emergencies.
- Purchase emergency and preservation supplies, and store appropriately.
- Create a realistic emergency plan that is frequently updated and reviewed.
- Collect contact information for all employees and designate their roles in recovery.
- Compile a priority list for the most significant collections and operational files.
- Develop a short-list of preservation options for damaged materials.
- Create a list of vendors and consultants who specialize in emergency preparedness for archival materials.

example, rolls of disaster plastic could be used to protect open ranges of materials if a sprinkler leak is discovered. All disaster kits should have waterproof cameras to help document the disaster and the recovery, notepads and pens, flashlights, plastic gloves, dust masks, and first aid kits. For water-based emergencies, archives should have mops, sponges, rubber boots, waterproof containers to hold damaged material, and blotting paper to dry wet materials (Forde, 2007). The disaster kit and equipment should be kept in an accessible location close to the collections.

The committee uses the survey to create a preparedness plan for the archives. This plan should include contact information for all employees, a list of disaster supplies, salvage priorities for the most significant collections and items, the roles that each archivist takes in the recovery process, and a short list of preservation options for damaged materials (Wilkinson, Lewis, and Dennis, 2010). In addition to saving collections, archivists should also account for the protection of their finding aids, catalogs, registers, donor files, accession records, and other vital information about the operations of the program (Forde, 2007). The details of the plan should also be incorporated in the academic library's preparedness planning.

When the unexpected happens, archivists must act quickly but cautiously. Discovery of a small leak can be remedied in a matter of hours, while damage from an electrical fire may take months for recovery. Safety of all employees is paramount to the success of a preparedness plan. Once the spaces are deemed safe for entry then the recovery process can begin.

A frequently updated disaster plan is the blueprint for reacting to an actual emergency (Matthews, Smith, and Knowles, 2009). Staying calm in the face of a disaster (i.e., walking into a collections storage space with two feet of standing water) is difficult, but necessary

---

Managing an Emergency in the Archives

- Remain calm.
- Ensure the safety of all employees.
- Follow the emergency preparedness plan when possible.
- Document affected areas and materials before recovery begins.
- Remove archival material from the affected areas.
- Communicate with all employees the recovery plan.
- Triage damaged materials for preservation or conservation attention.
- Consult other colleagues and other experts in the field.

to avoid further damage to the employees and to the collections. Documenting the disaster with photographs and detailed notes may in fact help a conservator save damaged materials. As the initial shock of a disaster recedes, the leader of the program coordinates a recovery strategy based on the preservation plan.

Next, archivists remove the damaged material and make informed preservation decisions (Forde, 2007). Preservation of damaged materials is made easier and more efficient if the disaster plan includes recommendations on how to approach the preservation of common formats. For example, there are numerous methods to drying paper-based materials, with air drying and blast-freezing the most common, but not all paper reacts well to these methods (Fortson, 1992). The preservation of formats such as photographic materials, magnetic tape, and objects are even more complicated and should be addressed in the disaster plan. Archivists should know what kinds of paper and photographic materials are in their collections and how to treat them in case of an emergency. Basic preservation skills can save many items during the recovery phase; however, archivists should consult with colleagues and conservators before making irreversible preservation decisions.

Small disasters may not deserve a detailed preservation strategy, but academic archivists should still document their response to the situation. For example, mold outbreaks are common in academic libraries and can have disastrous effects if not treated quickly. Mold and airborne fungi thrive in extreme temperatures and relative humidity, which makes it likely that an outbreak can occur following an even larger disaster, such as a flood (Fortson, 1992). As one method, isolating the affected materials and adjusting the climatic conditions usually eliminate the problem in a matter of weeks. Documenting preservation treatments and methods will make it easier to deal with reoccurring emergencies.

Full recovery from a disaster depends on the severity of the event and the types of materials damaged. Archivists may work with external companies and conservators for months following a flood, while smaller emergencies such as water damage to a box of books can be dealt with in-house in a matter of days. While it is impossible to predict a disaster, it is possible to anticipate how collections might be affected by certain kinds of emergencies. The keys to managing a disaster in an academic archives program are being prepared, staying calm, ensuring the safety of the people in the disaster zone, and having an updated strategy to deal with recovering and preserving archival collections (Matthews, Smith, and Knowles, 2009).

CONCLUSION

Academic archivists receive a range of new materials, all of which have unique origins. Collections of books, manuscripts, records, and photographs arrive on the loading dock in various states of organization. Archivists must first accession these collections to provide basic points of access. Following further investigation, archivists develop plans to organize each collection. From these backlog collections, archivists must determine processing priorities based on factors such as research usability, size and scope of the collection, and resources needed to complete the arrangement and description.

Processing collections involves an understanding of archival principles and realistic practices. Archivists must be strong organizers, with the ability to turn a box of random papers into a box full of well-organized folders in a logical sequence. Arranging and describing archival materials in a single collection may take weeks, months, or even years to complete. As the preferred access method for users, archivists create searchable finding aids using EAD, DACS, and other standards developed by archivists. A good finding aid demonstrates a clear sense of intellectual and physical control over the collection, and, in turn, leads users to the materials.

Managing the collections and storage spaces of an academic archives program takes an enormous amount of resources. Keeping track of hundreds or even thousands of boxes requires having a reliable system of storage and retrieval. Collections in academic archives are destined to be shelved in storage spaces under the program's supervision. Archivists manage their collections and spaces by providing security, monitoring and adjusting the environmental conditions, and following a clear tracking system for every shelf and every archival container. Protecting these collections from natural or human-made threats requires archivists to develop emergency preparedness plans and preservation strategies.

REFERENCES

Balloffet, Nelly, and Jenny Hille. 2005. *Preservation and Conservation for Libraries and Archives.* Chicago: American Library Association.

Bastian, Jeannette A., and Donna Webber. 2008. *Archival Internships: A Guide for Faculty, Supervisors, and Students.* Chicago: Society of American Archivists.

Boles, Frank. 2005. *Selecting and Appraising Archives and Manuscripts.* Chicago: Society of American Archivists.

Dewey, Barbara I. 1991. *Raising Money for Academic and Research Libraries*. New York: Neal-Schuman.

Fleckner, John A. 1977. *Archives and Manuscripts: Surveys*. Chicago: Society of American Archivists.

Forde, Helen. 2007. *Preserving Archives*. London: Facet Publishing.

Fortson, Judith. 1992. *Disaster Planning and Recovery*. New York: Neal-Schuman.

Greene, Mark A., and Dennis Meissner. 2005. "More Product, Less Process: Revamping Traditional Archival Processing." *American Archivist* 68 (Fall/Winter): 208–263.

Hunter, Gregory S. 2003. *Developing and Maintaining Practical Archives*. 2nd ed. New York: Neal-Schuman.

Khan, Miriam B. 1998. *Disaster Response and Planning for Libraries*. Chicago: American Library Association.

Kurtz, Michael J. 2004. *Managing Archival and Manuscript Repositories*. Chicago: Society of American Archivists.

Maher, William J. 1992. *The Management of College and University Archives*. Chicago: Society of American Archivists.

Matthews, Graham, Yvonne Smith, and Gemma Knowles. 2009. *Disaster Management in Archives, Libraries, and Museums*. Burlington, VT: Ashgate Publishing.

O'Toole, James M., and Richard J. Cox. 2006. *Understanding Archives and Manuscripts*. Chicago: Society of American Archivists.

Pacifico, Michele, and Thomas P. Wilsted, eds. 2009. *Archival and Special Collections Facilities: Guidelines for Archivists, Librarians, Architects, and Engineers*. Chicago: Society of American Archivists.

Pearce-Moses, Richard. 2005. *A Glossary of Archives and Records Terminology*. Chicago: Society of American Archivists.

Pitti, Daniel V. 1997. "Encoded Archival Description: The Development of an Encoding Standard for Archival Finding Aids." *American Archivist* 60 (Summer): 268–283.

Pyatt, Tim. 1999. "Cooperative Collecting of Manuscripts in the 'Old South.'" *Rare Books and Manuscripts Librarianship* 14, no. 1 (September): 19–25.

Ritzenthaler, Mary Lynn. 2010. *Preserving Archives and Manuscripts*. 2nd ed. Chicago: Society of American Archivists.

Ritzenthaler, Mary Lynn, and Dianne Vogt-O'Conner. 2006. *Photographs: Archival Care and Management*. Chicago: Society of American Archivists.

Roe, Kathleen D. 2005. *Arranging and Describing Archives and Manuscripts*. Chicago: Society of American Archivists.

Roth, James M. 2001. "Serving Up EAD: An Exploratory Study on the Deployment and Utilization of Encoded Archival Description Finding Aids." *American Archivist* 64 (Fall/Winter): 214–237.

Schellenberg, T. R. 1956. *Modern Archives: Principles and Techniques*. Reprint, 2002. Chicago: Society of American Archivists.

Society of American Archivists. 2007. *Describing Archives: A Content Standard*. Chicago: Society of American Archivists.

Swartzburg, Susan Garretson, and Holly Bussey. 1991. *Library and Archives: Design and Renovation with a Preservation Perspective.* Metuchen, NJ: Scarecrow Press.

Sweetman, Kimberly Burke. 2006. *Managing Student Assistants.* New York: Neal-Schuman.

Trinkaus-Randall, Gregor. 1995. *Protecting Your Collections: A Manual of Archival Security.* Chicago: Society of American Archivists.

Weideman, Christine. 2006. "Accessioning as Processing." *American Archivist* 69 (Fall/Winter): 274–283.

Wilkinson, Frances, Linda K. Lewis, and Nancy K. Dennis. 2010. *Comprehensive Guide to Emergency Preparedness and Disaster Recovery.* Chicago: Association of College and Research Libraries.

Wilsted, Thomas P. 2007. *Planning New and Remodeled Archival Facilities.* Chicago: Society of American Archivists.

8

Public and Research Services in Academic Archives

INTRODUCTION

Building a strong public presence and robust research services are key ingredients of a mature academic archives program. Public services for academic archives are much more than just providing in-person researchers with in-depth, personal reference assistance. The unique nature of material in academic archives makes the reference process more complex. Academic archivists must have deep knowledge of their collections and be able to deliver that information to researchers accurately and efficiently. Researchers using academic archives may have other needs, such as requests for high-quality scans of material, information about permission to publish, or online access to material for classroom purposes.

This chapter examines how academic archives develop and maintain their public and research services. An active reading room, a visible outreach program, efficient and effective reference services, and rich online resources are indications of a successful academic archives program. Academic archivists involved in public and research services must deliver efficient reference assistance, target researchers, prioritize their services, develop and assess instructional sessions, and create a public and virtual awareness for the program. All of these public interactions are prime opportunities for building archival advocacy and supporting the mission of the archives program. This chapter seeks answers to the following questions:

1. How do academic archives approach research services?
2. How do academic archives approach public outreach?
3. How do academic archives maintain a strong virtual presence?

RESEARCH SERVICES IN ACADEMIC ARCHIVES

Redefining Reference

Traditionally academic librarians and archivists have defined interaction with their patrons as "reference" work. This type of interaction simply means that there is a reference interview process where library patrons have questions that reference librarians attempt to answer. While this kind of reference work is still very much a part of academic libraries and archives, the definition of reference has expanded into a more service-oriented approach to include assisting virtual researchers, providing library instruction, and generally the idea of information literacy (Turcotte, 2006). Because of this expansion of the concept of reference, leaders of academic libraries and archives have redefined their reference and instructional offerings under the title of research services. Research is so much at the heart of the archives' reading room; therefore, it is important for academic archives to embrace the broader term of research services.

Research services encompasses traditional reference activities with researchers in the reading room, interactions with virtual researchers, instructional programs, campus outreach to students and faculty, exhibits and public programs, and community involvement (Turcotte, 2006). Quite simply, research services are the public face of archives. It is through research services that an academic archives program interacts with a majority of its supporters, researchers, and other constituents. Research services is responsible for the researchers, the exhibits, the policies, and the layout of the reading room, while also building useful virtual resources such as the website, online collections, and online reference services.

Academic archivists focused on public services, outreach, and reference activities are the core of a research services team. Having a

Goals of Research Services in Academic Archives

- Provide effective reference assistance to in-person and virtual researchers.
- Create enforceable and easily understood reading room policies.
- Promote access to collections while protecting those collections from theft or harm.
- Overlap with archivists responsible for acquisitions and processing.
- Plan, coordinate, and assess public events such as exhibits.
- Develop rich online resources and a user-friendly website.
- Develop relationships with other departments in the academic library.

coordinator for public-focused programs and services helps streamline and avoid duplication of efforts. An integrated team of research services archivists works in parallel with an acquisitions and processing unit to ensure effective delivery of material and information to researchers. The coordinators of these two units must make sure there is necessary sharing of information about collections, donors, researchers, policies, and programs. Figure 8.1 shows a common services model for academic archives, in this case a special collections and university archives unit.

Further, research services in academic archives should overlap with other reference, instructional, and research services within the academic library. For example, a coordinator of research services should be the contact point for requests from campus faculty and students about advanced bibliographic and collection-focused instruction. Commonly, faculty and students approach a reference librarian with such a request, and librarians should know to refer the researcher to a research services archivist. As another example, an archivist may join a reference librarian to help conduct a general session for undergraduates on doing research in the library.

The research services unit should comprise approximately half of the human resources of an academic archives program, with the other half

Figure 8.1
Services Approach for Academic Archives

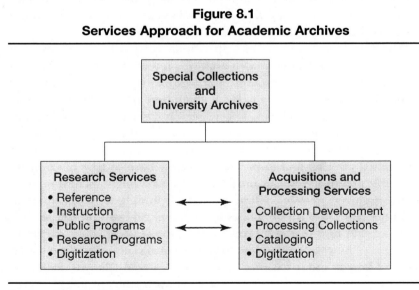

Source: Graphic by Marc Brodsky.

devoted to acquisitions and processing services. There should be significant overlap between these two units. For example, an archivist focused on processing materials should keep a reference desk shift and participate in public events when necessary. Likewise, the coordinator of research services should process a small amount of collections each year and may take a role in reviewing student-produced finding aids. This kind of overlap allows academic archivists to be focused on specific duties, while remaining current in other areas of archival work. A careful balance between the public and more behind-the-scenes activities keeps research services from receiving all of the attention and resources from external sources.

Classroom Instruction

While a departmental tour or a simple show-and-tell with original materials introduces many new researchers to academic archives, instructional sessions reach even greater numbers. Research services units in academic archives offer a range of instructional sessions for their researchers, and many programs have multiple archivists planning and teaching classroom sessions. The use of primary sources for instruction is not a new approach, but academic archivists now use a variety of pedagogical methods. Many archivists have taken on the role as educators by introducing audiences to the research process and primary sources through workshops, in-class visits, formal courses, hands-on activities, and online tutorials (Robyns, 2001).

The most common type of instructional session provides researchers with a basic introduction to archives, research, and the academic archives. For example, academic archives may offer a short 30-minute session for classes or groups to learn about how archival materials differ from other library materials, how to search for archival materials, and what kinds of collections are readily available in the archives (Johnson, 2006). This kind of session can be connected with another library instructional offering and does not necessarily have to take place in the academic archives. A longer introductory session might include a review of the archives' website, online searches of finding aids, and material from the collection for attendees to examine. All introductory sessions must explain how research takes place in the reading room, including the steps of how to register, how to request materials, how to use materials, and how to request copies or scans of material (Robyns, 2001). Introductory instructional sessions should demystify the purposes, services, and collections of academic archives.

A very common approach to introducing students and researchers to academic archives is to focus on primary sources. The use of primary materials is at the core of research. Demonstrating the importance of primary sources, the differences between secondary and primary sources, and the challenges of using original materials are useful ways to introduce students to archival research (Tally and Goldenberg, 2005). Using this approach also fits well with instructional efforts in academic libraries to create active learning exercises that are primarily designed to lead students to secondary sources. Primary source education works well with many disciplines, with programs in the humanities and the social sciences the most obvious

> **Designing Instructional Sessions**
>
> - Offer introductory and advanced sessions.
> - Describe the purposes of archives and how they differ from libraries.
> - Explain the research process and how scholars use archives.
> - Discuss access tools for archival materials, especially finding aids.
> - Review reading room policies and rationale.
> - Focus on the value of primary sources and when possible use actual examples.
> - Work with interested faculty in planning and improving instructional sessions.
> - Use technology for instruction and for making course materials available online.
> - Develop assessment tools for each session.

(Schmiesing and Hollis, 2002). Traditionally, the majority of collections in academic archives support academic programs in history, English, philosophy, and other disciplines that rely on original material for their research projects. Developing primary source sessions to reach students in the sciences, engineering, medicine, and more technical programs may take more planning and depend on the availability of original material.

More focused and detailed instructional sessions have become common offerings by academic archives. Because of the complexity of archival research and the variety of courses offered, these sessions are often devised by an archivist and a professor teaching collaboratively. For example, a historical methods class for graduate students focused on the French Revolution visits the academic archives for an instructional session. That session provides students a general overview and a hands-on exercise where original French newspapers from the 1790s are given to students for their examination. The archivist discusses with students the research challenges of their newspapers (i.e., translating, fragility of the material, understanding historical context), while the professor asks students to describe the content of specific articles in their newspaper.

Following such a session, the students are required to use primary sources found in the archives in their course research papers. If holdings on specific topics of the French Revolution are limited, students may be able to use other nearby archives or selected online primary sources.

Advanced instructional sessions require considerable time and commitment from the academic archives. To plan sessions, an archivist meets with interested faculty members to design the session and possibly an archives-based class assignment. Prior to the session, the archivist selects material and secures a classroom or a space in the academic archives. It may be possible for an archivist to do an advanced session in a classroom with a limited amount of original material and online access. For example, an archivist can display a digitized page from a 1455 Gutenberg Bible through a web connection, rather than bringing the actual Bible into the classroom. However, part of the session is to familiarize students with the location, policies, and archivists in the academic archives unit. Following the session there may be follow-up questions and research activity from the students. Placing research and research materials from the archives at the center of a class project requires careful planning and commitment from archivists, and the assignment reinforces the instruction (Schmiesing and Hollis, 2002). Over the course of the semester archivists may assist dozens, if not hundreds, of students working on class-based archival research projects.

Because of the commitment, academic archivists must evaluate the effectiveness of each instructional session in order to prepare for future sessions. Assessment can be done through a formal survey given to the students, and informally by talking with archivists, students, and faculty involved in the session (Yakel, 2008). Based on the responses, academic archivists may reconfigure their approaches to instruction. For example, an academic archivist and a faculty member devise an assignment for students in a small-sized English course on modernist literature to examine one of five unpublished manuscripts in the academic archives for their research papers. While the students made excellent use of the manuscripts and created strong papers, at the end of the course the

> **Target Audiences for Instructional Sessions**
>
> - General library users
> - Graduate students conducting research
> - Research methods courses in many disciplines
> - K–12 teachers and students
> - Academic librarians
> - Community groups
> - Genealogists and family historians

professor noted that there was not enough original material to support future classes. Adjusting the assignments and the instructional sessions to match the needs of each course is time-consuming, but it exposes students to the challenges of research, the value of primary sources, and, most important, the purposes of academic archives (Robyns, 2001).

Instructional sessions are not limited to on-campus students. Many academic archives work closely with their K–12 community to educate students about archives, research, and primary sources (Hendry, 2007). These sessions may be designed for a classroom assignment or to support programs such as National History Day. American history or social studies classes at different grade levels are the most obvious courses to target, but depending on the available collections it may be possible to work with other disciplines such as science and math. Academic archivists work with K–12 teachers to design the sessions and arrange for visits to the archives.

For in-class instructional sessions, archivists locate collections with wide appeal for the K–12 audience. For example, a manuscript collection from a noted scientist who was involved in the development of the atomic bomb at the Los Alamos Laboratories could be used for K–12 classes in history and science. The collections include handwritten notes about experiments, images of personnel, published articles, personal diaries, and a small amount of laboratory equipment. This material may support an assignment for students in a seventh grade history class to write an essay that considers the lives of the people who were part of the building of the atomic bomb. The same material, especially the notes about experiments, could be used by a high school chemistry or physics class learning about atomic subparticles. Finally, a group of sixth graders working on a National History Day project related to the bombing of Hiroshima may want to use images of Los Alamos from the same collection in their presentation.

Online access to preselected material is one way to reach more students without overwhelming an academic archives (Davison, 2009). For example a graduate course in the digital humanities may be focused on transcribing a collection of unpublished poetry. Instead of having ten students use the collection in the reading room and then make multiple photocopies from which to work, it may be easier to scan the entire collection and make it accessible through the website. Once the class has concluded their projects, the archivist may add the transcriptions to the finding aid, making the collection more accessible and searchable. Online access to material may be an even better way for K–12 students to access original materials for their assignments or projects (Gilliland-Swetland, 1998).

Genealogists, off-campus researchers, and other groups also benefit from instructional sessions. If there is a demand for assistance with archival research, academic archivists should tailor sessions to meet those needs. For example, members of a local historical society interested in the early history of their community wish to discover more information about the town's three founding families. Using manuscript collections associated with founding families, academic archivists design an instructional session for the group enabling them to better understand how to conduct research in the reading room. For genealogists, academic archives may want to sponsor basic genealogy workshops focused on locating primary, secondary, and online sources. Finally, faculty and staff in the academic library are an important group to target for basic instructional sessions. Explaining the basics of archival research to academic librarians in an instructional session fosters a much clearer understanding of how the academic archives program fits within the broader mission of the academic library.

No matter how large the academic archives program and the number of archivists devoted to instruction, it is difficult to host hundreds of classes and thousands of students each semester. Instead, a program of in-class and virtual instructional sessions should be built slowly with careful collaboration with academic faculty, the K–12 community, and other interested researchers and groups (Visser, 2006). One unique result of exposing researchers of all ages to academic archives and primary sources is the actual recruitment of future archivists. A high school student familiar with academic archives has a much greater chance of conducting archival research when they attend college, and some advanced students may know early in their academic careers that they want to be professional archivists. Exposing researchers of all ages and types to archival materials through instructional sessions promotes the profession, reaches first-time researchers, and increases public awareness about archives.

Online Projects and Virtual Interaction

Much like academic librarians, academic archivists working in a research services team use technology to work with virtual patrons. As mentioned earlier in this chapter, the most basic communication with virtual patrons is through an e-mail reference service. Questions are received through a designated e-mail account and then distributed to archivists. The goal is to reply within a few days with either an answer or an indication that the request will take much longer to complete. A few academic archives use a chat service for real-time interaction with patrons (Theimer, 2010).

The problem with this approach is that chat is intended to answer questions within a few minutes and many of the queries received by academic archivists may take hours to address. The complexity of archival research and original materials make a chat service for academic archives difficult to sustain successfully.

> **Using Technology to Enhance Virtual Interaction**
>
> - Select the right technology for the right purpose.
> - Use technology to improve communication, provide outreach, and create high-quality digital collections.
> - Use technology to provide greater access to archival materials.
> - Share resources and expertise when using technology.

Research services archivists also use social networking sites, blogs, wikis, RSS feeds, and Web 2.0 technology to connect with virtual researchers (Theimer, 2010). For example, a digital archivist can reach virtual researchers through a blog, a Facebook page, or with simple e-mail discussion and distribution lists. Announcements of upcoming events, new collections and acquisitions, recent publications that originated in the collections of the archives, and changing operating hours can be publicized through these virtual mechanisms as well (Whittaker and Thomas, 2009). Traditional print publications, such as brochures and exhibition catalogs, can be easily distributed through linking electronic versions to the website and other virtual outlets.

Developing virtual networks of supporters is a form of outreach to the research, campus, and local community. For example, a lecture series sponsored by a special collections department can be widely publicized through traditional methods such a direct mailing of announcements and posters, as well as through blog and website postings (Chute, 2008). There may only be a dozen attendees at the lecture, but there are numerous ways to reach virtual attendees. It may be possible to have a live Internet feed of the event or later upload a video of the entire lecture. Providing access to such events and adding additional content to the website provides an even richer experience for virtual researchers.

Using readily available technology to enhance online services and access is an inexpensive way to provide outreach (Theimer, 2010). Most emerging technologies are affordable for academic archives, especially if numerous departments in the library are committed to the same technology. Staff time is the greatest expenditure in creating a strong virtual network for academic archives, but archivists do not necessarily have to be experts on developing online tools. Larger academic libraries have dedicated staff for website and Web 2.0 development, which often means that the creation of content is the primary job of the archivist. A strong and cooperative library systems or information technology department makes developing virtual services and outreach much easier for academic archivists. One caveat is that academic archivists should not be solely independent in their efforts to develop the technology for virtual outreach tools. Working closely with other library professionals on developing and maintaining technology ensures that archivists are a mainstream part of the academic library.

THE READING ROOM AND THE SETTING FOR RESEARCH

The reading room represents one of the most important parts of an academic archives program. It is in this controlled space that in-person researchers consult collections, take notes, make copies, and request scans of particular items. The reading room is where scholarly books and articles begin, undergraduates learn about primary sources, and the public comes to view an exhibit. While the square footage of the space may be a very minor part of the entire footprint of the academic archives, the reading room is one of the most important parts of the program. The main activities in the reading room include collection research, in-person reference assistance, and direct interaction between archivists and the general public.

The location of the reading room influences the effectiveness and success of public services. Typically special collections are placed on the top or the bottom floor of the academic library (Pugh, 2005). In the former case, there is a disadvantage of being more isolated from regular library patrons and separate from other units. Similarly, in the latter case, the lowest floor of academic libraries is often located in a basement, which creates environmental concerns and isolation from the patrons who enter the library building through a main or ground floor entrance. Some academic archives are located in their own building and have more flexibility of available spaces. However it is common that "branch" library units, which often include stand-alone academic archives, are located on the periphery of campus or in a difficult to find location. Management of college and university buildings and interior spaces usually reside with the institution's administration and seldom with the occupants of the building. While academic archivists may have no real control over the physical location of the archives, it is important to understand which campus office or official makes decisions about the use and assignment of spaces for working, storing materials, and providing public services. Further, archivists should work closely with the librarian or administrator who is responsible for updating the signs in the building where the academic archives is located to enhance visibility.

Academic archivists do have control over the layout of their reading rooms. As mentioned in previous chapters, it is becoming more common to combine separate reading rooms (i.e., manuscript, archives, and rare book reading areas) into one central public research and service location. Researchers should immediately be in a reception area when entering the reading room. This space should have a registration point where researchers sign in, learn about the basic rules of the reading room, and deposit personal items in lockers or a secure location (Pacifico and Wilsted, 2009). Accessibility for researchers with disabilities should also be considered when designing the layout of the reading room and planning for services (Greene, 2010).

No food or drink should be allowed in the reading room. This policy applies to both archivists working the main reference desk or researchers walking in the front door. Most all academic archives allow researchers to bring notes, books, and laptops into the reading room, with some allowing scanners, copiers, digital camera, and other equipment (Pugh, 2005). The entrance and reception area should also serve as the exit for researchers. Security is greatly improved when there is only one entrance and exit for researchers to enter and leave the reading room (Kurtz, 2004).

Designing a Reading Room

- Have a separate reception area for registration.
- Have space for a small ready reference section.
- Provide researchers with computer workstations to access online materials, such as finding aids.
- Locate copiers, scanners, or any other duplication equipment within or adjacent to the reading room.
- Consider the needs of disabled researchers when selecting furniture and arranging spaces.
- Place researcher desks in direct view of reference archivists.
- Display materials in cases if space is available.

The Research Process

Research visits may last a few hours, several days, or even multiple weeks depending on the project and relevant material. Long-term research usually involves prior contact between staff and the researcher, frequently months in advance. With prior notice from researchers planning a multi-day visit, archivists can have material ready for use upon their arrival. More common, however, is the short-term researcher who may be unfamiliar with using academic archives. Archivists should plan their services for a variety of researchers, whether they are scholars with 30 years of experience or an undergraduate working on an English composition paper.

The next phase of the research process is for registered researchers to discuss their projects with archivists, answer basic questions, target possible collections, and prioritize their time. Reading rooms are commonly designed to allow the registration and preliminary reference interview to occur at the reference desk, rather than in separate locations. Many reading rooms have a "ready reference" area near the reference desk for researchers to browse and use during their visit. This reference collection may include copies of the institution's yearbooks, course catalogs, alumni directories, published local and state histories, and genealogical sources, in addition to reference tools that support the program's major collecting areas (Maher, 1992). Many times researchers can find answers to their questions in the ready reference area without having to request archival material or work closely with an archivist. A computer workstation should be located near the reference section for researchers to access online finding aids and digital collections. Twenty years ago, printed finding aids and inventories would have filled the ready reference area, but it is now more common for finding aids and inventories to be electronically available.

Much like academic librarians, academic archivists work with their researchers through a reference interview process. During the reference interview, the researcher is expected to explain the research project or topic, and the archivist suggests appropriate archival and secondary sources (Pugh, 2005). The archivist may take the researcher to a separate area (i.e., his or her office or a meeting room) to address complex reference questions that will require extended conversation. Once the discussion is completed, the researcher requests the relevant archival collections. Some archives have an automated request system for archival materials through a computer workstation that allows researchers to request material before or during their visit. This kind of system is most valuable when materials are housed off site and require advanced retrieval time. Most institutions will pull materials on demand, frequently employing students for this purpose.

Rules and Expectations of Conducting Research

Once the material has been requested the eager researcher takes a seat at a table in the reading room. There are variations of how to best arrange and design the actual research area of the reading room. For example, one repository may prefer a set of long tables for researchers to share, while another repository has individual desks for each researcher. Whatever the arrangement, the research space should have sufficient lighting, access to electrical outlets, sufficient work space, and enough room for researchers to work with a small number of boxes and folders (Wilsted, 2007). For security purposes, the tables should be arranged in such a way that the archivist at the reference desk can clearly observe all of the researchers in the reading room (Trinkaus-Randall, 1995). Larger programs may have security cameras operating in the reading room, but most academic archives rely on monitoring by staff.

When the material arrives, the archivist should remind the researcher of any use restrictions (e.g., none of the collection can be photocopied) and the basic rules of the reading room (Cox, 1992). It is standard practice for researchers to be allowed only pencils

Common Rules of the Reading Room

- Complete a registration form.
- Deposit personal items in a locker or secure area.
- No food or drink is allowed.
- Only pencils are allowed for taking notes.
- Work only at a researcher table in the reading room.
- Maintain original order of material and folders.
- Return folders to the correct boxes in correct order.
- Do not take original materials outside of the reading room.
- Minimize conversations.
- Expect an archivist to inspect materials at the end of a research visit.
- Sign out of the reading room.

when taking notes, as stray pen marks are irreversible and thus permanently damage archival material. Most archives request that researchers work with only one box at a time (in order to avoid misfiling of folders) and request that cotton gloves be worn when using photographic materials. Archivists should also instruct researchers to keep materials in the original order in which they find them. Careful handling is an important part of using archival collections, especially when materials are brittle and fragile. For some collections, archivists may need to explain special use instructions to the researcher. Staff should have the authority to restrict reproduction, types of use, or access based on the condition of the materials.

Once the researcher is working with the materials, the archivist may continue to search for relevant items in the collections. However, it is wise to discuss any further information with the researcher at an obvious break in the research, such as at lunchtime or at the end of the day. Some researchers are talkative and want to continue discussion with archivists or start up new conversations with other researchers, but the best advice is to limit these conversations in the reading room out of respect for others doing research. If researchers need to consult material in the open stacks of the academic library, then they should be allowed to leave their material at their desk.

Copies, Reproduction, and Scanning

During archival research patrons may discover an absence or a wealth of relevant material. In the former case, researchers may want to return to finding aids or an archivist to search for other possible collections. For the latter case, researchers are frequently interested in receiving photocopies or scans of relevant material rather than spending hours taking extended notes. The rules of obtaining copies of material vary by repository, but generally many archives allow self-service copying and offer in-house scanning services (Pugh, 2005). If self-service copying is available for researchers, then copy machines or overhead scanning equipment should be housed within or adjacent to the reading room. Some repositories complete the copying for researchers either on demand or within a few days of the researcher's visit. However, with staff and student employee time needed for other activities, it is more common that repositories allow researchers to complete their own copying, unless of course the material is too fragile or could be

> **Common Policies for Duplicating Materials**
>
> - Self-service photocopying for patrons when materials are stable, and for less stable materials on a case-by-case basis
> - Scanning and digital photography services made available
> - All duplication completed within the reading room
> - Delivery of digital copies through online pickup or through the mail

damaged by copying. Archivists can deliver scans to their researchers either by mailing a CD, e-mailing the file, or putting the file on an online pickup site where researchers can download the file.

It is inadvisable to allow researchers to leave the reading room with archival material in order to use duplication equipment in other parts of the library or on campus. For example, a researcher requests scans of blueprints in the archives for a senior thesis project and the archives does not have a map scanner. The researcher asks to take the material to his or her department where there is access to a map scanner. The archivist should recognize this request as an opportunity to work with another department, but only if the material is handled and transported by archivists, and not by the researcher. As another example, a researcher wants color copies of a photograph and the library's only color copier is in a room on a different floor. The archivist should either go with the researcher to make the copy or complete the copy for the researcher at a later time.

Charges for duplication services are as varied as the collections found in academic archives. Many archives charge the same rate for photocopies as that of their academic library. Revenue from copies or scanning is usually designed to cover costs of time, labor, and equipment, and not to generate income for the department (Pugh, 2005). In many library systems, copier money is collected from all departments (including the academic archives) and deposited in a general library or administrative fund. In an effort to keep funding within the department, a few repositories have waived all in-house copying and scanning fees in favor of recommending that researchers make a donation to support the archives program. A common result of this option is that donations are significantly larger than would be generated by reproduction charges.

Copyright and Permissions

All forms of reproduction (i.e., scanning, digital photography, and photocopying) are covered by copyright law. Frequent changes to copyright law make it imperative that academic archives are aware of the rules and consequences of possible violations. Ownership is the first factor in determining copyright. Generally speaking, archives own the physical components of their collections, but not necessarily the intellectual property. Most deeds of gift transfer the material to the archives and the copyright remains with the donor, family, or creator. Researchers, and not archivists, are responsible for contacting the copyright holders.

Official institutional records are often an exception to this rule, since technically the college or university archives has domain over the created documents and intellectual "property" of their institution. When an archival repository maintains the physical and intellectual ownership of a collection, it is up to the leader of the program or the director of the library to make decisions about copyright (Hunter, 2003).

The second factor in determining copyright is whether the material is considered in the public domain. The date of a document helps determine whether it is still under copyright protection. Much of the material in archives created before the twentieth century is out of copyright, but not all of it. In addition to date, copyright is affected by whether the material has ever been published or registered with the copyright office. Other considerations include format, authorship, country of publication, and a variety of other special cases (Hirtle, 2011). Materials in the public domain do not require specific permission for duplication or publication; however, researchers should always attempt a "good faith effort" to determine whether a copyright holder exists. For example a researcher wishing to reprint a diary from a Civil War soldier should first determine if a published version of the diary has ever appeared, and if any heirs or family members might still claim copyright.

Finally, the purpose or use for the material in question factors affects how to interpret copyright law. Simple use of archival material does not require a researcher to request any kind of permission or determine what is in the public domain, but making copies or scans of material for specific purposes beyond those allowed does involve copyright law. Researchers in academic archives frequently have an educational purpose connected to their reproduction or scanning request. As examples

---

Copyright and Permissions Granting

- Academic archivists cannot grant permission to reproduce material for publication purposes unless the institution holds the copyright or the deed of gift transferred copyright to the repository.
- In most cases, the burden of identifying the copyright holder and asking for permission to reproduce rests with the researcher.
- Fair use for educational purposes covers many duplication requests in academic archives, but not all situations.
- Academic archivists must encourage researchers to provide a clear citation attributing that the material is in the archives.
- Academic archivists should remain current on changes in copyright law, such as the limits of fair use and how to determine public domain materials.

of common educational uses of archival materials, a faculty member wants scans of ten documents to use in a course the following semester, a graduate student wants to copy a lengthy unpublished manuscript for dissertation research, or an undergraduate wants to include scanned images of campus buildings in a course presentation on the architectural history of the university. These scenarios fall largely within the educational exception in the copyright law known as "fair use." Determining if a duplication request falls within fair use depends on the purpose and character of the use, the nature of the copyrighted work, the amount of material used in relation to the entirety of the work, and the monetary effect of the use based on market value (Wherry, 2008).

The requests of many researchers fall outside of fair use for educational purposes. For example, a researcher writing a book for a commercial press wants permission from the archivist to publish a scanned image from a manuscript collection in the archives. If the publication of a book, article, or other format could result in financial profit the rules about permissions and copyright become more complicated. The archivist can supply the scanned image, but unless the archives holds the copyright, they cannot grant permission to publish the material (Crews, 2008). Instead, the researcher should make a good-faith effort to locate a copyright holder or to determine whether the material in question is in the public domain.

Archivists are frequently faced with the complexities of copyright law and should provide their researchers with basic guidance. Archivists should advise that permission to publish can be granted only by the copyright holder, which is seldom the archives. Accession files for each collection may include contact information for the donor or creator. Further, it is not the archivist's responsibility to determine who the copyright holder is. Without being ambivalent, archivists should leave matters of copyright and permissions gathering to the researcher. However, academic archivists must encourage researchers to provide a clear citation in their publication that attributes the archives as the repository for the material or collection that was referenced (Pugh, 2005).

Completing a Research Visit

Once a researcher has finished consulting archival material and made copies he or she prepares to exit the reading room. During this last phase of an in-person research visit, the researcher returns all archival material to the appropriate boxes and folders, leaving behind nothing on the desks but notes and copies (Hunter, 2003). Researchers usually signal to an archivist in the reading room that they are finished with the material and are ready to begin the checking-out process. During these discussions, researchers may ask to hold material for a visit in the following few days or may share their research experiences.

The final step of a research visit is for the researcher to sign out and to collect personal belongings from a locker or a secure space. Some archives have a policy to closely inspect any notes or materials that the researcher is taking with them. This inspection is not to imply that researchers are devious and trying to pilfer archival material; rather, it is common that first-time researchers accidently interfile archival materials or secondary sources with their notes. However, some researchers do in fact target archives and libraries for theft, so having a final level of security over researchers before they leave the reading room is a simple way to deter such illegal and sometimes hard to detect behavior (Trinkaus-Randall, 1995). This cycle of research continues with the arrival and departure of each researcher in the reading room.

THE VIRTUAL READING ROOM

The online presence of an academic archives program is just as important as its reading room. From the website, virtual researchers should be able to find basic information about the archives, its collections, and policies governing research. The website introduces online researchers to the activities and services of the program, such as the mission, vision, contact information, physical location, collection strengths, a contact list of staff, and direct links to more detailed pages (Pugh, 2005). A website for academic archives may also have extensive online resources of original materials for researchers to browse and search at their leisure. This kind of online reading room allows distant researchers to access original material, with many of them completing their research without needing assistance or to travel.

Websites for academic archives, regardless of complexity, attract a range of online researchers to the virtual reading room. To handle incoming reference inquiries, a majority of academic archives have a designated e-mail address for reference questions or a reference request form generated through the website. This practice streamlines the reference process, rather than requiring researchers to determine which archivist in the staff listing is most appropriate to contact. The initial reference e-mail from a researcher may lead to extensive communication with research archivists or the correspondence may be completed with a single response.

Academic archivists who are focused on reference services want their website to reach the three most common types of virtual researchers. The first group of virtual researchers completes research through their own independent searching without contacting an archivist. These researchers may be seeking an answer to a simple question, such as the exact date of the college's founding. This type of researcher may also want access to a specific source for the research project, such as an online image of the university's signature building. Academic archives with extensive online collections of material may be able to serve dozens if not hundreds of this type of online researcher each day (Stielow, 2003).

Crafting a logical, searchable, and straightforward website for the archives makes this kind of virtual reference interaction possible. It is difficult to track how the website either fulfilled or did not fulfill research requests because these kinds of reference activities are completed independently by the researcher.

A second major group of virtual researchers are those who contact the academic archives in need of

> **Virtual Researchers and Their Needs**
>
> - Online researchers only, who complete their research without contacting an archivist
> - Online researchers with basic directional or reference questions
> - Online researchers with more advanced reference queries, which leads them to request additional help from a reference archivist

basic assistance. This group may need general information, directional assistance, have questions about departmental policies, or need further information about collections. For example, a biology professor completing a history of his or her academic college needs the founding dates for specific departments in the college. An academic archivist responds by directing the professor to online course catalogs that are full-text searchable. The professor then accesses the online catalogs to find the information for the project. These reference queries are easily tracked and, as in the previous example, often these basic requests do not result in follow-up questions.

A third type of virtual researcher has more advanced reference queries, which leads to a request for help from a reference archivist. These researchers most often have a well-formed question or a sense of what would support their research. Researchers in this group may be scholars who are planning a visit to conduct research, genealogists searching for information about their family history, curious faculty interested in using specific collections, or someone in the campus public relations office searching for an early commencement program. It may be possible to assist these researchers by completing simple research for them, directing them to online collections, or referring them to another campus office or repository (Cohen, 1997). For example, a sports memorabilia collector wants more information about an image of the school's 1923 football team. A reference archivist may be able to supply the researcher the names of the players, but may refer the collector to the director of the school's sports museum for further information.

Whether virtual researchers are thousands of miles away or just across campus there are many who are unable or unwilling to arrange an on-site visit to the reading room. Each academic archives program should have a clear policy regarding completing research for off-site or online researchers (Pugh, 2005). The time it takes a reference archivist to track down obscure information or search for a specific document might be better used for other more pressing researcher needs. Many times on-campus requests, such as reference inquiries from the president's office or from a philosophy graduate student, are given priority over external nonaffiliated researchers. Whatever policies for virtual researchers are followed, academic archivists should be consistent about how they prioritize detailed off-site research requests.

An online reading room also serves as a contact point for other types of public services and programs for the academic archives. A website should announce recent news, upcoming events, public programs, new collections both received and processed for researcher use, and the addition of new online resources. For example, the website for an archives specializing in Civil War history would want to make multiple announcements about their activities, programs, and research collections that support the Civil War Sesquicentennial Commemoration. As events are completed, archivists should frequently update the website in

---

Basic Components of an Academic Archives Website

- Brief description of mission, collections, and purpose
- Ability for researchers to make an electronic reference query
- Announcements, events, and highlights
- Links to digital collections, finding aids, and other relevant online sources
- Contacts, location, directions, mailing address, operating hours, and other general information

order to keep the information current for new and returning virtual researchers.

The website is an important link to providing outreach to the campus and the community. For example, a high school teacher preparing students for participating in National History Day may visit numerous archival websites to determine which archives could support online research or host a class visit. The teacher may discover that a nearby academic archives program supports History Day projects with online tutorials, hands-on instructional sessions, and online primary sources. Teaching faculty may want to interact with these high school students both virtually and in the actual reading room to help refine their projects.

Just like the physical reading room, the virtual reading room reaches a broad audience. While the experience of actually visiting an academic archives' reading room cannot be replicated, a visit to the virtual reading room can be a rich experience. A well-designed website can provide virtual researchers with access to resources, online collections, and academic archivists focused on the research process. The virtual reading room supports traditional research, as well as the needs of the general public, the campus community, and on-campus constituents. The virtual reading room should include a list of contacts, especially if there is a designated archivist for public programs, instructional sessions, and exhibit planning (Pugh, 2005).

ANALYZING THE RESEARCH PROCESS

The research process, for both in-person and virtual researchers, triggers the recording of information about what material was requested, the affiliation or category of the researcher, and what services were needed. Archives should protect the actual identity of their researchers; however, the type of research conducted and the needs of the researchers inform a number of areas of the program. For example, a researcher studying African Americans in the Civil War brings a reference archivist's attention to a number of existing collections in the repository and the need to acquire more materials. And because that researcher is a faculty member teaching a course on African Americans and the military, there is an immediate need to consider the instructional needs of that faculty member and the students.

Academic libraries and archives record a variety of statistics for surveys, reporting, and other functions. The most useful kinds of data collected (i.e., what people are researching and who is using the material) can be used for collection development decisions, expanding services, and building new campus outreach programs. In many ways the research process indicates the future needs of the program and that information must be considered when archives programs are examining their mission, vision, and involvement in strategic planning.

EXHIBITS AND PUBLIC EVENTS IN THE READING ROOM

In addition to being the location for research activities, an academic archives' reading room can be a meeting place for supporters and those interested in the program. The reading room should be a vibrant place where scholars, students, and donors interact (Traister, 2003). Some reading rooms are large enough to feature exhibits, displays, and public events. The idea of using the reading room for multipurpose events is not a new concept, but as demand for public spaces in academic libraries has increased, there has emerged a stronger need to reconceptualize the uses of the reading room (Wilsted, 2007).

If designed well, a reading room can support a range of exhibits and displays for public viewing without sacrificing the security and traditional research purposes of the space (Finch, 1994). For example, if the registration point or the main desk of a reading room can be moved closer to the researcher desks, then the reception area nearest to the entrance can be used to display a small amount of material in cases or on shelves. Lockable or enclosed shelves provide sufficient security for the material on display. The rearrangement of the reception area allows multiple uses of the space, while still keeping the registered researchers and visitors in separate locations (Wilsted, 2007). For smaller research rooms, it is possible to have display cases built or moved into the reading room, perhaps close to the ready reference area. The cases should

Planning Exhibits and Events for Academic Archives

- Collaborate with others in the library and the institution to help share costs, resources, and spaces.
- Limit the amount of original materials put on display outside of the department.
- Connect the topics of exhibits and events with other shared activities on campus and in the community.
- Designate one or more archivists to plan, coordinate, and arrange exhibits and events for the department.

be located in a space that does not interfere with the operations of the reading room or distract researchers at their tables.

The most common exhibits in the reading rooms of academic archives focus on original material found in the department. These kinds of in-house exhibits are a good opportunity for archivists to display textual materials alongside realia, artwork, and photographs (Finch, 1994). For example, a college archives on a campus with a rich military tradition might design an exhibit of material on the school's cadet corps using existing collections and recently acquired papers from a retired ROTC (Reserve Officer Training Corps) commandant. The exhibit could feature early cadet uniforms and swords from previous donations alongside 1970s correspondence between the commandant and the president of the college from the most recent donation. Other sources to display could include images from the college's military photograph series and official publications of the Army unit on campus. A brochure or handout with information about the history of the cadet corps and the material on display is an inexpensive way to support the exhibit.

To make the exhibit even more relevant, the archives could schedule the exhibit to coincide with the seventy-fifth anniversary of the cadet corps and schedule library visits from the freshman corps members. It is important to promote the exhibit to the campus, local community, or regional groups through the archives' website, local media sources, and relevant listserves or online sites (Chute, 2008). Hosting an exhibit opening with a small reception and possibly a short lecture or set of speakers is an excellent opportunity to use the reading room for a public event to celebrate the donation and research. In most cases, the largest expense for such events is the amount of time that archives employees utilize to complete the project (Traister, 2003).

Larger and more elaborate displays and exhibits require archivists to consider using spaces near their reading room. It is also important to limit the amount of original, and thus irreplaceable, material displayed in spaces outside of the control of the academic archives. Displaying high-quality color copies of scanned original materials is a much safer and inexpensive way to share archival treasures with a large audience. For example, a traveling exhibit related to the history of the Underground Railroad sponsored nationally by the Smithsonian Institution consists of ten panels that are each eight feet tall and four feet long. With text, images, and facsimiles of original documents printed on each of the panels, the exhibit chronicles the amazing journey of 20 specific slaves from Maryland who made the difficult trek from slavery in the

Old South through the free states of the North and finally to freedom in Massachusetts. The topics in this exhibit would have wide appeal for the local community and the campus of a nearby historically African American university.

A reading room with a small amount of reception space would not be a suitable place for the Underground Railroad exhibit. Locating such an exhibit in a nearby library space would provide enough room for visitors, and involve other people and departments in the library in the planning of the exhibit. Just like an in-house display of material, larger exhibits are excellent opportunities to encourage community and scholarly participation. In the above scenario, archivists and librarians may collaborate with faculty in the African American studies and history departments, while also reaching out to a local chapter of the NAACP to support the exhibit. Exhibits can be supplemented with a series of public events, forums, lectures or gatherings, even with a limited budget. Figure 8.2 shows a small exhibit of material to support women's history month.

Figure 8.2
Reading Room Exhibit

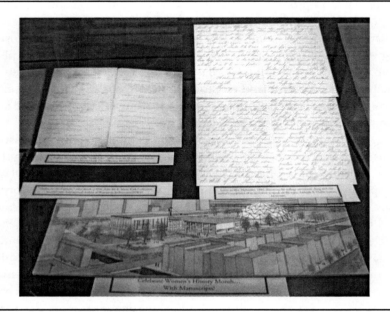

Source: Photograph by the author.

Supporting any kind of exhibit requires a time commitment from the department. At least one archivist should be focused on planning, coordinating, and arranging exhibits as part of their job responsibilities. For example, the lead reference archivist for the department may want to begin a lecture series to occur each spring semester. The thematically based series might feature between three and five speakers during the semester. Each lecture includes a presentation, a reception, and an adjacent exhibit related to the topic. This kind of event planning requires the department to have access to a public space where presentations can be held, usually somewhere in the academic library with close proximity to the academic archives. Some academic archives are fortunate to have their own presentation space, or they can reconfigure their reading room to accommodate small- to medium-sized audiences.

OUTREACH AND ADVOCACY

Building on the theme of the reading room as a place, academic archives can use their physical spaces for other kinds of campus and community outreach (Hunter, 2003). In the case of land-grant institutions, outreach may also be defined as service to the community and oftentimes the state. Many colleges and universities, both public and private, make service an integral part of the institutional mission. This broader kind of outreach should be considered when planning for services, events, and collaborations.

One of the easiest ways to get students, faculty, and researchers interested in the archives program is to offer tours of the department and host open house events (Pugh, 2005). Figure 8.3 shows a tour group of cadets to special collections. For decades, archivists decried the idea of offering stacks tours, largely for security reasons. As a result only other archivists may have had the privilege of a "behind-the-scenes" tour of other archives. Offering daily or impromptu tours to researchers helps break down barriers of access and

---

Making Outreach Part of Academic Archives

- Emphasize that the reading room is a place for researchers to meet.
- Emphasize that the academic archives is a place for the exchange of scholarly ideas.
- Offer tours of the stacks and the department.
- Offer spaces for relevant campus and community groups to hold meetings or events.

Figure 8.3
Cadet Corps Visit to Special Collections

Source: Photograph by Marc Brodsky.

misconceptions about special collections departments. Donors or potential donors to academic archives are particularly interested in seeing where their collections might be stored. Literally taking nonarchivists to the physical location of the material helps educate about the challenges of collecting, managing, and accessing collections.

Internal meeting spaces in academic archives have multipurpose uses. While the use of the reading room for events may be limited to after normal operating hours, a separate space has much greater possibilities. In these spaces, academic archives may sponsor dinners for select potential donors, host receptions for the opening of new collections, hold lectures by distinguished academic scholars, and teach basic sessions on how to conduct archival research (Wilsted, 2007). Even more practical, a meeting room can be used for departmental and library gatherings, planning sessions with faculty and students, and a space to discuss with donors the process of acquiring and processing collections.

Academic archives with a designated meeting area that is separate from the reading room have a distinct advantage to offer campus and community groups a useful meeting place. For example, academic departments at any sized school are always in need of meeting spaces for job candidate interviews, theses and dissertation defenses, lectures, and other functions. Such a meeting area can be used for classroom instruction using primary sources followed by actual class meetings. Beyond campus departmental uses, a meeting space in academic archives can be shared with community groups, such as a local historical society, a club that is connected to a collecting strength, or an alumni-based organization (Hunter, 2003). Academic archives should be selective about who can use their spaces, giving the highest priority to events that support the program.

Supporting the archives program through events in the reading room is a form of advocacy. Further, all public interactions and outreach should be seen as opportunities for promoting the purposes of the archives. While all segments of academic archives advocate the mission, vision, and purposes of the program, it is through in-person and virtual interaction with the public that the greatest amount of archival advocacy can occur (Hackman, 2011). Archival advocacy happens in visible and invisible ways, which may bring immeasurable positive effects to an archival program. For example, a public lecture from a Nobel laureate cosponsored by the academic archives may have little to do with the collections and research that takes place in the reading room on a daily basis, but the archives played an important role in planning and sponsoring the event. Attending the event is a noted scientist on campus, who three years later decides to donate papers to the archives and endow a position to support that area of collecting. Other attendees at the

> **Simple Advocacy for Archives**
>
> - Collaborate frequently with groups, campus departments, and other potential supporters.
> - Sponsor public events with the potential for a large audience.
> - Understand how decisions are made in the library and on campus, and find ways to collaborate with the decision makers.
> - Pay attention to politics and how local, state, and federal legislation affects archival programs.
> - Identify whom or which organization to ask for support.
> - Ask for support when support is needed.

lecture may appear in the reading room just days later to ask about services, collections, and how to make a donation.

While advocacy for archives most often unfolds on a national stage, it is important for academic archivists to recognize the value of local, state, and regional promotion of their archival programs. Advocating for archives starts in the reading room with researchers and continues throughout the academic library and across campus. Understanding how the institution's administration operates and who has the true ability to make changes on campus is central to spreading the good word about archives. While many archivists are resolved to remain apolitical, it is important that archivists understand politics in order to effectively advocate for their program (i.e., requesting new spaces, funding, and positions). For most archivists, being able to ask for such resources is usually more difficult than explaining the real value of archives.

CONCLUSION

The public side of an academic archives program encompasses reference services, the reading room, a virtual reading room, exhibits, public events, instructional sessions, and outreach. More broadly defined as research services, this part of academic archives is the most recognizable part of the program. Through research services, academic archives create public awareness for the program, attract supporters, collaborate with others in the library, and assist a range of researchers. The physical and virtual reading rooms may be the only part of the archives that researchers experience, which makes their design and ease-of-use imperative.

Academic archivists focused on research services have a range of responsibilities. They frequently interact with in-person and virtual researchers, offer researchers suggestions and services, monitor the actual and virtual reading rooms, guide groups on tours of the archives, host displays and exhibits, plan events, teach instructional sessions, build user-friendly and content-rich websites, and promote the academic archives program to a large audience. Both on campus and off campus, academic archivists promote their collections and services through collaborative projects.

The most successful academic archives programs have a recognizable public presence and robust research services. Academic archives create interest in their programs through outreach and collaboration, which results in advocacy for the archival program. Archives programs build research services by considering the needs of their researchers, knowing the content of their collections, and frequently assessing the effectiveness of their services. Research services are most successful when they are fully integrated in the other activities of the archives and the academic library. Emerging technologies allow academic archives to promote their services and collections to a range of researchers. But as the following chapter explains, technology and digital content creates challenges for academic archives and archivists.

REFERENCES

Chute, Tamar. 2008. "Perspectives on Outreach at College and University Archives." In *College and University Archives: Readings in Theory and Practice*, edited by Christopher J. Prom and Ellen D. Swain, 137–154. Chicago: Society of American Archivists.

Cohen, Laura B., ed. 1997. *Reference Services for Archives and Manuscripts*. Binghamton, NY: Haworth Press.

Cox, Richard J. 1992. *Managing Institutional Archives: Foundational Principles and Practices*. Westport, CT: Greenwood Press.

Crews, Kenneth D. 2008. "Perspectives on Outreach at College and University Archives." In *College and University Archives: Readings in Theory and Practice*, edited by Christopher J. Prom and Ellen D. Swain, 227–243. Chicago: Society of American Archivists.

Davison, Stephen. 2009. "If We Build It, Will They Come? Strategies for Teaching and Research with Digital Special Collections." *RBM: A Journal of Rare Books, Manuscripts, and Cultural Heritage* 10, no. 1 (Spring): 37-50.

Finch, Elsie Freeman. 1994. *Advocating Archives: An Introduction to Public Relations for Archivists*. Metuchen, NJ: Scarecrow Press.

Gilliland-Swetland, Anne J. 1998. "An Exploration of K–12 User Needs for Digital Primary Source Materials. *American Archivist* 61 (Spring): 136–157.

Greene, Mark A. 2010. "Improving Accessibility for People with Disabilities." *Archival Outlook* (November/December): 10–11.

Hackman, Larry J., ed. 2011. *Many Happy Returns: Advocacy and the Development of Archives*. Chicago: Society of American Archivists.

Hendry, Julia. 2007. "Primary Sources in K–12 Education: Opportunities for Archives. *American Archivist* 70 (Spring/Summer): 114–129.

Hirtle, Peter B. 2011. "Copyright Term and Public Domain in the United States, 1 January 2011." Cornell University, Copyright Information Center. Last updated January 3. http://copyright.cornell.edu/resources/publicdomain.cfm.

Hunter, Gregory S. 2003. *Developing and Maintaining Practical Archives*. 2nd ed. New York: Neal-Schuman.

Johnson, Greg. 2006. "Introducing Undergraduate Students to Archives and Special Collections." *College and Undergraduate Libraries* 13, no. 2: 91–100.

Kurtz, Michael J. 2004. *Managing Archival and Manuscript Repositories.* Chicago: Society of American Archivists.

Maher, William J. 1992. *The Management of College and University Archives.* Chicago: Society of American Archivists.

Pacifico, Michele, and Thomas P. Wilsted, eds. 2009. *Archival and Special Collections Facilities: Guidelines for Archivists, Librarians, Architects, and Engineers.* Chicago: Society of American Archivists.

Pugh, Mary Jo. 2005. *Providing Reference Services for Archives and Manuscripts.* Chicago: Society of American Archivists.

Robyns, Marcus C. 2001. "The Archivist as Educator: Integrating Critical Thinking Skills into Historical Research Methods Instruction." *American Archivist* 64 (Fall/Winter): 363–384.

Schmiesing, Ann, and Deborah R. Hollis. 2002. "The Role of Special Collections Departments in Humanities Undergraduate and Graduate Teaching: A Case Study." *Portal: Libraries and the Academy* 2 (July): 465–480.

Stielow, Frederick. 2003. *Building Digital Archives, Descriptions, and Displays.* New York: Neal-Schuman.

Tally, Bill, and Lauren B. Goldenberg. 2005. "Fostering Historical Thinking with Digitized Primary Sources." *Journal of Research on Technology in Education* 38, no. 1 (Fall): 1–21.

Theimer, Kate. 2010. *Web 2.0 Tools and Strategies for Archives and Local History Collections.* New York: Neal-Schuman.

Traister, Daniel. 2003. "Public Services and Outreach in Rare Books, Manuscript, and Special Collections Libraries. *Library Trends* 52, no. 1 (Summer): 87–108.

Trinkaus-Randall, Gregor. 1995. *Protecting Your Collections: A Manual of Archival Security.* Chicago: Society of American Archivists.

Turcotte, Florence. 2006. *Public Services in Special Collections.* Washington, DC: Association of Research Libraries.

Visser, Michelle. 2006. "Special Collection at ARL Libraries and K-12 Outreach: Current Trends." *The Journal of Academic Librarianship* 32 (May): 313–319.

Wherry, Timothy Lee. 2008. *Intellectual Property: Everything the Digital-Age Librarian Needs to Know.* Chicago: American Library Association.

Whittaker, Beth M., and Lynne M. Thomas. 2009. *Special Collections 2.0: New Technologies for Rare Books, Manuscripts, and Archival Collections.* Santa Barbara: Libraries Unlimited.

Wilsted, Thomas P. 2007. *Planning New and Remodeled Archival Facilities.* Chicago: Society of American Archivists.

Yakel, Elizabeth. 2008. "Managing Expectations, Expertise, and Effort While Extending Services to Researchers in Academic Archives." In *College and University Archives: Readings in Theory and Practice,* edited by Christopher J. Prom and Ellen D. Swain, 261–286. Chicago: Society of American Archivists.

9

Digital Frontiers and Electronic Challenges for Academic Archives

INTRODUCTION

During the past two decades, advances in technology have greatly changed the work of academic archivists. As modern communication has become more electronic and less paper based, an increasing number of electronic formats and digital issues confront archivists. The field of electronic records requires archivists to apply paper-based archival theories and develop new theoretical approaches to managing electronic materials. Because software, operating systems, equipment, formats, and file types change so quickly, archivists must remain connected to the information technology community.

Emerging technology has also allowed academic archivists to improve public services, program awareness, outreach efforts, and develop standard archival cataloging tools such as Encoded Archival Description (EAD) and Describing Archives: A Content Standard (DACS). Technological advances have allowed academic archivists to launch online digital projects and deliver digital renderings of their original materials to online users. Through successful digital projects, often grant funded and interinstitutional, academic archives have evolved into producers of electronic records.

As more information has become available electronically, academic archivists have adapted to technological shifts and developed new ways of conceptualizing archives and managing records. Their role in the academic library as digital curators of campus information will only grow in the coming decades. This chapter describes complicated technological issues faced by academic librarians and archivists including managing electronic records, participating in digital projects within the academic library, launching digital projects, providing access to archival collections, and collaborating with other information professionals. These challenges and opportunities set the stage for the future for academic archives. This chapter seeks answers to the following questions:

1. How do academic archivists identify, collect, preserve, and provide access to electronic records?
2. How do academic archives build digital assets that have long-lasting value?
3. How can academic archives use technology to better reach and meet the needs of their researchers?

ELECTRONIC RECORDS

Definitions and Concepts

The variety of electronic communications, materials, and formats has blurred the very definition of an electronic record. In paper-based environments an archival record is defined as recorded information with content, structure, and context that is preserved because of its enduring value (Hunter, 2003). However, electronic records are much more complex and require special considerations for preservation and long-term access. Unlike paper records, with electronic materials there is an ongoing challenge to preserve the storage media, the software and possibly the hardware needed to access the information, and the security and integrity of the recorded information (Saffady, 2009). Effective management of electronic records depends on a clear understanding of how those materials were created, stored, and made retrievable.

The concept of an electronic record begins with its creation. Campus electronic records are created by individuals, committees, departments, administrative offices, and students for multiple and sometimes overlapping purposes (Tibbo, 2008). The added challenge for academic archivists is to collect the scheduled official records and capture selected unofficial electronic records. A large majority of the electronic records created at colleges and universities are only needed for short-term purposes (i.e., simple communication between students, draft reports, and online class assignments). Only a fraction of electronic records generated by an academic institution should or must be kept. Too often, an unnecessary amount of electronic records are retained by the institution, simply because ample and inexpensive electronic storage space is available. As a result, academic archives become responsible for enormous sets of files and data sets with little archival or historical value. The academic archivist should remain focused on the electronic records that have long-lasting historical value or are scheduled by records management for retention (Bearman, 1994).

At this stage, the creator (i.e., a person, an institution, or even a computing system) generates data that is recorded within a specific electronic file type. These files may include spreadsheets, databases, word processing files, images, audio recordings, and e-mail messages (Saffady, 2009). The data within these files may be structured or unstructured. For example, a database file contains data in well-defined fields and would have a good deal of structure, while a word processing file with various kinds of text, numbers, or formatting would be unstructured. The data is electronically encoded as a file and then stored or saved for future uses.

After an electronic record has been created, it is stored on some type of media. Storage media can be magnetic, optical, or solid state depending on the type of file and computing system (Saffady, 2009). The most obvious place to store an electronic file is on the hard drive of the computer on which it was created. However, important files should be duplicated on to additional storage media in case the computer's hard drive fails or is corrupted. Common external media devices include removable hard drives, USB flash drives, recordable CDs, and, if created a decade or more ago, floppy disks. These storage media devices are popular because they are portable, have large amounts of storage space, and provide easy access to electronic files.

> **Characteristics of Electronic Records**
>
> - Created in the normal course of business or operations
> - Evidence of communication or a transaction
> - Created using hardware and software
> - May be structured or unstructured
> - Saved as a type of file on storage media
> - May be retrieved for further use
> - Management of files with long-term archival qualities by the archives

Since the beginning of campus computing, colleges and universities have backed-up their most valuable electronic records using mainframe computer networks. However, within the past two decades college and universities have relied on more localized networks and centralized servers to provide frequent back-up of electronic files (Dow, 2009). The most recent change to large centralized approaches to managing electronic records is the rise in cloud computing back-up methods. By using off-site electronic records storage options, colleges and universities avoid the frequent maintenance of computer hardware and software back-up systems. But relying on third-party sources for storage, maintenance, and retrieval brings into question the security of the data.

Once a file is created and stored, then it must be accessible for retrieval and further processing. For example, the president of a small college creates an assessment tool such as a campus scorecard to measure progress. The scorecard begins as a file on the president's computer and the master file is placed on a college server where it is frequently backed up. As the details and results of the scorecard change, the president's office will update the file. If the records of the president's office are scheduled and monitored properly, the original file and subsequent versions of the scorecard will be retained on college computer servers. Unlike paper records, electronic files need not be physically nearby to be usable. But wherever they are stored (i.e., a server on campus, a local network, or an overseas data storage company) they must be kept in a technologically secure environment to avoid damage, theft, or corruption of the data (Hunter, 2000).

Archivists are often involved in the creation of on-campus repositories, which are a likely location for electronic records. Within academic libraries there has been a concerted effort to create and maintain institutional repositories, where faculty and departments can deposit their electronic files for scholarly access. Behind the public side of an institutional repository there is a preservation plan and a back-up system to ensure the security and longevity of the electronic records in the repository. Academic archivists are also involved in institutional and interinstitutional efforts to create "dark archives" to house the master files on multiple servers (Dow, 2009). Dark archives project are designed to store master files of multi-institutional projects on secure servers that have very limited access. Large-scale efforts such as book scanning, grant-funded digitization initiatives, and online journals frequently rely on a dark archives approach to preservation. These projects are designed to place master files in multiple locations

---

Electronic Records in Academic Archives

- Official records from scheduled department
- Other records from campus and off-campus sources
- Legacy electronic files
- Digital assets created by the academic library

to ensure longevity and preservation of significant electronic files and digital assets.

The numerous storage options for electronic records on campus challenge academic archivists to remain connected to the offices, departments, and faculty that they serve. Further, the rise of electronic communication services has resulted in colleges and universities with multiple departments and individuals outside of the library who are responsible for campus information management. Archivists may seek alliances with the school's chief information officer, records manager, or computer science faculty who are developing new technologies, to help identify archival electronic records and ways to provide secure long-term storage of those files (Dearstyne, 2002).

In addition to considering how to handle new electronic records, academic archives face the problem of storing and retrieving legacy electronic records. Archival collections are littered with obsolete storage media and unreliable equipment needed for retrieval of the files. Figure 9.1 shows an array of obsolete electronic storage media found in academic archives. Simply putting dozens of computer disks in a box at the end of

Figure 9.1
Obsolete Storage Media Found in Academic Archives

Source: Photograph by the author.

an archival or manuscript collection is not an effective approach to managing and preserving electronic records. This all too common practice in academic archives has resulted in millions of inaccessible electronic records rapidly deteriorating in already processed collections.

Even new collections coming from donors have electronic records that are difficult to retrieve and preserve for researchers. For example, manuscript collections coming from contemporary writers may feature hundreds of unpublished short-stories, all of which reside on eight-inch floppy disks. Faculty papers are another common source of mixed media collections, which may include ten boxes of files covering the first two decades of their career and five boxes of computer disks that cover the last decade of their career. While not official records of the institution, these kinds of electronic records are unique electronic resources that should be included in the larger electronic records management plan for the academic archives program (Davis, 2008).

A Management Plan for Electronic Records

The management of electronic records on campus and in pre-existing collections requires academic archivists to be more proactive and technologically savvy than when working with paper records. Unlike boxes of textual records that arrive according to records schedules or donor visits, the planning for electronic records must take place often before those materials are even created (Dollar, 2000). Defining who has created or will be creating the records is the initial challenge of managing electronic records. Once those creators and their collections have been identified, the archivist must appraise the electronic records and decide which materials to acquire for the archives. Next, the electronic records plan must define a storage and retrieval component that ensures preservation, security, and long-term sustainability. Finally, an electronic records management plan must consider how researchers will access the material.

IDENTIFYING RECORDS CREATORS ON CAMPUS

A management plan for electronic records begins with the same kinds of archival theory (e.g., appraisal, evaluating research use, and possible access restrictions) and approaches used for paper-based collections. The first step in creating this plan is to identify key electronic records creators on campus. These records creators can be administrators, faculty, campus departments, and students. Official records are the primary grouping of electronic records to consider. If a records management program is in place and records schedules exist for many campus offices then it is likely that electronic records are already being collected and backed-up on institutional servers. However, the academic archivist needs to take an active role in designating which electronic records from official records groups are classified as archival (Bearman, 1994). These decisions may resemble the same kind of paper-based archival materials already scheduled for the archives, such as final reports, official correspondence, and selected committee minutes. And just like paper records, electronic files may contain personal, legal, financial, and personnel data. That information should be handled carefully, many times excluded from selection, or deleted or destroyed according to the records schedule (Saffady, 2009).

The unscheduled and unofficial electronic records created across campus may in fact be more voluminous and complicated than the official electronic records. These types of electronic records are often part of existing paper-based collections already in the archives. For example, the forestry department has a long relationship with its university archives and has been sending paper records to the archives for dozens of years. In the past five years, most of the faculty activity reports, the department's annual report, bi-annual newsletters, and official syllabi for courses are stored electronically. The archivist and the department head should decide which of these kinds of formats and files have long-term value and how those materials can be safely transferred to the archives. Taking all files from servers just because it is an easy process and storage space is plentiful is a poor approach. Instead, collective decisions between the leader of the unit and the academic archivist about what materials possess archival value will make the later steps of managing these records much more efficient.

Selecting Electronic Records for Archives

- Identify record creators and other sources of material.
- Select any material that is mandated by law to be retained permanently and others that have value.
- Work with records managers and department heads to target material.
- Include material from diverse groups with unique perspectives.
- Evaluate potential research uses.
- Consider file types, formats, and the equipment needed to retrieve the information.
- Cooperate with campus information technology to plan for long-term storage.

An electronic records management plan must account for existing and future digital assets as well as legacy electronic records already in processed collections (Hunter, 2000). The academic library itself is the most obvious source of existing electronic records for archivists to consider. Academic libraries create large amounts of digital files, whether as electronic texts, online journals and newsletters, webpages, the online catalog, and administrative files. Like other campus departments, only a small portion of the electronic records created and managed by the library should be selected for the archives.

While academic libraries are centers of information, not all of that information is the responsibility of the academic archives. For example, digital files created by the library, such as scanned photographs, books, and other unique resources, are likely candidates for long-term electronic record storage. Electronic files from library administrators and faculty, such as annual reports, collection statistics, and scholarly publications, are another possible collecting area. On the contrary, many of the main reference resources of an academic library, such as proprietary databases and subscription-based online journals, represent third-party digital assets that are inappropriate choices for the archives and may violate license agreements. Thinking about long-term uses, academic archives may choose to save snapshots of the library's website, selective e-mails regarding important announcements, files from significant library committees, or electronic material that documents a major library initiative (Dow, 2009).

Outside of the academic library there are numerous campus sources of valuable electronic records. Departments, programs, and campus organizations that are not scheduled through records management may have significant electronic assets with potential historical value. For example, the faculty women's club at a large university has been in existence for decades and has been a frequent donor of paper-based material to the archives. However, the organization's leaders have been documenting the past decade of their activities using a digital camera and a laptop. In this case, the archivist may encourage the creators of the electronic files to do some initial selection, or appraisal, before transferring the most significant images and files to the archives. Perhaps the most difficult part of working with these kinds of records creators (i.e., periphery individuals and groups who would not be scheduled under a full records management program) is the reality of limiting these records in favor of electronic materials coming from other campus sources.

The unexpected or surprise electronic records creators may be the most problematic. For example, an archivist acquires a small collection of material from an alumna documenting her work as a reporter for the campus newspaper during the early 1990s. The donor, now a professional journalist, donated five boxes of research notes, page-proofs, and drafts specifically related to her coverage of a controversial decision to tear down a historic campus building to make way for a new athletic facility. During the accessioning process, the archivist discovers that there are several dozen labeled computer disks with files of unpublished articles relating to the controversy. Since the files are unpublished and the content is not in printed form within the collection, the archivist must decide how to preserve these electronic materials on a more reliable storage media. Collections with mixed formats are common in academic archives and those collections frequently contain electronic records with unique content possessing archival value (Roe, 2005).

Appraising Electronic Records

It is the responsibility of an academic archivist to evaluate, or appraise, incoming or potential collections of archival material. Appraisal is the process of selecting material that contains important historical evidence with potential research value for addition to the archives. Archival appraisal for official records, manuscripts, family papers, electronic materials, or any kind of potential donation can be done at the collection, creator, series, file, or item level (Pearce-Moses, 2005). Because each collection is unique, academic archivists must determine which level of appraisal is most appropriate. The scope, size, and significance of the collection help determine how to appraise a collection. Archivists must also consider the availability of storage spaces, staff time for processing, needed equipment and software to access the electronic materials, and what kind of access points will be needed for researchers to effectively use the collection.

Depending on the type of academic institution and how that college or university is funded, there are rules regarding which electronic records must be permanently kept in the archives. Legal mandates may also require an archives program to retain certain kinds of records from specific campus units (McLeod and Hare, 2006). For example, a state-funded university is governed by a gubernatorial-appointed board of trustees. The minutes, records, and official files generated by the board of trustees may stretch back 100 years and the paper-based materials are the largest record groups in the school's archives. State law may require the archives to keep the records of the school's board of trustees permanently. The addition of electronic records to the record group represents an ongoing commitment from the archives to document the activities of the board of trustees.

Archivists adapt paper-based archival theories and practice into realistic approaches to managing electronic records, especially in the area of appraisal. When appraising electronic records, archivists select more broadly and usually with less examination than when appraising paper-based records. Because of the enormous volume of electronic material, archivists often appraise electronic records at the collection or series level (Pearce-Moses, 2005). At these top levels, the resulting inventories may list the name of the creator of the materials, followed by a simple list of file names. As a result, the description of the records may be very brief.

In many cases, appraisal of electronic records is merely the

> **Appraisal of Electronic Records**
>
> - Consider scope, size, and significance of the collection.
> - Choose an appropriate level of appraisal, usually at the collection or series level.
> - Determine the potential research uses.
> - Avoid taking large sets of data and files without some kind of content analysis.
> - Create a basic inventory of selected files with some description of content.

process of transferring the files from campus units to the archives, with no real examination or sampling by the archivist. In the case of official records that are scheduled for the archives, there is little need to select and de-select material since the files coming to the archives have already been designated as archival. The unofficial electronic materials coming from other campus and noncampus sources pose the problem of varying formats, file types, and storage devices. Appraising electronic records on computer disks manufactured more than thirty years ago may be difficult since the hardware and software needed to access the files may no longer exist (Saffady, 2009). Another factor to consider is that collections often contain identical documents or items in both paper and electronic formats. Deciding which format to keep can be difficult and often the archivist retains both versions.

Because of these realities many academic archives have massive collections of electronic records that have never been closely examined or prepared for researcher use. This kind of limited appraisal evolved because of the practicality of the acquisitions process for electronic records. For example, acquiring 300 gigabytes of data can be done easily because electronic storage space is inexpensive, whereas an archivist would avoid taking a 30-box collection without closer examination of the contents.

But in both cases, there is an investment of time and resources to manage and provide access to these materials. Accepting 300 gigabytes of electronic material for the archives represents a commitment to store, migrate, and preserve the data in perpetuity.

When archivists take in large amounts of electronic files, there should be a basic level of appraisal. Without an understanding of the content within the files, processing archivists will have a difficult time creating useful descriptions for researchers and understanding the structure of the data. Through a closer examination of the files, archivists can recognize important contextual information and the relationships between different files (Guercio, 2001). Basic appraisal of electronic records should also attempt to identify files that are damaged, compressed, or collapsed. Over time the structure of electronic records may change, so archivists must ensure that the content of the files is authentic, accurate, and secure. Applying some level of appraisal to electronic records will improve the arrangement and description of the materials, their long-term preservation and migration, and access by researchers.

Storing Electronic Records

Once records and their creators have been identified and materials selected, the archivist must plan for the storage needs of the electronic materials. Before transfer of material to the archives, electronic records exist as files on a variety of storage media. For official records, files usually begin on individual computers and then are backed up on servers or tape drives maintained by the institution. The unofficial records coming from unscheduled departments or from individuals on campus may only exist on the hard drives of individual computers or on external drives. Other electronic files identified as having archival or historical value may only exist on CDs, flash drives, or outdated floppy disks. The electronic records that have not yet been created may pose unique storage challenges, especially because storage options and back-up systems are frequently changing.

The transfer of electronic files from department, office, group, or individual to the archives is similar to the donation process for paper-based records. For official files, there is usually some kind of paperwork in need of review and signatures (Shepherd and Yeo, 2003). The unofficial files may require a simple deed of gift form to complete the transfer of ownership to the archives, especially when electronic files are part of a larger collection of paper, images, publications, and other traditional archival formats. Archives acquire electronic files through multiple methods using different storage options. Files may be transferred electronically from one server to another server, they might be uploaded to a secure website for downloading, they may arrive on an external hard drive, or they might be on floppy disks left in a large box outside of the door of the archives.

When archives acquire new electronic records the archivist must first assess the existing storage media and determine a long-term

> **Working with Selected Electronic Records**
>
> - Secure transfer or deed of gift document for materials.
> - Identify formats and file types.
> - Decide how to best store and retrieve electronic files.
> - Migrate files on unstable media to more reliable storage devices.
> - Attempt to identify files that are damaged, compressed, or collapsed.
> - Monitor the security and stability of electronic records.

storage solution. It is the archives' responsibility to maintain the original content, context, and structure of electronic records (Saffady, 2009). Storage solutions for electronic records must account for preservation, migration, deterioration of data, security, and long-term sustainability. Different types and formats of electronic records may in fact have different storage solutions. For example, three series of electronic records from a past university president would likely be stored in a frequently backed-up repository, while five years of electronic publications from the anthropology department on ten floppy disks could be transferred to a library storage server. Access to resources, legal liability and obligations, and the strength of campus technology are other important factors in finding long-term storage solution for electronic records. However, there are a few common storage options available at most colleges and universities.

Relying on campus servers is the first option for long-term storage of electronic records. Even the smallest academic libraries have their own computer servers or access to campus servers to host such standard information resources as the library catalog, websites, and local or subscription databases. Receiving space on the secure part of the server is the most challenging, since the master files will need to be protected from unauthorized access. It is common for academic libraries to use multiple servers. In this approach the first server serves as a secure production area, where master files are housed and authorized users (i.e., catalogers and web developers) can update or add new files. This first server may in fact be backed up to an external institutional server on a routine basis. The production server also communicates with a public or access server, which houses copies of the files, the user interface, webpages, and the databases that users access when they use the library's electronic resources.

There are distinct advantages of placing electronic records with archival value on library or institutional computer servers. If managed correctly, the multiple server approach allows for preservation, security, routine back-ups of master files, addition of new material, and separate access for researchers (Saffady, 2009). This approach also encourages close cooperation between archivists and other information professionals. It is not uncommon for archivists to keep the original storage devices containing the files, but once those files are copied to a secure server then their focus is to work with others to ensure the migration and ongoing maintenance of the files on the server.

One of the most recent approaches to electronic records storage is reliance on some kind of repository, often a shared institutional repository where numerous departments, faculty, and campus units store their electronic material. An institutional repository is a centralized approach to managing and accessing the digital assets of a college or university (Zach and Peri, 2010). Repositories are built on a multiple-server system, and their strength is that they allow numerous creators to manage their own digital files and provide different levels of access for the users and the creators. For example, a medium-sized state university has an institutional repository where faculty, staff, and administrators can share short-term materials (i.e., course materials, campus-wide memoranda, and announcements) with the campus, while also saving more important digital files (i.e., syllabi, departmental policies, and staff evaluations) into a more secure part of the repository. Institutional repositories also allow numerous creators to easily add materials, which results in digital content documenting a wide range of activities, topics, and functions—some that have long-term archival value and some with only short-term uses.

Often the academic library is the host or a key player in the operation of an institutional repository. Traditionally, academic libraries and archives have served as the repository for their institution's paper-based materials. In the digital age, academic libraries and archives collect the digital assets and publications of their institution. Across all types of academic institutions, the once print-only publications, such as course catalogs, theses and dissertations, student and faculty handbooks, yearbooks, and newsletters have become predominantly electronic. Because these and other electronic publications need to be accessible to the campus and community, the library is an obvious place to store, preserve, and mitigate access to these materials. Further, academic libraries have become producers of digital collections, supporters of freely accessible digital content, and sponsors of electronic scholarly publishing (Yiotis, 2005).

An institutional repository approach offers academic archives a manageable and flexible virtual space for electronic records. This system allows archivists to upload legacy electronic records from archival collections, highlight online collections, and provide greater access to frequently requested digital files (Zach and Peri, 2010). In particular, institutional repositories are most useful for storing and providing access to official and unofficial institutional records. Because institutional repositories are designed to mirror their institution's administrative and academic structure, digital files are stored and arranged according to the office or department where they were created. For example, an oceanography professor uploads digital images, scans of handwritten research notes, and an unpublished manuscript related to his career-long study of the effects of oil spills on the Gulf of Mexico ecosystem to the university's institutional repository. Those files will become part of the digital materials for the earth sciences department in the college of science. An archivist may designate portions of the professor's files as having archival value and recommend those files for long-term storage.

> **Storage Options for Electronic Records**
>
> - Multiple server method to provide secure storage and access
> - Institutional repository
> - Multi-institutional servers such as dark archives
> - Third-party systems, such as cloud computing models

Academic libraries also participate in repository projects involving other institutions. These repositories are designed to store common digital files, which are needed by numerous libraries, and master files from many institutions. For example, a journal scanning project between six small colleges results in online access to three dozen student literary magazines. A repository, based at one of the institutions, hosts the common files that all participating institutions can access and manages the master files on a secure server. Other interinstitutional repository projects, known as "dark archives," are designed to only store master files and other important electronic records in a secure electronic environment (Dow, 2009). Many grant-funded digitization projects rely on a dark archives approach as the main digital preservation plan for their master files.

The advantages of collaborating with others on campus and with other institutions are much greater than an academic archives program attempting to internally manage all of its electronic materials. Instead of building separate storage systems, academic archives should take full advantage of nearby resources. A solid library systems department, campus information technology units, or colleagues at other institutions are much better equipped to manage long-term digital files than a single academic archives program. By working with other departments and experts, the archives program becomes a more known and valued part of the electronic footprint of the campus, the profession, and the scholarly community.

There are also off-site and off-campus options for storing electronic records. The most recent development of cloud computing allows large amounts of electronic files to be uploaded through an Internet connection into a multiple servers operated by third-party data companies. While this approach is somewhat inexpensive, if not totally free, the lack of security and oversight of the data makes it a dangerous option for storing official records and legacy electronic records. A more secure, albeit more expensive option is to contract with an external vendor or company to store and manage the master files and other digital content. But again, there are always common dangers of placing official records and other electronic files in the custody of external organizations, no matter how secure their storage systems and servers might be.

The least reliable storage solution for electronic records is to keep the files on their original storage media (i.e., external drives or disks) and not copy the information to a more recent storage format, such as a CD. While this simple step seems obvious, it is important to remember that all storage and media devices deteriorate and will eventually fail. Creating high-quality duplicates of the original files on the most recent technology and media helps migrate the data to a more stable environment (Stielow, 2003). Migrating digital files is more than simply moving files from old to new servers. Rather, it requires an understanding of the structure of the data, how to preserve legacy software within different electronic environments, the institution's information architecture, the level of security for servers, and back-up mechanisms and schedules.

Wherever and however an archives program stores its electronic records and digital assets, the storage approaches should ensure preservation, security, and long-term sustainability. The ease of retrieval is an important aspect when considering storage options for electronic records. The process of retrieving files from a repository, a server, or a tape drive directly affects how the files will be migrated to newer technology and storage media (Dollar, 2000). The ongoing migration is crucial to sustaining the content, context, and structure of the digital material and preserving the information in the original file. Archivists want to not only store and preserve electronic records they want their researchers to have access to the information in those files.

Planning for Researchers

Once an appropriate storage solution for the electronic records has been identified, the electronic records plan must define how electronic records can be retrieved and accessed for use (Hunter, 2000). As noted above, the electronic records plan must consider how archivists can retrieve and update stored digital assets. How researchers will be able to retrieve and view the electronic records is also part of this planning. During all stages of electronic records management and systems design the academic archivist must keep in mind the needs of the researcher. The expected needs of researchers affect other parts of the electronic records management plan including records appraisal, public access, and delivery mechanisms.

During the selection of electronic materials archivists must consider the research potential of records. Official, unofficial, and other electronic records contain information that may document a transaction, provide evidence, or record some kind of event or activity (Hunter, 2003). Appraisal of electronic records is often a more automated process than the appraisal of paper-based materials. Because of the sheer volume of electronic files, it is common for archivists to examine only a small percentage of files. However, with certain types of structured electronic records it may be possible to search for specific content. Some structured records, such as database files, can be sorted and sampled easily if the native software used to create the files is available.

Archivists should not only appraise electronic records for specific content, but also consider how individual documents relate and connect to other documents (Roe, 2005). For example, a set of electronic correspondence from the religion department may appear routine and not worth retaining. However, at the time those files were written two professors in that department had resigned in protest of the college's decision to eliminate the faculty senate. As a parallel, correspondence files created by the tenth president of the college have initial value, but when those files are paired up with the correspondence from the religion department, these records have a much greater informational value. This example demonstrates the importance of historical context and the need to represent multiple perspectives in the holdings of an archives program. Reexamination of files in large record groups, especially in scheduled official materials, may also occur over time as new topics and research areas emerge.

In addition to appraising electronic records for potential research needs, academic archives must consider how to provide public access to electronic records without compromising the security and integrity of those files (Pugh, 2005). One approach is to have dedicated workstations available in the reading room for researchers to access electronic records. These computers are directly connected to servers where copies of the electronic files are retained. Other times electronic records workstations have specific software and hardware needed to access certain kinds of electronic records. Using the above example, a dedicated computer workstation in the reading room provides access to a database of official correspondence created by the tenth president of the institution (those files are located on a library-maintained server) and the computer can also read files from the religion department (those files were stored on Zip disks and a CD use copy has been created for access). The workstation approach improves security of the files while allowing in-person researchers access to electronic files.

Electronic Records and the Researcher

- Select material that has the greatest potential for researcher use.
- Recognize historical context and interrelationships between documents.
- Consider how the information in files can be searched, sorted, and sampled.
- Develop finding aids, guides, or other tools to assist the search process.
- Designate a workstation or an online location for researchers to access the files.
- For legacy records, provide the equipment and software needed to access the information.
- Create a user-friendly interface with strong searching capabilities.

More commonly, academic archives provide access to electronic records through online mechanisms, such as web portals, online databases, and digital projects. Creating such online access requires a content management system (CMS). These systems are either developed in-house as open source software programs or by purchasing a proprietary software package. In the former case, academic libraries are involved in numerous open source initiatives and often the software and programs are readily available. However, dedicated programming and technical staff are needed to make an open source CMS usable and reliable. The commitment of staff and other resources make a proprietary CMS an attractive option for academic libraries and archives to collaborate especially when a number of institutions are involved in purchasing an external software system and can share costs. The CMS system must protect online electronic files from harm and restrict any files that need to be suppressed from viewing.

Whether files are accessible through the web or through a workstation in a reading room, researchers should be able to easily search and retrieve electronic content. The interface and search functions allow researchers to explore digital collections through common keyword, title, author, subject, and name searching. The ability to browse files according to creator, subject, time period, or other delimiters will improve search results. Other traditional archival tools such as finding aids and inventories should also be connected to the searching process and the interface of the CMS.

Often researchers walk into the reading room with a topic that requires the use of electronic files. Academic archivists help guide the researcher to the appropriate record groups, unofficial electronic files, and other digital assets. They introduce researchers to the available search tools for electronic records (i.e., finding aids, databases, and search engines) and explain how to access these electronic materials (Pugh, 2005). The use of electronic records for research is increasing as the volume of electronic material acquired by academic archives rises. While the challenges of storing, preserving, and migrating electronic records is daunting, the need for long-term access to these materials will only increase.

DIGITAL PROJECTS AND ACADEMIC ARCHIVES

In the past two decades, academic libraries of all sizes have invested resources in the development of unique digital assets. Unlike official records originating in campus departments, these electronic files are created or managed by the academic library or archives for the purpose of research. Often the files become part of a digital collection focused on a specific topic, such as a collection of historical documents related to Native American treaties of the nineteenth century. Digital collections may start as a campus pilot-project, a grant-funded initiative involving multiple institutions, or as a result of research by a faculty member. The content from each digital project becomes part of the library's collection of digital assets. Academic libraries are defined as the creator of these digital materials, some of which are digital renderings of original sources or new born-digital materials.

Digital files created by academic libraries are a class of electronic records with great relevance for academic archives. For many academic libraries, their archival holdings are what define the library's unique physical and thus digital assets. Through digital projects, archival collections become accessible to countless researchers, students, and other academic libraries. Participation in digital projects helps meet the larger mission of access and outreach for the archives program. Further, the involvement of academic archivists in these digital projects is in fact part of campus electronic records management. Academic archives and archivists play a vital role in the development, production, maintenance, and long-term preservation of digital library projects.

Planning a Digital Project

The first phase of a library digital project is conceptualizing an online collection of material that directly supports a research or instructional need (Hazen, Horrell, and Merrill-Oldham, 1998). While access is an important principle of library and archival work, the deeper needs of researchers should drive the planning and discussions. Available unique archival materials are integral to developing digital projects. The materials found in archives (i.e., manuscripts, diaries, photographic images, and correspondence) have a direct influence on what kind of digital project can be developed. The formats themselves can define a digital project, such as an effort to scan newspapers during a certain period in a school's history or to digitize all of the yearbooks or course catalogs. The condition and frequent use of these formats may make a digitization project an attractive option to improve and increase access (Smith, 2001).

Too often, however, online projects are unfocused because leaders of the initiative do not equally and concurrently consider the needs of researchers and the availability of materials. For example, a group of historians, scholars, and librarians on a small college campus propose the idea to provide online access to original material related to the founding of their school's town. While the concept is sound, the college archives has only a small amount of original material for such a project and the original courthouse documents from that period were destroyed by fire. Broadening the scope of the project, searching for available archival materials at other repositories, and partnering with other institutions may be the only way the digital project can move forward.

Frequently librarians and archivists decide to digitize materials without working with specialists in the field or with on-campus faculty or departments. Such a project may result from the research interests of an archivist who wants to highlight specific items in their collections. Over time these various digital assets become part of a general digital collection, which may have little focus, appeal, and limited research interest. For example, over a five-year period a university archives digitizes a group of nineteenth-century senior theses, school pamphlets related to World War I, photographs of the renovation of the main campus library, and a dozen handwritten letters from students on campus during the 1950s. Individually these digital collections may have research potential, but combining them into some larger unfocused digital collection related to university history will only decrease the chances of researchers finding them. While creating access to the inaccessible collections in archives may create research use, building digital access for unclear audiences and unclear purposes is a poor use of resources (Hazen, Horrell, and Merrill-Oldham, 1998).

Having the right partners and stakeholders involved at the beginning of a digital project is just as important as understanding the needs of the researcher and what collections are available (Smith, 2001). While every digital library project that uses original material is unique, there are key individuals and perspectives to include in the planning group. Within the library there should be representatives from the archives, members of the cataloging or technical services department, select subject librarians depending on the scope of the project, and technicians from a systems or digital library department. The planning groups should also include campus representatives, including faculty with relevant subject expertise, teaching faculty who want to use the digital collection for in-class instruction, technical specialists from the information technology unit, and relevant faculty from the education department, especially if the project is designed for the K–12 audience (Hughes, 2004). Many digital projects involve off-campus representatives from other institutions, such as museums, other types of archives, government agencies, and professional organizations.

Defining Digital Projects

- Identify research or instructional needs.
- Select specific collections that support demonstrated research.
- Include a wide range of campus participants and experts during planning.
- Develop a clear list of objectives and outcomes for the project.
- Determine technical needs, available resources, and challenges.
- Secure the resources needed to produce and maintain digital content over time.

Some digital projects rely on subgroups or subcommittees to determine important matters such as technical standards, content selection, interface design, and educational outreach. During the planning stage the number of participants on the project may swell to over a dozen members before decreasing in size when the actual production begins.

Producing and Delivering Digital Content

The next phase of a project is the actual production of digital content. Having a coordinator for the project and a detailed work plan are the keys to effective production. A coordinator, who may be an archivist, manages the daily activities of the project and carries out a specific plan of work. This work plan includes the responsibilities of all the participants and subgroups, with target dates for completion of certain parts of the project (Hughes, 2004). There should also be funding to hire student or part-time employees to do the majority of the scanning. The process of scanning, working with digitized images, and applying metadata schemas is time consuming and requires a great deal of focus and workspace. The work plan should list any needed technical, human, office, and computing resources to complete the project's objectives.

Digital projects begin with a set of objectives (i.e., digitize 2,000 images from a heavily requested campus photograph collection) and often expand or contract according to the research demands and available resources (Stielow, 2003). Digitization projects are directly affected by technological developments, changing standards, and new approaches by academic libraries to provide electronic content to researchers. Because of these shifts, digital projects often develop in phases. In fact, many digital initiatives in academic libraries begin as pilot-projects and over time gain depth as new content and access tools are added. The idea of scaling or growing digital collections over a long period often means selected digitization from numerous collections rather than scanning large single collections in their entirety.

Academic archives programs play an important role in the creation of digital content. In addition to having unique materials, archives programs often serve as the actual location for the digitization and creation of digital files. Academic archives are logical locations for a production laboratory, which includes computers, book scanners, digital cameras, and other high-end digitization equipment. Keeping the original material within close proximity of the equipment improves security and decreases the chance of misplacing items. Locating such a digitization center within an academic archives department also builds on the strengths of academic archivists.

Academic archivists serve digital projects in multiple ways. First, their knowledge of the collections makes them both contributors and stakeholders in digital library projects. Archivists originate many of the concepts for digital projects because they know what materials exist and which collections receive the most attention from researchers. Such expertise often results in archivists selecting material to be digitized during the production phase. Even if an archivist has little

Managing a Digital Project

- Create and follow a plan of work.
- Designate a project coordinator.
- Hire student or part-time employees to do the majority of the scanning.
- Search for campus partners and collaborators at other institutions.
- Approach digital projects in phases.
- Keep current on technological shifts and new developments.
- Include archivists, especially during the selection, scanning, and contextualization of material.

knowledge of certain collections, they often know of faculty and scholars who are experts and can help assess the potential of collections for digitization. Archivists use this collective knowledge to help select collections and specific items for digitization.

The selection of material for digital projects is a subjective process that requires some level of oversight. Most projects rely on one or two experts, often archivists, to select material from archival collections for digitization. Those experts must understand the audience and goals of the project, while having a firm grasp on collection provenance and historical context (Stielow, 2003). For example, a digital project focused on antebellum politics in Missouri requires an expert who knows both the collections and the historical details of the period. Archivists are good choices for the role of content selector because they understand the needs of researchers, their collections, and the realities of digitization. The fragility and format of material, any possible restrictions on use of the collection (i.e., there is no deed of gift, the collection contains personal information, or the copyright holders are reclusive), and unclear provenance are common considerations when selecting archival content for digitization (Hoffman, 2001). Selectors should be wary of selecting material that is not original (i.e., photocopies or microfilm) and instead focus on the authentic and unique items contained in the archives. Finally, the process of digitizing the material, including the needed equipment, software, or technical expertise, is an important factor is selecting one document over another.

Throughout the planning and production phases of digital projects, leaders must not only solidify and adapt technical standards but also apply those standards to the actual work of digitization (Hughes, 2004). Archivists collaborate with others in the library and on campus during digital production, but frequently archivists are the technical experts as well as the project managers. They develop metadata schemas, search terms, and other tools to improve the ability to search digital collections. Archivists also oversee the scanning of material by determining technical standards for scanning, establishing practices and workflows, training staff and students on procedures, and ensuring that there is some level of quality control for digital assets. Finally, archivists are responsible for locating, retrieving, and returning all selected material to the archives.

Because archivists are involved in the technical details of creating digital assets, many archivists assist in the development of the public interface for digital projects. From the researcher's perspective, the quality of a digital collection is only as good as the ability to search and locate digital files. The design of the website, interface, search engine, and display options for a digital collection has a tremendous influence on connecting researchers with research materials (Hazen, Horrell, and Merrill-Oldham, 1998). Systems or digital library units are often the designers of the online public face for their libraries. However, archivists are frequently part of the project's team responsible for planning how digital projects will be presented.

All digital projects connected to an academic archives program should have a range of online tools to enhance the experience of the virtual researcher (Hughes, 2004). Those tools should support and complement the online content, without overpowering the purpose of the project. The ability to search across all digital projects, finding aids, and other online content from an academic archives program is perhaps the most powerful tool available for virtual researchers.

Special Funded and Multi-institutional Digital Projects

While many digital projects begin as internal academic library initiatives, expanding the effort to include other institutions often improves the quality of the digital content. Multi-institutional digital projects help connect the topics, people, and events in multiple collections that may be deposited at archives that are geographically disparate. From the perspective of a researcher, the ability to access multiple collections found at different archives represents enormous searching and research power. Similarly, archivists benefit from projects that include material from other repositories, especially when they are processing new collections, trying to determine provenance, and creating access tools for their researchers. Such interinstitutional digital projects are very attractive to granting agencies, which provide funding for equipment, staff, and other costs for worthwhile projects (Hughes, 2004).

Digital projects that involve more than one institution rely on the same principles of planning an internal or campus-based initiative. The institutions and the primary participants must collaborate, cooperate, and communicate. Technological collaboration between librarians, archivists, and programmers at different institutions is needed throughout a digital project. Similarly, archivists must work together to determine the overall content of their collections. Academic archivists have a unique perspective on what their researchers want and what collections exist. When archivists share this information with archivists at other institutions, clear patterns and shared objectives often emerge related to possible collaborative digital projects.

For example, an archivist at a small New England college may have a collection of photographs from a retired faculty member related to archaeological excavations in the 1950s at a site in Montana. Similarly, an archives program at a large university in Montana has a collection of photographs and documents related to the same excavations. In this fictitious example, both institutions have nationally known archaeology departments and there is constant research demand for the material at each archives program. Because of the overlap and the fact that the material is not duplicated elsewhere, archivists at each institution decide to create online access to both collections through one web-based project.

In addition to questions about selecting content, the two academic archivists work with web developers and technology support departments in their libraries to make sure they are building an online project that meets the technological requirements of their programs. Together, they pick the same metadata schema, or mark-up language, for scanned materials. They also make collaborative decisions about the design of the website or web portal, what kind of database will exist for the content, what kind of searching will be possible, which institution will virtually host the project, how each institution will add or update content to the project's site, and how digital files will be preserved or backed-up (Stielow, 2003).

Getting initial support from the administration, at both the library and institutional levels, is crucial to launching a successful collaborative digital project. Already existing consortiums of academic libraries may make collaborative projects between institutions much easier. Even with

> **Indicators of a Successful Multi-institutional Digital Project**
>
> - There is clear commitment of staff and resources from each institution.
> - A solid funding source, such as a federal or state grant, exists.
> - Digital collections are drawn from original sources at each institution.
> - Digital collections can be searched, sorted, and browsed in multiple ways.
> - The digital collection meets the research and instructional needs of many audiences.
> - Project leaders understand and use cutting-edge technology to provide access.
> - There is a clear preservation plan in place to protect and migrate the digital assets.
> - The project follows a promotion and outreach plan.
> - The project is updated and adjusted according to measured researcher needs.

a great range of expertise and support coming from collaborating institutions, there are other resources needed to support interinstitutional digital projects. Small collaborative digital initiatives may be able to work with little or no additional funding, instead relying on the reallocation of current staff and equipment. Other times, institutions designate or award funding to digital projects to help offset the costs of running a digital production unit. To save on costs and make the most of available resources, it is common for institutions to divide the responsibilities of hosting a server, operating a scanning center, and maintaining the web interface.

Many interinstitutional digital projects are funded by external grants. Federal and state agencies award millions each year to library-based projects that provide online access to original archival materials. The most attractive grant applications include multiple institutions (including not just academic, but private and government institutions as well), a focused but yet broad set of original materials, an effective educational outreach program, an assessment plan, and an approach to preserving the resulting digital master files (Hughes, 2004). Federal agencies such as the Institute of Museum and Library Services (IMLS), the National Endowment for the Humanities (NEH), and the National Historical Publications and Records Commission (NHPRC) have grant programs aimed at providing online access to original primary sources. Each state also has historical boards, other agencies, and statewide library programs with intermittent funds for digitization projects. These agencies fund projects that result in online collections of textual documents, museum pieces, objects, printed pieces, and photographic images, from the collections of museums, archives, historical societies, and private individuals.

Digitization grant projects require a great deal of time to conceptualize and propose. Participation from multiple institution means that the goals of the project must be clearly communicated and adjusted collectively. Once project leaders have identified the audience, the purpose of the project, and the likely collections to digitize, there is an intense period of assembling a grant application. It takes multiple drafts and close work with research offices on different campuses to prepare a grant proposal. The budget is perhaps the most difficult, sometimes contentious, and time-consuming piece of the application. A well-written narrative of the project and a realistic plan of work are essential parts of a grant application. Likewise, the personnel involved in the project (i.e., programmers, archivists, and subject experts) affect the strength of the proposal.

Just like internal projects, grant-supported digital efforts require careful planning to complete the work and ensure the long-term uses of the resulting collection. Many granting agencies require a detailed plan for creating access tools for a wide range of researchers. Using the previous multi-institution example, a project focused on three significant archaeological excavations in Montana during the early 1950s primarily provides researchers the ability to search and browse the digital collection. But the online project has much broader appeal with the addition of an online exhibit, links to K–12 lesson plans using selected materials, historical narratives about the excavations written by subject experts, present-day images of the locations, and a list of museums and archives with related material. The website allows archivists to announce events, publications, and project updates related to the virtual collection.

Promoting and Evaluating Digital Collections

Researchers are central to designing and improving digital collections. Guidance from the academic and research community should be a significant factor in the planning and management of online projects (Hazen, Horrell, and Merrill-Oldham, 1998). The needs and preferences of researchers influence the creation and maturation of digital collections. The creators of digital projects can better understand their intended audience by interacting with researchers through promotion, outreach, and ongoing assessment efforts.

Improving access to original materials through online access is important, but unless the scholarly and research communities are aware of the project there may be little use of the collection. Without some level of outreach and promotion, projects run the risk of becoming idle and unused. For example, an academic archives program creates an online collection of 500 printed pamphlets related to the five years prior to the American Revolution. The selected materials are rare, historically significant, and not previously available online. Project leaders create a complex full-text searching system to access the materials and quietly release the collection through the main academic archives' website. Within a few weeks the website and project has only attracted a handful of researchers and after six months of availability the usage statistics and reference requests reveal that the project is the most infrequently used online collection sponsored by the archives. Projects with high-quality content may be discontinued or halted simply because researchers have taken little interest.

> **Keeping Digital Projects Relevant and Active**
>
> - Develop and follow a promotion plan that targets many audiences.
> - Announce, advertise, and promote the project.
> - Create an assessment plan that involves targeted researchers.
> - Measure quality and usability of the project.
> - Use researcher feedback to make adjustments to the project.
> - Track the overall outcomes of the project, for both the users and the scholarly community.
> - Add new content and learning tools to the project.

Active promotion must accompany digital projects to make them viable resources for potential researchers. The first step is for project leaders to write a basic overview of the project that can be conveyed and reused through several outlets. At the department level, academic archives generate general announcements, newsletters, webpages, and targeted mail and e-mail lists for collections updates (Hackman, 2011). Promoting a new online collection through one of these methods is an effective and inexpensive way to increase awareness about digital resources. Many academic libraries have outreach librarians who communicate with the campus public relations office. Through that office, information about the digital project may become part of a press release, a radio interview, an announcement in a campus publication, or displayed prominently for a brief period on the institution's website. Both on-campus and off-campus publications are always in need of content to fill their pages, so seeking out newspaper columnists, editors of academic journals, and freelance writers is an easy way to promote the project. Finally, the creation of small online exhibits, featuring highlights from the digital materials, may appeal to researchers who want to browse the major contents of a collection.

Outreach is one aspect of promoting the project. All colleges and universities provide some level of campus and community outreach. Broadly defined, outreach allows the archives program to promote their collections and services directly to intended audiences (Pugh, 2005). With digital projects, academic archives can create strong relationships with teaching faculty, students, and the nearby community. For example, a small college archives creates an online project of campus and town buildings constructed during the 1930s by the Works Progress Administration (WPA). The collection includes original architectural drawings, printed and handwritten documents related to each building, images of construction, and correspondence from the WPA offices in Washington, DC. Programs in architecture and history will directly benefit from this collection, as well as members of the town council who are struggling with downtown redevelopment and historic preservation plans. Project leaders should connect with these audiences through events, classroom instruction using the collection, digital exhibits, and presentations to each group.

Measuring the quality and usability of online resources is a staple of academic libraries and archives. This concept of assessment is an important part of creating and refining digital projects. A common approach to assessing the quality and usability of digital collections is using focus groups and feedback surveys. The focus group approach randomly selects researchers to complete a pre-test, an online assignment using the digital collection, and a post-test to measure their ability to use the online project. This kind of evaluation tool can be part of the project's website and be open to anyone who wants to offer feedback. More targeted approaches involve selecting experts, scholars in the field, and advanced students for evaluation and their feedback. This method is particularly important when expanding a digital project, as archivists want to know which topics are of the greatest interest to researchers.

Outcomes-based assessment is another approach that tracks the results of how digital projects affected lives and patterns of researchers. For example, an online project related to the role of women in World War II attracts significant usage from K–12 history students working on National History Day projects. Outcomes-based assessment is designed to see how the K–12 students not only used the materials from the collection in the creation of papers and posters, but more important, how the project changed viewpoints and attitudes about gender roles in the classroom. This kind of evaluation involves long-term interaction with researchers, and has become a common requirement of grant-funded digital projects.

Overall, digital projects should have a well-defined audience and be centered on the needs of actual researchers. A dialogue between researchers and project leaders must occur in the early stages of developing a project and continue throughout the enhancement of a digital collection. Part of that dialogue is measuring the affects of a digital collection on the scholarly, campus, K–12, and local communities. Carefully planned events, promotional efforts, instructional sessions, and online tutorials are just a few approaches to generate a strong public awareness for digital projects (Pugh, 2005). Publicizing a digital project is more than just telling researchers about the collection; it is about demonstrating the usefulness of the project in the lives of many researchers. Ultimately, if a digital collection is not reaching an audience and has created little intellectual stimulation, then perhaps the resources needed to maintain and update the project would be better utilized elsewhere.

Long-Term Access to Digital Content

Once digital files are available for online researchers, archivists work with other members of the project team to provide long-term access to those materials. Like other electronic records, archivists must balance access with security of the files. The master files may become part of a dark archives or a secure server, while lower-resolution versions of the files are created and placed in a publicly accessible database of digital materials (Dow, 2009). When a researcher requests a high-resolution of an image, it is usually the responsibility of an archivist to grant that permission and retrieve the file. Thus, archivists should be well aware of the location of the electronic files, understand the protocol for handling copyright or permissions requests, and have selected an acceptable storage and retrieval plan (Stielow, 2003).

Long-Term Archival Considerations for Electronic Records

- Provide ongoing access to digital assets.
- Store digital master files in a secure and backed-up location.
- Migrate electronic records to the appropriate software and storage conditions.
- Ensure that the information in electronic records is secure, uncorrupted, and authentic.
- Be familiar with copyright and permission policies and procedures.

Because digital assets produced by an academic library are a kind of electronic record, the long-term management and preservation of these files falls under the purview of academic archives. Too often, the completion of a digital project leads project leaders to focus on other digital initiatives and quickly leave the ongoing maintenance of the files to the archives. Even more problematic for archives is that the master files for many of the first digital projects launched by academic libraries are housed on CDs or floppy disks, rather than backed-up on servers. All digital projects, whether they concluded 20 years ago or are being updated weekly, should be preserved in the archives.

Creating unique digital assets requires large investments of time and funding. The expectation of those involved in such digital initiatives is that their project will promote research, reach a large audience, and generate publicity for the library and the institution (Hughes, 2004). Just like archival collections, each digital project is different and will appeal to different audiences. Some projects will receive national attention, while others only get noticed by a handful of researchers. No matter how successful and popular digital projects become, they can become stagnant without promotion and careful attention to changes in software, file structure, technical standards, and needs of researchers (Hughes, 2004). Archivists play an important role in not only preserving master files of unique digital assets, but keeping digital projects updated and relevant.

CONCLUSION

Technological advances have brought great challenges and opportunities to academic archives. The shift from paper to electronic communication has resulted in a larger number of electronic files and formats arriving in archives. Thus, academic archivists must consider how to select, classify, preserve, and provide access to these digital materials. In the case of official electronic records, archivists must work closely with record creators, campus information technology experts, records managers, and department heads to ensure the retention of records with archival value. Archivists must also take responsibility for identifying and collecting unofficial electronic records that document the history of their institution. In addition to the problem of software and hardware obsolescence, archivists must find ways to migrate and preserve electronic files without sacrificing the authenticity and integrity of those records.

Digital assets created by an academic library are an important group of electronic records for academic archives. In many cases, academic archivists are involved in the creation of these digital files, especially when original materials (i.e., manuscripts, photographs, and diaries) from archival collections are scanned, encoded for searching, and made accessible through an online portal. Archivists serve as subject, collection, and technology experts on many digital projects. Their understanding of researcher demands, collection management, and the historical significance of materials under their purview, makes archivists key players in the creation of digital projects. Within the academic library, archivists can play a crucial part of planning for the curation of unique digital resources created by faculty, students, and staff. Further afield, many digital projects led by archivists stretch far outside of the academic library to include other campus units and archivists at other institutions.

Academic archives use technology to manage and build collections for a diverse audience of scholars, students, and supporters. In collaboration with other archivists, information professionals, and technology experts, academic archivists have developed national standards for managing electronic records, searching digital assets, and structuring discovery tools, such as online archival finding aids. Their efforts have resulted in proven approaches to identifying, capturing, migrating, preserving, and providing access to electronic records. Electronic records programs, collaborative online projects, and institutional repositories sponsored and led by academic archivists have put academic archivists on the forefront of the digital frontier.

REFERENCES

Bearman, David. 1994. *Electronic Evidence: Strategies for Managing Records in Contemporary Organizations.* Pittsburgh: Archives and Museum Informatics.

Davis, Susan E. 2008. "Electronic Records Planning in 'Collecting Repositories.'" *American Archivist* 71 (Spring/Summer): 167–189.

Dearstyne, Bruce W. 2002. *Effective Approaches for Managing Electronic Records and Archives.* Lanham, MD: Scarecrow Press.

Dollar, Charles M. 2000. *Authentic Electronic Records: Strategies for Long-Term Access.* Chicago: Cohasset Associates.

Dow, Elizabeth H. 2009. *Electronic Records in the Manuscript Repository.* Lanham, MD: Scarecrow Press.

Guercio, Maria. 2001. "Principles, Methods, and Instruments for the Creation, Preservation, and Use of Archival Records in the Digital Environment." *American Archivist* 64 (Fall/Winter): 238–269.

Hackman, Larry J., ed. 2011. *Many Happy Returns: Advocacy and the Development of Archives*. Chicago: Society of American Archivists.

Hazen, Dan, Jeffrey Horrell, and Jan Merrill-Oldham. 1998. *Selecting Research Collections for Digitization*. Washington, DC: Council on Library and Information Resources.

Hoffman, Gretchen McCord. 2001. *Copyright in Cyberspace: Questions and Answers for Librarians*. New York: Neal-Schuman.

Hughes, Lorna M. 2004. *Digitizing Collections: Strategic Issue for the Information Manager*. London: Facet Publishing.

Hunter, Gregory S. 2000. *Preserving Digital Information*. New York: Neal Schuman.

———. 2003. *Developing and Maintaining Practical Archives*. 2nd ed. New York: Neal-Schuman.

McLeod, Julie, and Catherine Hare. 2006. *How to Manage Records in the E-environment*. New York: Routledge.

Pearce-Moses, Richard. 2005. *A Glossary of Archival and Records Terminology*. Chicago: Society of American Archivists.

Pugh, Mary Jo. 2005. *Providing Reference Services for Archives and Manuscripts*. Chicago: Society of American Archivists.

Roe, Kathleen D. 2005. *Arranging and Describing Archives and Manuscripts*. Chicago: Society of American Archivists.

Saffady, William. 2009. *Managing Electronic Records*. 4th ed. Lenexa, KS: ARMA International.

Shepherd, Elizabeth, and Geoffrey Yeo. 2003. *Managing Records: A Handbook of Principles and Practice*. London: Facet Publishing.

Smith, Abby. 2001. *Strategies for Building Digitized Collections*. Washington, DC: Digital Library Federation and Council on Library and Information Resources.

Stielow, Frederick. 2003. *Building Digital Archives, Descriptions, and Displays*. New York: Neal-Schuman.

Tibbo, Helen. 2008. "The Impact of Information Technology on Academic Archives in the Twenty-First Century." In *College and University Archives: Readings in Theory and Practice*, edited by Christopher J. Prom and Ellen D. Swain, 27–51. Chicago: Society of American Archivists.

Yiotis, Kristin. 2005. "The Open Access Initiative: A New Paradigm for Scholarly Communication." *Information Technology and Libraries* 24, no. 4 (December): 157–162.

Zach, Lisl, and Marcia Frank Peri. 2010. "Practices for College and University Electronic Records Management (ERM) Programs: Then and Now." *American Archivist* 73 (Spring/Summer): 105–128.

Part III

The Future of Academic Archives

10

Emerging Trends and the Horizon for Academic Archives

INTRODUCTION

Making predictions can be dangerous, especially when changing technology and the availability of resources affect those forecasts. For archivists, there is a great deal of uncertainty about the future of the profession and the nature of archival work itself. At the beginning of the second decade of the twentieth century, the archival profession is faced with how to build programs and meet the demands of researchers during periods of unpredictable support, a host of unanswered questions about electronic records, and the transition of professional leadership from one generation to the next. These and other challenges are shared across the profession, and those challenges become more nuanced depending on the type of archival program.

Academic archivists, those who work in archives programs based in colleges and universities, represent one of the largest groups of the profession. Despite their great numbers and significant contributions to the profession, there is still great ambiguity and lack of unity in the subfield of academic archives. Few archival sources and leaders have articulated exactly who academic archivists are, what academic archivists do, how academic archivists are similar and different from other types of archivists, and what academic archival work may become in the future.

This chapter builds on what we know about today's academic archives and archivists and offers a glimpse into the future. At present a set of emerging trends have direct implications for academic archives and all professional archivists. Those trends help academic archivists make educated guesses, rather than predictions, about the future. By analyzing these developments this chapter confronts the complex question of:

"What will academic archivists and academic archives programs look like 20 years from now?"

PAST GUIDANCE

For more than 30 years academic archivists have relied on just a handful of sources for professional guidance. The first focused work on academic archives appeared in the late 1970s as a manual of basics for college and university archivists (SAA, 1979). Notable archivists, such as Ernst Posner, Maynard Brichford, and Nicholas C. Burckel, wrote more than a dozen chapters for the book. This work served as one of the few sources specifically for academic archivists until the publication of William J. Maher's comprehensive guidebook to managing college and university archives (Maher, 1992). Maher's book provided great detail about the basics of starting and managing a college or university archives program. While the book continues to have relevance, Maher devoted only a few dozen pages to the issues of electronic records and using technology to provide access to archival collections, which even in the early 1990s seems inadequate.

In the mid-2000s, a group of archivists in the Society of American Archivist's College and University Archives Section began work on an updated book of essays for academic archivists. That manual, published in 2008, nearly 30 years since the first reader, added important new voices and topics to the scant literature on working in college and university archives (Prom and Swain, 2008). At the same time, the College and University Archives Section also sponsored an online set of campus case studies, which continue to be added, to discuss issues with born-digital records (SAA, 2011).

While other sources on topics in academic archives exist, most notably Helen Willa Samuels's *Varsity Letters* (1992), academic archivists have often turned to more general

Standard Printed Sources on Academic Archives
• SAA's *College and University Archives: Selected Readings* (1979)
• William Maher's *The Management of College and University Archives* (1992)
• Helen Samuels's *Varsity Letters: Documenting Modern Colleges and Universities* (1992)
• Christopher Prom and Ellen Swain's *College and University Archives: Readings in Theory and Practice* (2008)
• "Campus Case Studies" (2008–present)

works on archives for answers to their questions. Academic archivists have also relied on literature in other fields such as records management, leadership, information and data management, library science, special collections librarianship, rare books and manuscripts, and computer science to supplement their work in the academic environment. What is missing in all of these focused and tangential works is a sense of the academic archives of the twenty-first century and the emerging trends that will affect academic archivists in the coming decades.

GUIDANCE FOR THE FUTURE

Today's academic archives programs are a vibrant part of their campuses and the archival community. The strongest of these programs contribute to the development of new technology, services and outreach in academic libraries, national archival standards, integrated library and campus functions, and documentary techniques to better understand their institution's history. The leaders of these programs have a wide range of skills, education, and a vision to better integrate their programs into the life of their campus, community, and profession. As a growing and influential subfield of the archival program, academic archives are setting the pace for other archives, library, and record management programs. The responsibilities of academic archivists are broad and reach across their program, their academic library, their institution, their profession, and their community (Figure 10.1).

Many of today's academic archives programs are contributing to the future of the field. Tomorrow's academic archives programs will be even more focused on developing and providing access to unique collections, services, and tools for their researchers, libraries, and institutions. Changing technology is a significant factor that will help redefine the possibilities of access and connectivity for archives programs. The need to better manage and share resources is another important factor that will allow archives programs to thrive, even during the worst of times. Programs that are able to demonstrate their relevancy, purpose, importance, and financial sustainability have the greatest opportunities to succeed. Advocacy, developing new technological skills, effective promotion, educating the public, and building programs with a clear strategy are just a few of the ways to overcome the challenges of the coming decades.

Recent trends in archives, libraries, and the academic environment point to clear directions and new possibilities in the field of academic

Figure 10.1
Overlapping Areas of Responsibility for Academic Archivists

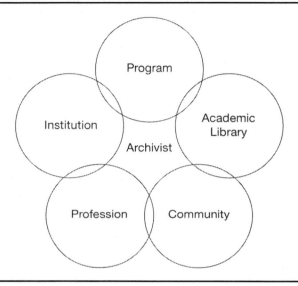

Source: Graphic by Marc Brodsky.

archives. The areas with the most potential may in fact offer the greatest challenges to academic archivists. The changing profile and responsibilities of academic archivists provide great opportunity for new leadership within academic libraries and the profession. While there are many emerging trends affecting all archivists, a handful of specific developments have the greatest potential to redefine the field of academic archives.

Archival Values

In 2012, there is a growing awareness of a shift in archival thinking and practice. This ongoing movement, known as "Archives 2.0," represents the systemic and interrelated changes in the archival world during the past two decades (Theimer, 2011). Some of the key points of Archives 2.0 include a focus on users, technology, assessment, standardization, engagement, advocacy, and openness (Theimer, 2011). In only the past few years, Archives 2.0 concepts have become mainstream values for the archival profession. The wide acceptance of Archives 2.0 demonstrates the evolution and maturation of the profession in reaction to changing demands (Theimer, 2011).

The attitudes and practices of tomorrow's archivists will build upon the already strong concepts of Archives 2.0. In particular, the next generation of archivists will be better collaborators (not cooperators), technical specialists (not generalists), entrepreneurs (not participants), teachers (not instructors), and activists (not promoters). Archivists will also be responsible for measuring the effectiveness of collections, services, and programs by assessing the outcomes of the research, rather than just collecting statistical data on reading room and collection usage. In the process, these values will result in yet another paradigm shift for the profession, which will focus even more on the needs of researchers and less on the needs of archivists.

These evolutions in the profession will be seen most readily in the ranks of the next generation of academic archivists. One example to illuminate shifting values is that academic archivists of the future will work closer with faculty, students, and researchers in the sciences to develop online collections, teaching modules, and

> **Next Wave of Archival Values**
>
> - Collaborators, not cooperators
> - Technical specialists, not generalists
> - Entrepreneurs, not participants
> - Teachers, not instructors
> - Activists, not promoters
> - Measuring outcomes, not statistics
> - Looking outward more than inward

research partnerships. The ability for archivists to become more involved in the work of scientific research on their campus creates limitless possibilities. With skills as digital technicians and content curators, academic archivists can become a crucial part of grant-funded research projects at college and universities, which will result in new resources for the archives program and the academic library. Collaborative projects will allow academic archivists to emerge as teachers of important content, such as digital curation and preservation and even subject areas represented in their collections. Archivists will advance the work of library assessment by effectively measuring the research experience and the outcomes of the completed research. Beyond grant and campus opportunities, archivists will become more entrepreneurial in their collaborations, seeking new external ways to support their programs and collections. In the process, academic archivists will take on a new role as activists for their program and the profession.

The Uniqueness Factor

The uniqueness of academic archives is an important part of understanding the future. Academic archives are unique for a variety of reasons. First, collections in academic archives are unique, rare, and one-of-a-kind resources. As academic libraries have become somewhat homogenous with their holdings of books, journals, and electronic database subscriptions, the materials in their special collections and archives units have defined the uniqueness of each academic library (Dooley and Luce, 2010). Certainly there is overlap in the collecting areas of special collections departments, but the need to document somewhat undocumented areas of social and cultural history—rather than just documenting the history of the institution—will result in an expansion of the kinds of original and unique material available to researchers in academic archives. As more unique collecting areas emerge, the types of research and researchers will expand and further define the uniqueness and unique holdings of each academic library.

In the future, newly acquired collections will be overwhelmingly electronic-only and academic archivists will have the responsibility to collect, preserve, maintain, and provide access to these digital materials. These future digital acquisitions will include not only official records, but research material, publications, data sets, and other historically significant material. The many challenges of dealing with new electronic formats will require archivists to develop unique skills to become an active part of the creation, management, and long-term preservation of digital materials (Walters and Skinner, 2011). At the same time, paper-based collections in academic archives will attain even more unique qualities and will be in constant demand from researchers. That reality will make digitization services a central part of the operations of all academic archives, and the practice of sharing paper-based collections with other nearby or topically similar archives programs. Academic archivists will manage their unique collections with a new array of digital tools to provide researchers with unprecedented access to, searching options for, and contextualization of archival materials. Storage of unique materials will become a balance of managing physical and electronic spaces.

The need to effectively manage and facilitate access to the unique resources of academic libraries will advance the trend of centralizing or merging individual archival units into a singular special collections department. As academic libraries further realize the potential of their unique archival materials for instruction, research, fundraising, and international prominence, special collections will become even more of the centerpiece for their library (Dooley and Luce, 2010). Academic archivists, who have a broad range of skills and understanding of academic libraries, will direct these special collections departments and take the lead in defining the uniqueness of their collections, departments, libraries, and institutions. Advancing technology, centralization of services, new collecting areas, the proliferation of born-digital materials, and the broadening of the mission and skills of academic archivists, will create much more unique academic archives programs of the future.

Preparation for Academic Archives

The question of education and training for archivists is a frequent topic of debate. There are still leaders in the archival profession who discount the value of a master's of library or information science degree for archivists, instead arguing for a subject master's degree or significant experience that cannot be learned in a classroom environment. While these arguments are common, within academic libraries an ALA-accredited master's degree in library and information science is the standard. Some libraries are willing to consider candidates who hold a doctorate in a related field rather than a library degree, while other libraries do not. Many job postings for academic archivists require either a library degree or a degree in a related field; however, in practice most academic library search committees eliminate candidates from their pool who do not hold a library degree. There is no indication that baseline standard qualification for a professional position in an academic library (i.e., a master's degree in library and information science) will change in the near future.

Graduate programs in library and information science take different approaches to education, with specialization as a growing trend. Some programs provide students with a generalist approach to all manners of library work, and yet other graduate library programs focus students in certain

> **Common Traits of the Next Generation of Academic Archivists**
>
> - An ALA-accredited master's degree in library and information science, with a specialization in archives
> - Additional training sponsored by professional organizations
> - Significant work experience in an archival setting
> - Additional graduate work in a subject-based or technology field
> - Designation as a special collections archivist

"tracks" to make them more prepared for a specific subfield of librarianship. While there are no specific graduate programs focused on academic librarianship, most all library and information schools offer courses on working in an academic library. Because of the crisis of leadership and direction in academic libraries there is a strong possibility that graduate library programs will work with professional organizations such as the Association of Research Libraries (ARL), the American Library Association (ALA), and Association of College and Research Libraries (ACRL) to create specialized programs in academic librarianship.

A specialization in archives and records management is a growing area of library school education. Over a dozen institutions claim to offer an archives track for students wanting to become professional archivists. The best of these programs provide the general knowledge of library school (i.e., courses on reference, cataloging, information structure, and emerging technology) while offering a focused curriculum of archival courses and practical working experiences. During the past two decades these specialized training programs in library and information schools have produced a large number of academic archivists.

Although professional groups such as the Society of American Archivists (SAA) have frequently developed graduate curricula for training archivists in library and information programs, there is no indication that those suggestions will be universally implemented. For such a curriculum to gain favor, there must be much closer communication between practicing archivists and archival educators. As one possible solution, many archivists have pushed for a professionally recognized master's or a doctoral degree in archives (both of which exist in Canada and other countries); however, these efforts are still in their infancy. For archivists in training wanting to work at a college or university it is more important to understand that entry into the academic library's ranks will require an ALA-accredited master's degree in library and information science first. Possessing a second graduate degree in a subject specialty, a technology or technical field, or possibly in archival science, is what will set apart candidates for academic archives positions.

With so many library and information graduate programs offering specializations in archival work, the next generation of academic archivists will come from these focused programs. The strongest of this next generation will have additional degrees or specializations in historical, technical, and content areas, in addition to graduate training in archives. Academic archivists have traditionally had backgrounds in the humanities, but what will be new is the combination of that subject expertise and technology into skills that resemble the emerging areas of digital humanities. With a large number of digital humanities centers on campuses, archivists will be liaisons between those units and the academic library (CLIR, 2009). Technology skills will be needed to develop new systems to manage and preserve electronic records and to provide new ways of accessing archival materials in a virtual environment.

The next wave of academic archivists will possess the skills of a librarian, an archivist, a scholar with a subject specialty, and a digital technician. Within another 20 years, college and university archivists will no longer have the same responsibilities and titles that they do now, simply because their work will expand to include other critical areas of their special collections department. To reflect these broader trends, the presence of these skills, and their location within the academic library, a majority of academic archivists will be designated with the new and more appropriate title of special collections archivist.

The Archives and the Academic Library

Because the majority of academic archivists work within an academic library, there is an even greater need to understand the emerging trends in academic librarianship. In some institutions archivists are not well connected to their academic library colleagues. Historically the standard work of librarians (i.e., working with faculty and students, selecting library resources, and answering basic reference questions) has had more in common with special collections librarians, who also select material and build print and manuscript collections. Because archivists have traditionally focused on acquiring, arranging, describing, processing, preserving, and providing access to archival collections, their work has often been on the periphery of the academic library and in many ways separate from other departments.

But in the past few decades, the lines between reference and instruction librarians, special collections librarians, manuscript curators, and academic archivists have blurred significantly, and brought the purposes of archives departments closer to the objectives of the academic library. Further, the recent interest in special collections and original research materials by leaders of academic libraries has rekindled an interest in the work of archivists. More practically, the tightening of resources in academic libraries has resulted in closer attention to the actual costs (including storage space, acquisitions funding, needed supplies, and wages for employees) of an archives department. For these and other reasons, academic archives units have become more blended or merged with larger units in the academic library, such as a special collections department. Likewise, the services and outreach activities in an archives program now resemble and overlap with other library departments and initiatives. This overlap will continue as groups of academic librarians will both cross-train and retrain to work within special collections and archives departments.

The seclusion of academic archivists is waning, as archives programs are becoming more dynamic and integrated into the mission of the college or university

> **Academic Library and Archives Overlap**
>
> - Use of technology to work with virtual audiences
> - Units merged into larger departments
> - Cross-training of employees for multiple tasks
> - Reading rooms more like an information commons for more collaborate research
> - Space for collections at a premium
> - Picking and then managing electronic resources
> - Emphasis on a research library concept
> - Digital curation

library. As a future trend, academic archives programs will develop stronger connections to library instruction and assessment efforts. Technology will allow academic archivists to provide much more than access to materials. Instead, new technology will enable archivists to create scholarly networks, learning tutorials, online forums for a greater interaction with researchers, evaluative tools to measure the results of instruction, and pedagogical methods that focus on the researcher. As the work of archivists becomes more understood and integrated into the daily operations of the academic library, traditional archival access tools such as finding aids and how to conduct research using original materials will become a standard part of library instruction.

Ironically, the interest in archives and unique primary materials is a return to the research library concept that dominated much of the first half of the twentieth century. The research library rests on the principle of building an in-depth collection of primary and secondary sources in a variety of formats for researchers. But unlike that golden age of American libraries, today's research library concept is even broader and uses technology to provide scholars and students access to a vast range of materials at many institutions. Digitization projects are just the beginning of creating online portals to original material from research libraries where researchers can discover, share, and add value to digital assets. Research by scholars and students is at the heart of a true academic library, which makes the original and unique materials in academic archives vital to developing programs and services for library researchers.

The public services portion of academic archives departments will be located within the main campus library building. That centralized location will allow archivists to be an active part of the library's faculty and fully integrated into the programs, services, and outreach efforts of the academic library. Within the main library, special collections departments will operate a centralized reading room with access to all collections, basic sources, subject experts, and multipurpose use spaces. Rather than just a room for quiet individual research, tomorrow's special collections reading room will look much like an information commons found in many academic libraries. In addition to the traditional space for individual research, the reading room will include classroom space to accommodate large groups, research rooms with cutting-edge technology for use by multiple researchers working on group projects, rooms with capabilities for virtual interaction with other scholars, digitization workstations, and spaces for exhibits and programs. These spaces will be used for basic and advanced instructional sessions on the use of primary sources and research methods, with more emphasis on reaching the K–12 community. The presence of staff, improved instruction on how to consult and handle archival materials, and enhanced security systems will allow researchers in any of these spaces to simultaneously access and consult a much wider range and volume of original material.

Additional archival facilities, usually located off-site and outside of a traditional academic library building, will house processing operations, backlogs, processed collections, and some digitization work. Because the collections will be centralized and are not accessible to researchers, the storage spaces can be better designed for climate, security controls, and maximum efficiency of space. The trend of multiple academic libraries sharing and storing materials in centralized off-site locations will be repeated by academic archives. To save on costs and to better share resources, academic archives will store their collections in large off-site facilities, often operated by several institutions with efficient courier or shuttle services for the collections and the staff. To improve access to large paper-based collections, many academic archives will loan material to other nearby repositories for use by researchers or for selected digitization. Archivists working in these off-site centers will focus greater attention on the preservation of their holdings and reprocessing projects.

Although the collections and spaces may be far apart, the employees of tomorrow's academic archives will work at each of these locations as well as complete their work in the virtual environment. Academic archivists will become better managers of their digital content. The role of academic archivists as curators will require them to manage the creation, storage, and preservation of reformatted and born-digital content. Academic archivists will take an active role in the design of storage systems, information architecture, and preservation strategies. In collaboration with other professionals, academic archivists will establish new standards to manage electronic records for long-term storage and access.

Academic libraries are becoming more closely involved with the creation of digital content on campus, more connected to classroom instruction, and more concerned with the curation of digital materials (CLIR, 2010). As the academic library shifts away from a repository to a collaborative center of information and scholarly communication, academic archivists have an opportunity to become digital curators (Walters and Skinner, 2011). This new role means that archivists will be involved in the creation and dissemination of digital scholarship by working with faculty, staff, and students. Digital curation will require knowledge of how to manage, preserve, and provide long-term access to digital content. That role will demand that academic archivists reconsider electronic records appraisal, migration practices, and repository management.

Academic archives have much to contribute to the research library approach to academic libraries. In addition to selecting and scanning original material, academic archivists can also contribute electronic records and other digital historical materials to virtual collaborations. As these electronic resources are combined with standard electronic library resources (i.e., databases, full-text online journals, and e-books), it re-creates a virtual version of the campus research library, but without the limitations of library hours and an actual visit to a building or reading room. In the process of building virtual research library collections, academic archivists will play an important role in designing projects, selecting material, managing digital files, and making active contributions to institutional and multi-institutional repositories. It is possible that academic archivists will help establish new stand-alone campus departments outside of the library to manage digital and information assets for the library, campus departments, administrative units, and other contributors.

Academic Archivists as Library Leaders

The rapidly changing academic and information environment makes it imperative for academic archivists to expand beyond their traditional archival roles. Academic archivists have the ability to redefine themselves in the areas of special collections librarianship, academic librarianship, digital librarianship, and records management. Each of these emerging areas directly affect the growth of the academic library and offer academic archivists opportunities to take an active role in determining and leading that direction.

The consolidation of individual library units into larger departments has brought many academic archives programs into the special collections world. While special collections represents many groupings of materials and formats, the emphasis on original sources makes this environment an ideal setting for academic archivists. With a base in a special collections department, an academic archivist can do much more than collect official records and document institutional history. Instead, an academic archivist working in special collections can develop skills in the tangential areas of manuscripts and rare books librarianship. With a greater command of print and unpublished materials and a stronger understanding of book and printing history, academic archivists can integrate even more primary materials into instructional sessions. While broadening their understanding of existing collections, academic archivists can play an active role in adding new materials through expanded work with donors and fundraising efforts. Development and outreach for special collections offers much greater opportunities than just focusing on alumni and campus units.

The emergence of digital librarianship relates directly to a new conceptualization of special collections. In many academic libraries, academic archivists are already an active part of digitization efforts. As selectors of materials, creators of metadata, experts on technology, and managers of digitization units, academic archivists have stepped forward as leaders of digital library initiatives. Often those digital projects are based within special collections departments and are coordinated by archivists. Because of their familiarity with the formats and the structure of information in archival collections, archivists are often the leaders in determining digitization, metadata, and technical standards for their library.

As part of building digital resources, archivists have continued to use technology to improve access to original archival materials. Contributions by archivists to digital efforts will result in more widespread use of access tools such as EAD (Encoded Archival Description) and EAC (Encoded Archival Context). Mature digital collections and projects will increase archival access and have much clearer intended outcomes and audiences. Another component of digital librarianship that relates to the work of academic archivists is the management of electronic records and legacy files. These born-digital archival materials offer great challenges (i.e., collecting, migrating, and preserving) for academic archivists, but the rich content and connections between digital materials make the effort worthwhile. As access improves, these electronic collections will become some of the most frequently used resources, both digital and non-digital, in academic libraries.

> **Library Leadership Qualities for Academic Archivists**
>
> - Effective manager of people, spaces, and collections
> - Developer of instructional and reference services
> - Builder of collections
> - Successful with donors
> - Records manager in an electronic environment
> - Leader of digitization projects

Because electronic records represent future unique collections in academic libraries, archivists must not only better understand the field of records management but also become involved in the planning for campus electronic records management. Academic archivists can contribute to these campus and professional discussions by sharing their understanding of technology, information architecture, access tools, researcher needs, and how paper-based archival practices can and cannot be applied to digital materials. The costs of operating separate records management and archival units will result in many institutions combining the two related functions, and most likely these merged programs will be part of an academic library. On some campuses, academic archivists will assume the responsibilities for records management, especially for digital records, while at other institutions archivists will continue to work collaboratively with records managers. Whatever the administrative relationship, academic archivists must take a more active role in records management in order to provide their researchers with archival and historical material.

While many professional archivists detest administrative duties and prefer their daily processing and reference duties, the closer integration of academic archives into the mission of the academic library opens up leadership opportunities for academic archivists. At the department level, archivists have a tremendous amount of influence on staff, student, and part-time employees. Academic archivists serve as trainers, coordinators, and supervisors for other members of the archives unit. Even the largest academic archives have relatively small hierarchies of management, which means that many of the responsibilities of the archives program are shared among professional archivists. Academic archivists at all levels, whether entry-level, middle manager, or director, serve as valuable departmental leaders.

Academic archivists with significant experience building and leading successful archival programs have emerged as the next generation of leaders for academic libraries. A consistent issue in academic library administration is a noted lack of training for new deans and directors. For decades, the path to the top of the academic library has often depended on having the right connections and experiences, which has resulted in only a small group of qualified deans and directors. In an effort to remedy this problem, several professional organizations have created leadership training programs. However, these approaches have simply not yielded enough future leaders of academic libraries. Because leading academic archivists have such a solid understanding of the direction of collections, technology, researcher needs, spaces, and fundraising, many are poised to assume greater administrative and managerial roles in the academic library. Within the next decade a significant number of deans and directors of academic libraries will come from the archival ranks.

Now more than ever before, experienced academic archivists are using their talents to lead academic libraries. Academic archivists have a clear understanding of the research process and are familiar with making decisions based on the needs of researchers. Within their library, academic archivists have the skills to contribute to discussions and decisions about collection development, acquiring electronic resources, designing learning spaces, conducting assessment, improving the reference experience, creating virtual access tools, conducting instructional sessions, purchasing or creating emerging technologies, and promoting the concept of a research library. Perhaps most significant, academic archivists have much to contribute to digitization and digital projects, both based in the library and in campus units.

Academic Archivists as Fundraisers

There will never be enough institutional resources available to support all of the initiatives of an archives program. Whether the archives program is private, government, or academic, the levels of funding and staffing have consistently proven inadequate. Despite such a reality, archivists have created tremendous collections, services, and programs, and they will continue to do so no matter what levels of support are available. The ability for archivists to find solutions when faced with lack of resources will only grow stronger in the coming years.

The recent trend of being frugal and efficient in difficult economic times will result in academic archivists becoming more enterprising and assertive in their efforts to support their programs. The lessons of the current economic recession will result in the leaders of archives programs concentrating on building large endowments for collection building and staffing costs. Cultivation of donors (both private individuals and organizations) will become a top priority for archivists, with the expectation of financial donations to accompany the donation of original material. Archivists will host an increased number of dinners, events, and other programs targeted at raising both awareness and resources for their archives programs. Parents of students, alumni and reunion groups, and external organizations will be the new target audiences for these events. This kind of direct fundraising will take place through the work of the employees of the archives, rather than through a centralized campus development office or officer. In addition to direct donations, many programs will rely on private funding, rather than just federal or state granting agencies, for special projects such as selected digitization.

For academic archivists there is an obvious strength in the area of fundraising and development. The need to fund new initiatives and to offset the loss of funding from state, federal, or external sources has made fundraising campaigns a common part of the academic environment. Colleges and universities, both public and private, have launched and will continue to launch multimillion and even billion dollar development campaigns. Academic libraries most often are part of these campaigns and frequently rely on special collections and archives departments to promote the uniqueness of their holdings. These departments are steeped in the process of donor work, especially because so many collections are acquired from alumni, campus contributors, and external donors.

In recent years, academic archivists have taken a more proactive role in institutional development. The acquisition of material is the most significant part of donor work; however, it will become even more common that an archivist, not the dean of libraries or an assigned library development officer, asks for funding to support the donation of material. Rather than asking for a general amount of funding, academic archivists must ask donors for specific amounts to help cover the costs of processing, which include student or staff wages, archival supplies, storage, preservation, and conservation. Sharing with donors the actual costs of space, time, supplies, and long-term storage is an effective strategy to secure a financial donation.

Fundraising Strategies for Academic Archives

- Be more enterprising, assertive, and entrepreneurial.
- Work closely with the library and the institution's development office.
- Communicate with known and potential donors.
- Speak to new groups of potential donors about the archives program.
- Suggest that donors of material also donate funding to support the processing and long-term storage of their collections.
- Provide donors many options for how their financial donation could be used to support the archives program.
- Consider private groups and other institutions as potential donors.

Other times archivists work with donors only interested in making a financial contribution, and it is even more important to have specific concepts and costs for these donors. For example, a past contributor to the library wants to build a collection of nineteenth-century cookbooks. The archivist should determine how much of an endowment will be needed to support the yearly purchases of these books, and how much would be needed to support a full-time staff or faculty position devoted this collecting area. Archivists should think "big" about these kinds of opportunities and consider naming spaces for the donor, such as the reading room, the department, or new learning spaces. While there are limitations on what could be named, the spaces in even the smallest academic archives have naming potential.

In the next 20 years, academic archivists will be even more involved in development for their institution. That work will expand far beyond acquiring new collections and funding to support those materials. Instead, development for academic archivists will include working with donors to secure resources to support programs and services in both the library and the department. In addition to working with individuals and recognized alumni, academic archivists will also seek support from organizations and private groups. Development will also involve securing resources for projects by sharing responsibilities and costs with other institutions, such as historical societies and other academic libraries.

Academic Archivists and the Academic Environment

Greater involvement by academic archivists in the activities of their campus have resulted in a stronger role for archives programs. Public programs, events, exhibits, and instructional sessions are the most obvious manifestations of campus outreach, but there are also other areas of opportunity for academic archivists. When academic archivists have subject expertise, such as in the humanities or a social sciences field, there are often direct connections to academic departments. For example, an archivist with graduate training in anthropology will have much in common with their college's anthropology department. Reaching out to the chair of the department or working with specific faculty may result in teaching or research opportunities.

The emerging role of academic librarians and their relationships to the programs that they serve is a relevant model for archivists to consider. While classroom teaching is not a common requirement for academic librarians, many are embedded in their departments. As part of that integration, librarians often have a second office near the academic programs that they serve; they attend faculty meetings in certain departments; they serve as external readers on thesis and dissertation committees; they serve on search committees; they advise students about library resources and career opportunities in the information field; they may be asked to teach or co-teach a course related to their subject specialty; and finally, they provide introductory library instructional courses to students. Academic archivists can effectively adapt this kind of embedded librarianship into their campus outreach efforts.

Strong connections between an archives program and an academic department may also create partnerships that help overcome shrinking resources. For example, an English department at a large university has worked closely with the library's special collections department to build up an impressive amount of twentieth-century American literary manuscripts. One result of this partnership is that most of those collections are unprocessed and require a processing archivist with an English background to provide a solid level of arrangement and description. To solve this problem, the library and the English department conduct a search for an archivist with a subject specialty. The successful candidate works in the library processing collections, but they are funded by a shared appointment between departments. The joint appointment also makes it possible for the candidate to teach courses in archival research for the English department, and to recruit student

> **Archivists Outside of the Archives**
>
> - Integration into academic departments
> - Classroom teaching responsibilities
> - Community activism
> - Active scholars with academic reputations

employees in the department to assist with the processing. Shared appointments for archivists can also occur at multiple institutions, especially when specific skills and training are needed by more than one college or university.

Academic archivists should consider their local community as an important part of the academic environment. First, archivists work with members of the local community to help support the archives program. They organize programs, make presentations, offer preservation advice, accept donations for the archives, and assist with individual research. But perhaps more important, academic archivists have developed strong relationships to their community that do not necessarily relate to their archives program. While archivists should take an unbiased and apolitical approach to their daily work, many have emerged as community leaders. Participation in community governance, organizations, and awareness activities by archivists will become even more common. Some archivists contribute to their communities by holding elected offices, serving on school boards, and chairing local task forces. The growing numbers of "activist archivists" will only increase in the coming years.

Outside of their college or university setting, academic archivists have multiple connections to scholars, experts, and faculty at other institutions. Archivists serve not only as a contact point for researchers, but as a conduit for understanding what is available in archives across the world. Because of that knowledge of resources and scholarship, many archivists are active in professional organizations and groups related to their subject specialty. Those archivists also contribute to the scholarly community by publishing chapters, articles, and books in fields outside of archives and library science. While many archivists do not consider themselves traditional scholars, their active study of many fields (i.e., subject strength, technology, information science, academic librarianship, and archives) provides them with a broad understanding of the academic environment.

Academic archivists are proven contributors to the academic and scholarly community. No longer can archivists relegate their professional responsibilities and duties only to pulling materials, answering reference questions, and processing collections. While those are important services that archives programs must provide, there is a growing obligation for academic archivists to be proactive scholars, contributors to intellectual discussions, and activists for many causes. These converging trends have pushed archivists much more into the mainstream of their campus, communities, and the profession.

Academic Archivists and the Profession

Despite shrinking budgets, the archival profession has expanded significantly in the past few decades. Membership in state, regional, and national archival organizations continues to rise as the membership in organizations for other professionals has become static or declined. The subfield of academic archives has steadily grown in terms of the number of archivists who identify themselves as academic archivists. Academic archives have become a budding subfield with a growing membership, expanding literature, training programs, and a collegial network of professionals.

The relationship between academic archivists and their professional archival organizations has great implications for the profession as a whole. Only government archivists can claim larger numbers than those who work on college or university campuses, which makes the contributions of academic archivists to local, state, regional, national, and even international archival organizations so significant. Professional leadership by academic archivists has been a constant and will likely continue into the future. However, because of shrinking resources and new expectations it is likely that academic archivists will rely more on local, state, and regional archival organizations, rather than national and international groups.

In the next decades, the Society of American Archivists will continue to retain and attract new members and lead the profession. However, the greatest opportunities for training, networking, and sharing new ideas will most likely occur at the regional level. Strong regional archival organizations, such as those in the Midwest, the Mid-Atlantic, New England, Southwest, and Pacific Northwest, will become the organizations of choice for reasons of costs, effectiveness, and relevance. State library and multi-institutional groups will also provide archivists

Professional Directions for Academic Archivists

- Ongoing commitment to the Society of American Archivists
- More participation in archival organizations at the local, state, and regional levels
- Increased involvement in consortiums and multi-institutional projects
- Greater connections to government archives and archivists
- More political involvement
- An increased number of collaborative electronic records project
- More archival leadership from the National Archives and Records Administration

at various levels new opportunities for leadership, especially in the areas of digitization, electronic records projects, and grant writing. Academic archivists are already active in the state and regional groups and their involvement will only increase in the future.

Over the next few decades, academic archivists will create new and stronger connections with their colleagues who work in both state and federal government archives. Part of that trend relates to the importance of government support in the activities and operations of colleges and universities. Public institutions have a direct connection with their state's legislature and all schools have some kind of connection to the federal government. Understanding the political process and landscape has become a crucial part of securing resources for higher education. At that same time, archivists both in government and higher education have become more politically aware and adept. The combination of activist archivists and well-connected government archivists will form an effective group to lobby for more support on behalf of statewide archival programs that benefit all state residents.

In addition to rallying support for archives, academic and government archivists have access to the kind of resources needed to solve electronic records challenges. These resources include new technology, funding, technical experts, and large numbers of archivists with expertise. Collecting electronic records from state agencies is very similar to the challenge of capturing electronic records from departments and units on campus, which makes this kind of collaborative project between archivists in government and on campus a natural fit. The sharing of resources and ideas between government and academic archivists (the two largest groups of professional archivists) will only advance the profession in fields such as electronic records management.

At the federal level there is great opportunity for academic archives. The National Archives and Records Administration (NARA) employs the largest number of archivists in the United States and operates dozens of archival facilities across the nation. The connection between academic archives and the National Archives became even clearer in November 2010 when NARA became a member of the Association of Research Libraries (ARL, 2010). Partnerships between academic archives and NARA will most likely develop in the areas of technology, electronic records management, and leadership development. Further, academic archives will benefit from programs and grant-funded initiatives sponsored by NARA.

Academic Archivists as Innovators

Through partnerships and new collaborations academic archivists are at the forefront of innovation. Since the 1990s academic archivists have played a significant role in the development of EAD, DACS, EAC, and numerous digital projects that have supported both archives and libraries. Academic archivists have established themselves as a vital part of their school's digital landscape, especially with their work in implementing institutional repositories and electronic records management programs at their college or university. Continuation of this work will lead academic archivists to create more reliable preservation strategies for electronic records, enhance digital collections, and invent new ways to connect technology to the research process.

Archival collections will continue to be paper-based so archivists must continue to experiment with minimal approaches to processing. However, the increasing amount of electronic files will affect the traditional approaches to arrangement and description, and appraisal. A more technologically savvy generation of academic archivists will lead the profession toward an improved way to process collections with born-digital and traditional archival materials.

Electronic records are the next wave of "hidden collections" that will attract attention from academic libraries. In an effort to meet that challenge, academic archivists will develop new appraisal methods for electronic records. While a minimal approach to managing electronic records is not a new concept, there is much to learn about electronic records appraisal from the experiences of the "More Product, Less Process" (MPLP) approach to processing paper-based archival records. The improvement of information systems and greater abilities to search and

---

Greatest Innovative Opportunities for Academic Archivists

- Adapt paper-based archival principles to the electronic collections, especially in the areas of appraisal, arrangement, and description.
- Create reliable preservation strategies for electronic records.
- Promote and provide access to electronic collections through enhanced online reading rooms.
- Build richer digital collections that satisfy multiple research groups.
- Decentralize physical spaces and digital collections.
- Document the diversity of society and the academic institution by collecting material with multiple viewpoints.
- Meet the needs of researchers with nontraditional research projects.

sort content (i.e., arrangement and description) will benefit both archivists and researchers. Such changes will allow academic archivists to focus less on how to capture and manage electronic records, and much more on how to promote and provide access to digital research materials.

Access to electronic archival materials will improve with more elaborate and enhanced online reading rooms, which will provide access to mature digital collections of primary and unique sources. Collaborative and interinstitutional digitization projects will continue with a new emphasis on scanning complete collections of material and including those files in multiple national digital library initiatives. Further, academic archivists will become involved in working with already existing campus digital projects, especially digital humanities centers, to migrate, preserve, and provide access to rich scholarly digital sources (CLIR, 2010). At the institutional level, electronic records will become a vital part of the reading room and the research experience. Legacy files, born-digital materials, and other audiovisual media will become some of the most frequently requested material in academic archives.

As academic libraries have redesigned their spaces to be more accommodating to groups and made better use of technology for learning, academic archives will also mirror this shift and become smarter with the management of their physical and virtual spaces. The era of new, separate archival buildings for special collections will end, and many academic archives will desire a stronger presence in the main campus library (most commonly in the form of a main reading room) in order to be closer to their researchers and their information colleagues. Instead of having one centralized location for all components of the program (i.e., reading room, collections, offices, and work spaces), archives programs will have multiple facilities focused on public services, collection management, and digitization. Likewise, the virtual spaces controlled by academic archives (i.e., webpages, digital collections, storage locations for electronic files) will also be decentralized and distributed.

Building on the past demands for diversity of material from archivists and historians, academic archivists will push even further to acquire collections that document multiple perspectives. While official records will retain an institutional importance, academic archivists will collect a much larger amount of unofficial materials to support a more diverse historical record of society and their campus community. A diversity of collections will allow academic archives to contribute more to interdisciplinary research and meet the needs of researchers with more nontraditional projects (i.e., documentary filmmaking, multimedia creations, digital portfolios, and graphic design). Collecting different groups of material and supporting new kinds of research broadens the mission of academic archives. No longer can academic archivists focus only on documenting the history of their institution through the collection of official materials; they must consider other sources, uses, and purposes for their programs.

CONCLUSION

A bright future exists for academic archives and for the archival profession in general. The mission of academic archives has broadened to reflect the needs of researchers, the demands of the academic library, and the realities of working in an academic environment. The future of academic archives will involve forward-thinking leadership from academic archivists in many colleges and universities. The majority of academic archivists work in a special collections department, which most commonly consists of merged archives and specialty units from an academic library. The traditional definition of an academic archivist as a university or college archivist has grown to include other library and information professionals. In the next 20 years, the roles and responsibilities for academic archivists will be shaped by an emerging set of archival values, which emphasize a more outward, and less inward, approach to leading archives programs.

Predicting an accurate future depends on understanding the past, the present, and emerging trends. Academic archives programs are presently situated to make significant contributions to their institutions, their libraries, the profession, the academy, their campus, and their communities. Technology is the greatest variable in understanding how research and archival work will be conducted in the coming decades. From managing electronic records to communicating with virtual researchers, technology offers academic archivists the greatest challenges and opportunities to redefine the profession. While academic archives programs will develop in their own way, technological changes will affect all programs in similar ways. Likewise, the next generation of academic archivists will combine traditional archival skills with emerging technologies to provide original and primary materials to the researchers of the future.

REFERENCES

Association of Research Libraries. 2010. "National Archives and Records Administration Becomes Newest Member of ARL." Association of Research Libraries. Last modified November 22. http://www.arl.org/news/pr/NARA-nov10.shtml.

Council on Library and Information Resources. 2009. *Working Together or Apart: Promoting the Next Generation of Digital Scholarship*. Washington, DC: Council on Library and Information Resources. http://www.clir.org/pubs/reports/pub145/pub145.pdf.

———. 2010. *The Idea of Order: Transforming Research Collections for 21st Century Scholarship*. Washington, DC: Council on Library and Information Resources. http://www.clir.org/pubs/reports/pub147/pub147.pdf.

Dooley, Jackie, and Katherine Luce. 2010. *Taking Our Pulse: The OCLC Research Survey of Special Collections and Archives*. Dublin, OH: Online Computer Library Center. http://www.oclc.org/research/publications/library/2010/2010-11.pdf.

Maher, William J. 1992. *The Management of College and University Archives*. Chicago: Society of American Archivists.

Prom, Christopher J., and Ellen D. Swain, eds. 2008. *College and University Archives: Readings in Theory and Practice*. Chicago: Society of American Archivists.

Samuels, Helen Willa. 1992. *Varsity Letters: Documenting Modern Colleges and Universities*. Chicago: Society of American Archivists.

Society of American Archivists. 1979. *College and University Archives: Selected Readings*. Chicago: Society of American Archivists.

———. 2011. "Campus Case Studies." Society of American Archivists. Accessed September 20. http://www2.archivists.org/publications/epubs/Campus-Case-Studies.

Theimer, Kate. 2011. "What is the Meaning of Archives 2.0?" *American Archivist* 74 (Spring/Summer): 58–68.

Walters, Tyler, and Katherine Skinner. 2011. *New Roles for New Times: Digital Curation for Preservation*. Washington, DC: Association of Research Libraries.

Index

About the Author

Aaron D. Purcell is professor and director of special collections at Virginia Tech. He earned his PhD in history from the University of Tennessee, his master's of library science from the University of Maryland, College Park, and his master's degree in history from the University of Louisville. Purcell has also worked at the National Archives and Records Administration, the National Library of Medicine, and the University of Tennessee.

Purcell is an active scholar, writing in the fields of history and archives. The University of Tennessee Press published his first academic book, *White Collar Radicals: TVA's Knoxville Fifteen, the New Deal, and the McCarthy Era*, in 2009. Purcell is completing an edited book on New Deal and Great Depression historiography for Kent State University Press, he is the editor of *The Journal of East Tennessee History*, and he is finishing a book on Arthur E. Morgan, the first chairman of the Tennessee Valley Authority. He has written articles on archival topics for the *American Archivist*, *Archival Outlook*, *IMJ*, and the *Journal of Archival Organization*. Purcell is an active member of the Society of American Archivists, the Mid-Atlantic Regional Archives Conference, and the Southern Historical Association.

He lives in Blacksburg, Virginia, with his wife, Laura, son, Samuel, and daughter, Caroline.

CPSIA information can be obtained at www.ICGtesting.com
Printed in the USA
LVOW071840130113

315504LV00004BA/421/P